DOMESTIC SERVICE AND GENDER 1660-1750

WOMEN AND MEN IN HISTORY

This series, published for students, scholars and interested general readers, will tackle themes in gender history from the early medieval period through to the present day. Gender issues are now an integral part of all history courses and yet many traditional texts do not reflect this change. Much exciting work is now being done to redress the gender imbalances of the past, and we hope that these books will make their own substantial contribution to that process. This is an open-ended series, which means that many new titles can be included. We hope that these will both synthesise and shape future developments in gender studies.

The General Editors of the series are *Patricia Skinner* (University of Southampton) for the medieval period; *Pamela Sharpe* (University of Bristol) for the early modern period; and *Penny Summerfield* (University of Lancaster) for the modern period. *Margaret Walsh* (University of Nottingham) was the Founding Editor of the series. Books already published in the series include:

Imperial Women in Byzantium 1025–1204: Power, Patronage and Ideology
Barbara Hill

Masculinity in Medieval Europe
D.M. Hadley (ed.)

Widowhood in Medieval and Early Modern Europe
Sandra Cavallo and Lyndan Warner (eds)

Gender and Society in Renaissance Italy
Judith C. Brown and Robert C. Davis (eds)

Gender, Church and State in Early Modern Germany: Essays by Merry E. Wiesner
Merry E. Wiesner

Manhood in Early Modern England: Honour, Sex and Marriage
Elizabeth W. Foyster

English Masculinities 1660–1800
Tim Hitchcock and Michèle Cohen

Disorderly Women in Eighteenth-Century London: Prostitution in the Metropolis 1730–1830
Tony Henderson

Gender, Power and the Unitarians in England, 1760–1860
Ruth Watts

Practical Visionaries: Women, Education and Social Progress, 1790–1930
Pam Hirsch and Mary Hilton (eds)

Women and Work in Russia, 1880–1930: A Study in Continuity through Change
Jane McDermid and Anna Hillyar

The Family Story: Blood, Contract and Intimacy, 1830–1960
Leonore Davidoff, Megan Doolittle, Janet Fink and Katherine Holden

More than Munitions: Women, Work and the Engineering Industries 1900–1950
Clare Wightman

Women in British Public Life, 1914–1950
Helen Jones

Women and the Second World War in France, 1939–1948
Hanna Diamond

A Soldier and a Woman: Sexual Integration in the Military
Gerard J. DeGroot and Corinna Peniston-Bird (eds)

DOMESTIC SERVICE AND GENDER 1660–1750

Life and Work in the London Household

Tim Meldrum

An imprint of **Pearson Education**

Harlow, England · London · New York · Reading, Massachusetts · San Francisco
Toronto · Don Mills, Ontario · Sydney · Tokyo · Singapore · Hong Kong · Seoul
Taipei · Cape Town · Madrid · Mexico City · Amsterdam · Munich · Paris · Milan

Pearson Education Limited
Edinburgh Gate
Harlow
Essex CM20 2JE
England

and Associated Companies throughout the world

Visit us on the World Wide Web at:
http://www.pearsoneduc.com

First published 2000

© Pearson Education Limited 2000

ISBN 0 582 31207 8 (CSD)
ISBN 0 582 31208 6 (PPR)

British Library Cataloguing-in-Publication Data
A catalogue record for this book is available from the British
Library.

Library of Congress Cataloging-in-Publication Data
Meldrum, Timothy.
    Domestic service and gender, 1660–1750 / Timothy Meldrum.
        p.   cm. — (Women and men in history)
    Includes bibliographical references and index.
    ISBN 0–582–31207–8 (alk. paper) — ISBN 0–582–31208–6 (pbk.: alk. paper)
    1. Domestics—England—London—History—17th century.   2.
Domestics—England—London—History—18th century.   3. Working
class—England—London—History—17th century.   4. Working
class—England—London—History—18th century.   I. Title.   II. Series.

HD6072.2.G72   L666   2000
331.7′6164046′09421—dc21   00–021674

Typeset by 35 in 11/13pt Baskerville MT
Produced by Pearson Education Asia Pte Ltd.
Printed in Singapore

To my parents, Brenda and Michael
Meldrum, for their love and support

CONTENTS

CONTENTS

LIST OF TABLES

ACKNOWLEDGEMENTS

This book's long gestation has ensured that a number of debts have accrued in its writing. The LSE's Economic History department fostered my nascent interest in early modern history, and my greatest debt is to Peter Earle, whose teaching and practice as a historian have always inspired my own. He has been a marvellous intellectual stimulant and support for a decade, supervising the PhD thesis on which this book is based, and reading the entire manuscript with his usual critical acumen.

Fellowship at the LSE was provided by Dudley Baines, Paul Johnson, Max-Stephan Schulze and Linda Sampson. The Institute of Historical Research allowed me to benefit from the wisdom in particular of Penelope Corfield, Vanessa Harding, Negley Harte, Tim Hitchcock, Derek Keene, Patrick O'Brien, David Ormrod, Bob Shoemaker & John Styles. University College Northampton houses supportive colleagues without which this book would never have been completed, and Julia Bush, Wolfgang Diecke, Peter King, Heather Shore, Cathy Smith and Liz Tingle deserve my thanks. Other friends who have directly or indirectly influenced this book include Paul Griffiths (who read chapter three), James and Deborah Ryan, Pam Sharpe, Richard Sheldon, Garthine Walker and Joe Ward.

I must also thank the staffs of the University College Northampton Library, Goldsmiths' Library, the British Library, the BLPES at the LSE, the Guildhall Library, the Corporation of London Record Office, and most particularly the London Metropolitan Archive. The book's research was greatly assisted by an ESRC Studentship, a Scouloudi Research Fellowship from the IHR, a bursary from the Centre of Metropolitan History's Achievement Project, and a sabbatical from UCN, for all of which I am grateful. It would never have made it onto the shelves without the persistence of the publishers, and Hilary Shaw and Elaine Richardson at Longman (Pearson Education) have both encouraged and cajoled in well-judged measure. My final debts lie with my parents, and with my wife Louisa, whose love and encouragement ensured the book's completion. All errors that remain, of courses, are entirely my responsibility.

The publishers are grateful to the following for permission to reproduce copyright material: Macmillan, for 'London domestic servants from depositional evidence, 1660–1750' from T. Hitchcock, P. King & P. Sharpe, eds., *Chronicling Poverty: The Voices and Strategies of the English Poor, 1640–1840* (Basingstoke, 1997); and Cambridge University Press, for 'Domestic service, privacy and the eighteenth-century metropolitan household' from *Urban History* 26 (1) (1999). Permission has been sought for Table 2.1, 'Distribution of Servants in Two City of London Parishes, 1690s', reproduced from P. Earle, *A City Full of People: Men and Women of London, 1650–1750* (London, 1994); we would be grateful for information that will help us to trace the copyright holder of this.

CHAPTER ONE

Introduction

If we could examine the intimate documents of any age, we should probably find it had its own particular domestic problems, for the relationship of master and servant is never easy to solve with entire satisfaction to both . . . It may be that the servant problem, in its modern aspect dated from these eighteenth-century controversies [over wages and insubordination], or more possibly that its seeds were sown in Restoration England . . .[1]

[T]he resurgence of waged domestic labour within contemporary Britain . . . signifies a highly traditional reconstruction of domestic work on class lines and opens the door to the construction of contrasting class-based femininities.[2]

A butler who stole from his employer to finance the life of a *bon viveur* which culminated in an alcohol, drugs and sex binge in Europe, was yesterday facing a prison sentence . . . [he] was given a Coutts bank card for household expenses, but while [his employers] were away in 1995, he entertained regulars from his local [Belgravia] pub to a lavish meal and fine wines at his employers' home. He even employed a butler and cook to give the impression the house was his.[3]

---

1   D. Marshall, 'The domestic servants of the eighteenth century', *Economica* **9** (25) (1929), 15–16.
2   N. Gregson and M. Lowe, *Servicing the Middle Classes: Class, Gender and Waged Domestic Labour in Contemporary Britain* (London, 1994), p. 235.
3   *The Guardian*, 23 July 1997.

A servant can have no unfeigned respect for his master, as soon as he has sense enough to find out that he serves a fool.[4]

The historical importance of domestic service

During the summer in which most of this book was drafted, a mercifully short-lived burst of home improvement involved lifting and replacing some of the floor-boards in the bathroom. Our small flat nestles in the roof of a typical converted late-Victorian London semi and had until then never threatened to become a 'theatre of memory'[5]; yet a few tugs on the crowbar revealed to Mick, Lou and me the wire pulley and wheel for a servant's bell. It had probably been installed in the last decade of the nineteenth century, some years before the First World War began the process of erosion in which domestic service shrank from being the largest single sector in the British labour market to one of the smallest by mid-century.[6] The thrill of discovery fortunately obscured the irony that an over-priced 'desirable two-bedroom edge-of-conservation area apartment in a sought-after leafy location' had been the building's least salubrious floor, where the servants were housed.

The presence of these shadows haunted the writing of a text about their late seventeenth and early eighteenth-century forebears and has hopefully served both to bring servants to life, but also to render them distant. This concrete discovery made service suddenly tangible: here, only yards from the word processor, a London domestic servant — probably a young migrant woman new to the metropolis — would have been dragged from sleep by the incessant tinkle of her employer's summons. But the bell was mechanical, not electrical; the room in which it would have rung was heated by coal dragged aloft from the cellar; and if the limp water pressure today is anything to go by, the water in which she washed her face was brought up by jug rather than pipe. The gulf separating us from that experience seems much wider than the difference in the historical contexts of servants' lives several hundred years apart.

Yet two of the quotations in the epigraph above suggest that at the turn of the twenty-first century British society is haunted once more by domestic

---

4   B. de Mandeville, 'An essay on charity, and charity schools', in his *The Fable of the Bees*, ed. P. Harth (Harmondsworth, 1970), p. 296.
5   R. Samuel, *Theatres of Memory* vol. I: *Past and Present in Contemporary Culture* (London, 1994).
6   M. Anderson, 'The social implications of demographic change', in F.M.L. Thompson, ed., *The Cambridge Social History of Britain 1750–1950* vol. 2, *People and their Environment* (Cambridge, 1990), p. 64.

service. This occupation has remained of vital importance throughout the twentieth century in African, Latin American, and Asian societies, something in which British expatriates living in them have also participated. But in Britain itself, a post Second World War hiatus in servant-employing divides Marshall's address to her 1920s academic readership on 'the servant problem' — in the knowing tones of one employer of domestic servants to others — from the small but significant minority of British middle-class households at the end of the twentieth century who elect to hire domestic labour for cleaning and childcare.[7]

Of course, the long history of problematic relations between servant and employer has frequently been characterised by manipulation, loaded negotiation, tension and conflict. While few employers of servants now have the resources or desire to allow their domestics to live within their households (let alone misuse a Coutts bank card), it is fair to say that recent developments have brought a version of 'the servant problem' to the fore once more, although this time a consideration of the 'employer problem' of servants is also likely to feature. In particular, anxieties generated by the employment of staff when high proportions of women are returning to work after childbirth — especially the employment of nannies — have been a persistent theme in the debate on gender and the 'future of work'.[8] Gregson and Lowe go so far as to posit that the *fin de siècle* return of domestic labour within many middle-class households has re-opened class divisions which some historians argue were originally forged between mistress and servant in the eighteenth century, although there is little attempt by these researchers to historicise their late twentieth-century sociological findings.[9] They have succeeded, nonetheless, in amplifying an echo of the past which had seemed irrelevant.

Domestic servants certainly haunt the ancient streets and houses of old London. If we turn back to the period embraced by this book, far from being 'ubiquitous but invisible'[10], their presence was felt, heard, seen and (thankfully for the historian) widely documented in the late seventeenth and early eighteenth centuries. They leap off the contemporary stage, shine out of canvases, and steal forth from the criminal records. This should not be

---

7   Marshall, 'Domestic servants of the eighteenth century'.

8   *The Guardian*'s Women's pages are a fruitful source of such discussion, e.g. K. Viner, 'Give us this day our daily', 14 January 1997; Suzanne Franks's *Having None of It: Women, Men and the Future of Work* (London, 1999) is a valuable contribution to the recent debate.

9   Gregson and Lowe, *Servicing the Middle Classes*. Chapter Four in this book explores the eighteenth-century debate.

10 Cf. D.A. Kent, 'Ubiquitous but invisible: female domestic servants in mid-eighteenth century London', *History Workshop Journal* **28** (Autumn, 1989).

in the least surprising: the institution of service was a cornerstone of pre-modern English life. The master–servant dichotomy informed economic negotiation and dispute, and in a semantic sense at least, did so until well into the nineteenth century. Social interaction was vertically cross-cut by the obligation and authority implied in hierarchical relations of service, it being the clearest way to characterise the social distance between the propertied and the propertyless.

However, this cultural paradigm did not always go uncontested by contemporaries, particularly in periods of intense political upheaval, and Christopher Hill has explored the way the conjunction of service and servility was challenged by new forms of 'freedom' during the Civil War.[11] Nor was the term 'servant' ever synonymous with 'the poor' to an extent that ruled out free labouring and independent cottage-dwelling, getting a living from (dwindling) common resources by gleaning from others' fields, foraging in woodland or grazing livestock on common pasture largely in the absence of the master–servant relationship. But servants had an importance in the society and economy of the seventeenth and eighteenth centuries that defied their lowly status: the widespread experience of life-cycle service in one form or another in adolescence and young adulthood explains the demographers' conclusions that some 13 per cent of the population of English communities (obviously with local variation), and more particularly up to three-quarters of those in the 15–24 age cohort, may have been servants.[12] This sheer scale affirms both the historical significance of domestic service, and the distance between it and today's concerns. But the slender bridge that now spans service's past and its present ensures that a book such as this seems more relevant than it did even when research for the PhD thesis from which it has emerged began in the early 1990s.[13]

Historiographical outlines

Such relevance notwithstanding, there are a number of reasons for penning a book on London domestic service between 1660 and 1750. The first is

---

11 C. Hill 'Pottage for freeborn Englishmen: attitudes to wage labour in sixteenth and seventeenth century England', in his *Change and Continuity in Seventeenth-Century England*, rev. edn (New Haven, 1991).

12 P. Laslett, 'Mean household size since the sixteenth century', in Laslett (with R. Wall), *Household and Family in Past Time* (Cambridge, 1972), p. 152; his *The World We Have Lost Further Explored* (London, 1983), pp. 262–3 and n. 17, p. 279 and n. 75.

13 T. Meldrum, 'Domestic service in London, 1660–1750: gender, life cycle, work and household relations', unpublished University of London PhD thesis (1996).

highlighted by the words of Dorothy Marshall, first professional historian of eighteenth-century domestic service, in the epigraph above. Her identification of a historical 'servant problem' is an unwitting acknowledgement that histories written about the subject in our period have taken an employer-made standpoint, the definitive master-narrative that now demands a corrective. This is not to dismiss the pioneering work done by Marshall herself, who dragged the subject from the gloom of neglect in two publications either side of the Second World War, in the first focusing on the eighteenth century and in the second surveying domestic service from the sixteenth to the nineteenth centuries.[14] Jean Hecht, too, wrote a valuable but now very dated study in which he employed 'the usual quarries of the social historian' using the 'descriptive or impressionistic method'; he claimed to have dealt with the inherent 'class bias' in his chosen documents — memoirs, correspondence, newspapers, travellers' accounts and so forth. 'Thus', he wrote optimistically, 'although it is largely through the eyes of the employer class that servants are viewed in this study, it is by no means a one-sided presentment that emerges from the assembled facts'.[15]

Nevertheless, a recent critic rightly observed that Hecht relied 'entirely on material generated by employers of servants in large establishments', and he consequently failed to live up to his own stipulations, reflecting 'the social concerns and prejudices of his sources'.[16] It would be churlish to criticise historians of an earlier generation without acknowledging that the range of sources for the social historian has expanded vastly since the 1960s; so it would be perfectly reasonable to expect the first major publication on the subject for forty years to offer something new. Yet Bridget Hill's book on eighteenth-century domestic service, a collection of essays rather than a monograph, fails to capitalise on the sophisticated progress of recent social history. Like her earlier text on women's work, it is heavily slanted towards the late eighteenth and early nineteenth centuries (and strangely enough, she admits she has 'allowed in material of the later nineteenth and even early twentieth centuries'), while her range of sources is very similar to Hecht's. An exception in terms of source material is her interesting and elegantly-written chapter on a woman who went into service in London in 1799 (at the age of twelve) and left an autobiography nearly half a century later. But the book as a whole reassures the reader with grand theories about change over the 'long' eighteenth century — the development of an

---

14 Marshall, 'Domestic servants of the eighteenth century'; her *The English Domestic Servant in History*, Historical Association General Series 13 (London, 1949).

15 J.J. Hecht, *The Domestic Servant Class in Eighteenth-Century England* (London, 1956), pp. xi, xii: the publishers failed to explain why the word 'class' was dropped from the 1980 reprint.

16 Kent, 'Ubiquitous but invisible', 112.

increasingly contractual and waged, feminised and isolated domestic service — which remain asserted yet far from proven.[17]

The concentration of historical writing on domestic service in the nineteenth and twentieth centuries colours Hill's essays too deeply, and provides further impetus for a new book on the earlier period. Publication (sociological as well as historical) on domestic service after 1800 in Europe, the USA and Latin America has largely focused on the construction of class, gender and racial discourses forged especially in relations between mistress and maid within the modern household. Research has tied the growth and feminisation of the domestic service sector to urbanisation and modernisation in general, and much of the work has been driven by the theoretical concerns of Marxism and feminism: the use of Davidoff and Hall's concept of 'separate spheres', locating these changes in the middle-class English household around the turn of the nineteenth century, has been particularly widespread. Such ideas have proved attractive to historians working on French domestic service before 1800, for whom the French Revolution serves as a watershed for the *bourgeois* employment of (particularly female) domestics. However, revisionist work within the last fifteen years has questioned the statistical usefulness of the nineteenth-century British censuses, the basis of much of the modernisation evidence, and has begun to investigate the nature and class basis of modern domestic service with much closer scrutiny.[18] These criticisms merely add to the perils in dragging theses about modern service backwards in time, and consequently these ideas (thanks to their influence in the historiography) will have to be addressed and challenged later in this volume.

If 'invisibility' fails to characterise domestic service in terms of contemporary sources, it is relevant — in the light of the plethora of publications on modern service — to the relative historiographical myopia evident for the period before 1800.[19] Nevertheless, other historians have been working on related fields which deserve consideration here. The writing of Zemon Davis drew historians' attentions to the activities of youth groups in late medieval and sixteenth-century France,[20] and an ensuing literature on the history of

---

17 B. Hill, *Servants: English Domestics in the Eighteenth Century* (Oxford, 1996), p. 18 and Chapter 10; for further remarks upon the slender historiography of pre-modern domestic service, see the Bibliographical essay.
18 L. Davidoff and C. Hall, *Family Fortunes: Men and Women of the English Middle Class, 1780–1850* (London, 1987); the publication in this series of Patricia Seleski's volume on London domestic service in the late eighteenth and early nineteenth centuries is eagerly anticipated. This literature is discussed further in the Bibliographical essay later in this book.
19 Here, Kent is undoubtedly right: 'Ubiquitous but invisible', 111.
20 N. Zemon Davis, 'The reasons of misrule', in her *Society and Culture in Early Modern France* (Stanford, 1975).

youth in early modern Europe has established a clear, relatively discrete and fairly lengthy period during adolescence marking a transition between childhood and adulthood, in which service played a significant defining role. Two works deserve particular mention at this stage, those of Ben-Amos and Griffiths. Both authors analysed aspects of service from their different perspectives on early modern youth but paid far more attention, largely through the nature and availability of their source material, to male apprenticeship than to domestic service. Gender is dealt with in both of their books — it is an unavoidable paradigm when writing social history at the end of the twentieth century — but it is not a key organising concept for either of them.

Ben-Amos made admirable use of diaries and autobiographies to re-construct adolescent lives, but only three of the seventy she employs were identifiably written by women: partly as a result, her brief account of domestic service leaves her overall story somewhat unbalanced. Griffiths rightly stresses that service was a prevalent but not universal experience for youth, and acknowledges early on the importance of bringing in 'the experiences of male and female servants and parish apprentices' in order 'to signpost their different expectations and fortunes'. Yet it is not a concern at the fore of his mind, and tucked away in a footnote in his concluding chapter is the pointed remark that 'gender is, of course, only one potential distinctive experience'.[21] This rather misses the point: 'gender' is not a 'distinct experience' but rather the social configuration of sexual difference, a process that colours most if not all distinct experiences. This book hopes both to fill in the gap left — understandably in some respects — in histories of youth by giving domestic service concentrated attention. But it is also intended to demonstrate the centrality of gender to an understanding of contemporary service in the wider sense.

Principal sources

The core source for the thesis is the collection of witnesses' depositions made at the London Consistory court between 1669 (the first year of surviving post-Restoration depositions) and 1752 (the final year bound in the book of depositions which straddles the eighteenth century's mid-point). All

---

21   I.K. Ben-Amos, *Adolescence and Youth in Early Modern England* (New Haven, 1994); P. Griffiths, *Youth and Authority: Formative Experiences in England, 1560–1640* (Oxford, 1996), pp. 10–11, p. 391 n. 6, p. 392.

the depositions of those witnesses in that period known to have been in domestic service when deposing (henceforth 'current servants'), or at some time before that point ('former', or 'ex-servants'), were selected for inclusion in a machine-readable relational database. These records were complemented by a selected rather than random sample of domestic servants' depositions at three other church courts, the Prerogative Court of Canterbury, the London Commissary Court, and the Court of Arches, to produce a total of 1,500 biographies of individual servants (1,181 female and 319 male).[22] In addition, a small number of domestic servants who appeared as witnesses in apprenticeship disputes at the City of London's Mayor's Court were sampled for comparison.[23] The provenance of these sources is listed below:

1. London Metropolitan Archive (LMA), series DL/C, vols 236–73 and 631–8, Bishop of London Consistory Court depositions series, 1669–1752.
2. Guildhall Manuscripts (GHMS), series 9065 A/9 to 11 inclusive, London Commissary Court depositions.
3. Lambeth Palace Library (LPL), series Eee 9 to 11 inclusive, Court of Arches depositions.
4. Public Record Office (PRO), series PROB 24/34 to 61 inclusive, Prerogative Court of Canterbury depositions.
5. Corporation of London Record Office (CLRO), series MC/6/111–71, Mayor's Court depositions, 1661–4.

The courts of the ecclesiastical jurisdiction have been the subject of some scrutiny in the last few decades, though only a few works have dealt with London or the period after 1660. They have demonstrated the early modern popularity of these courts, especially for the prosecution of defamation and matrimonial disputes, but also their decline (in terms of the volume of business) in the late seventeenth and eighteenth centuries. Despite this decline, the surviving records contain thousands of depositions given by an extremely wide range of Londoners, and canon law (embodying many of the principles of Roman law) ensured that testimony given in private was

---

22 I am grateful to Dr Peter Earle for sharing some of his data from the Prerogative and Commissary courts and the Court of Arches; his selection procedures are detailed in his *A City Full of People: Men and Women of London, 1650–1750* (London, 1994), pp. 263–77. For servants as church court witnesses, see L. Stone, *Road to Divorce: England 1530–1987* (Oxford, 1990), pp. 220–30.
23 For this source, see M. Pelling, 'Child health as a social value', reprinted in her *The Common Lot: Sickness, Medical Occupations and the Urban Poor in Early Modern England* (Harlow, 1998).

transcribed longhand by the clerk. Witnesses were usually asked, in order to establish their social 'credit', for a range of biographical details — how old they were; where they were born; where, for whom and for how long they had worked within the previous seven years; and so on — and often provided rich information on their labour (if they worked) and on relations within their households and in the wider London neighbourhoods in which they lived. The research for this book has therefore involved the construction of a prosopography of a significant part of London's working population.

The historian who has worked most extensively on these records to reconstruct the society and economy of early modern London, Peter Earle, has affirmed that they give a fair representation of the female population of the metropolis, but less so the male.[24] Yet there is reason to believe that both male and female domestic servants are particularly well represented in the depositions: the broad 'middling' status of the bulk of those bringing cases to the church courts in the metropolis, and the fair smattering of gentry and higher-status litigants (particularly in matrimonial disputes at the London Consistory court), ensured that most litigants employed domestic servants. The classes of case that were brought to these courts — predominantly defamation, matrimonial, and probate in order of frequency — took place in, around or near servant-employing households, and usually involved matters (extra-marital affairs, domestic violence, slander) that servants could hardly fail to witness.[25] Problems created by the coaching of witnesses by lawyers hardly arise in Chapters Three and Four, but are addressed where they might intervene in the analysis of household relations.

Rich though the church court depositions are, they are not without their drawbacks, like all sources for early modern social history. The need for witnesses to possess a minimum of social 'credit' suggests that the youngest and very poorest servants, particularly the poorest women and girls, may have been absent;[26] the preponderance of matrimonial disputes in wealthy families in the early eighteenth-century Consistory court meant that well-paid servants in the larger London households, especially menservants, were over-represented in that period. It is nigh impossible to verify the general plausibility or representativeness of the sources, since nothing precisely

24   P. Earle, 'The female labour market in London in the late seventeenth and early eighteenth centuries', *Economic History Review*, **42** (3) (1989); his *City Full of People*, pp. 269–73.

25   T. Meldrum, 'A women's court in London: defamation at the Bishop of London's Consistory Court, 1700–1745', *London Journal* **19** (1) (1994), 2, Table 1; Earle, *City Full of People*, p. 266 and *passim*.

26   Earle, *City Full of People*, p. 269. A similar problem was noted for the York depositions in the late medieval period: P.J.P. Goldberg, *Women, Work and Life Cycle in a Medieval Economy: Women in York and Yorkshire c.1300–1520* (Oxford, 1992), pp. 168–72.

comparable exists for the social and economic history of early modern London; but it is possible to verify the internal consistency of the characteristics of witnesses from the various church courts, as Earle has done with far larger samples.[27] The largely self-selecting servants found in quantifiable numbers in parish settlement examinations have been useful, but their bias towards older, more static and possibly poorer London domestic servants (not to mention the paucity of information on their working lives) serves to highlight the comparative adequacy of the church court depositions rather than the reverse.[28] Through sensitive use, the latter yield quantitative and qualitative data of incomparable depth for the period.

Structure of the book

This introduction has sought to establish the importance of London domestic service in the period under scrutiny, introduce the historical literature on the subject, and offer working definitions of the book's subjects. While domestic service had a significant impact on pre-modern life, the historiography retains a dated feel about it, utilising a limited range of sources, presenting gentry-made perspectives on the subject, and recently being over-determined by the concerns of historians of nineteenth- and twentieth-century service. The history of early modern youth has offered the most promising departures, but while these authors' passing interest in domestic service is understandable, less so was their relative lack of concern over gender. Contemporary definitions, explicitly or implicitly, took gender differences on board regardless of the alleged 'feminisation' of service that historians of modern service assume; but they also demonstrated an understanding of a distinct category of explicitly domestic servants well before such historians would allow.

Gender and life-cycle themes are central to this book, and its chapters will tackle the story of domestic service in London between 1660 and 1750 in the following manner. Chapter Two examines the social and economic context of London as an undeniably exceptional environment in the period, but also in some senses a microcosm of urban western European life; as such, the discussion leads on to the question of domestic service's definition. Chapter Three outlines the contemporary literature describing and prescribing the nature of service, the ideal nature of authority in the households

27 Earle, *City Full of People*, pp. 266–8.
28 Kent, 'Ubiquitous but invisible'.

in which servants lived, and their roles relative to their masters and mistresses. It examines the relevance of notions of patriarchy to an understanding of service and mastery, and the attempts employers and the state made to control the overwhelmingly young people who populated domestic service at this time. The fourth chapter focuses on the nature of relationships between servants and their employers that seem to have been prevalent in the metropolis in the late seventeenth and early eighteenth centuries. Did the ideal rhetoric of the early modern inclusive 'family', which embraced servants as much as blood kin, have any real purchase, or were domestic servants cast outside an increasingly 'private' nuclear family? Chapter Five examines domestic service as work, trying to identify the ways the occupation may be seen as a collection of economic as much as social relations. The degree to which gender and variation in household size affect the nature of domestic labour will swiftly become apparent as service work is sifted into drudging 'housewifery' and the 'idle luxury' performed in the largest households. The sixth and last substantive chapter considers remuneration, and the extent to which domestics participated in a moral economy of service in which mixed forms of earnings — wages as well as perks and vails, or tips — retained their importance. In conclusion, the book is drawn together by discussing the fortunes of those who left service; it is completed by a Bibliographical essay in which the literature on domestic service is discussed thematically for those who wish to pursue the subject further. But next, Chapter Two considers the metropolitan context.

CHAPTER TWO

Metropolitan service: the London context

London's economy

London provides the focus of the present study not simply through record availability (although this is important), but because it was the acknowledged centre of domestic service in Britain in the period under study.[1] The demographic and spatial expansion of the metropolis involved migration-fuelled population growth that nearly trebled the number of London's residents over the seventeenth century from some 200,000 in 1600 to over 550,000 by the beginning of the eighteenth century, and which resulted in a female majority at least from 1695. By then, London's population constituted some 11 per cent of England and Wales's total, with the next largest town, Norwich, only housing approximately 30,000 people: it is true that urban Britain would expand over the eighteenth century, but in 1700 London's pre-eminence was indisputable.[2]

As the English centre of manufacture, commerce and mercantile wealth, as well as of government, law and professions, London in the late seventeenth and early eighteenth centuries is credited with the making of a

---

1   B. Hill, *Servants: English Domestics in the Eighteenth Century* (Oxford, 1996), p. 4: she insinuates that I fail to see the exceptional nature of London as a place of employment for domestic servants (p. 41), but of course it is precisely because of its unique qualities that it is worth studying. However, until further local studies are conducted, there is nothing to suggest that some of the conclusions reached in this book do not have wider applicability upon early modern urban domestic service.

2   V. Harding, 'The population of London, 1550–1750: a review of the published evidence', *London Journal* **15** (2) (1990), 112, Table 1; P. Corfield, *The Impact of English Towns 1700–1800* (London, 1982), pp. 10, 15, 66, 99.

vibrant middle class. A resurgent literature on the economic and cultural history of consumption has offered convincing demand-led explanations for the increasing significance of both the 'middling sorts of people' and the more frequently resident gentry and nobility in Augustan London. It should come as no surprise that one repercussion of expansion and wealth-generation was a new and increasingly repressive rhetoric of control, with legal and institutional machinery to back it up, developed in London between 1689 and 1750 and often aimed at servants. But even if some contemporaries viewed servants as the enemy within metropolitan households, undoubtedly one way in which these metropolitan middling groups consumed was by hiring and retaining domestic servants. Indeed, this was arguably an essential component in the construction of middling identity in London.[3]

If the story so far has stressed rapid change, recent work on the structures of female employment in particular in London has highlighted long-term continuities. Schwarz concurs with Earle's work on the London female labour market when comparing the structure of female labour exhibited in the 1851 census to that apparent from church court depositions in the period 1695–1725, writing that 'the significant point is that there has not been much change from the eighteenth century'. Domestic service remained the largest sector of working women's employment across those 150 years, and while the evidential security of such assumptions is shaky, Bennett's work on female labour in London at the time of the 1381 poll tax suggests that the city housed a substantial number of young women in recognisable forms of domestic service even then.[4]

How many domestic servants were there, then, in London in the period under scrutiny? Gregory King, one of London's first great statisticians, gave a figure for London (calculated from the Marriage Duties' assessments of 1695 for the City of London, but embracing the whole metropolis) of 68,000

---

3   P. Earle, *The Making of the English Middle Class: Business, Society and Family Life in London, 1660–1730* (London, 1989), Chapters 1, 2 and 8; P. Earle, *A City Full of People: Men and Women of London, 1650–1750* (London, 1994), p. 124 and *passim*; J. Brewer and R. Porter, eds, *Consumption and the World of Goods* (London, 1993); J. Beattie, 'London crime and the making of the "Bloody Code", 1689–1718', in L. Davison, T. Hitchcock, T. Keirn and R.B. Shoemaker, eds, *Stilling the Grumbling Hive: The Response to Social and Economic Problems in England, 1689–1750* (Stroud, 1992).

4   L.D. Schwarz, *London in the Age of Industrialisation: Entrepreneurs, Labour Force and Living Conditions, 1700–1850* (Cambridge, 1992), p. 17: see also p. 16, Figure 1.5, and p. 24, Figure 1.8; P. Earle, 'The female labour market in London in the late seventeenth and early eighteenth centuries', *Economic History Review*, **42** (3) (1989), 341–2, and his *City Full of People*, pp. 115–16; J. Bennett, 'Medieval women, modern women: across the great divide', in D. Aers, ed., *Culture and History 1350–1600: Essays on English Communities, Identities and Writing* (Brighton, 1992).

servants, or 13 per cent of the metropolitan population, a figure that clearly included apprentices and some journeymen as well as domestic servants; this contrasts with his findings for 'other cities and great towns', at 11 per cent, and for 'villages and hamlets', at 10 per cent. However, Jonas Hanway estimated in 1767 that one-thirteenth (7.7 per cent) of the total population of London, or 50,000 people, were in exclusively domestic service at that time: for comparison's sake, adding together indoor and outdoor servants found in London's 1851 census gives a proportion of 8.5 per cent. Earle has estimated that at the turn of the eighteenth century, the proportion of London's population in domestic service, male and female, was also around one-thirteenth, or 7.7 per cent, and this seems plausible as far as it is possible to tell with any certainty. Taking the benchmark of a minimum population figure at 550,000 for 1700, this generates a base level of between 35,750 and 49,500 individual servants, and even a conservative estimate of population for the mid-eighteenth century means many more than that by 1750.[5]

This proportion may be compared with those from other English urban populations in the seventeenth century: Goose's findings for Cambridge (like London, an economy with a large service sector) from listings in the 1620s is closest at 7.86 per cent, whereas studies by Souden using Marriage Duties' assessments in the 1690s for Bristol, Gloucester, Leicester, Lichfield and Southampton fall between 7.9 and 11.6 per cent. Similar studies for London in 1695 also using the Marriage Duties' assessments have emphasised the City of London's distinctive household structure — fewer resident children but larger overall household size — and shown that servants formed between 20.9 and 23.5 per cent of the population. These last proportions fall well outside contemporary estimates, and a few notes of caution must be sounded here: the sources used in these findings only very rarely distinguish between types of servant, and male apprentices were not excluded; and they deal with the City of London rather than the metropolis as a whole, most notably excluding the domestic servant-saturated West End. But these historians have assumed, fairly, that most female 'servants' in urban households would have been domestics, although it would be most unwise to rule out some female, especially parish, apprentices. One-

---

5   G. King, *Natural and Political Observations upon the State and Condition of England*, reproduced in
    J. Thirsk and J. Cooper, eds, *Seventeenth-Century Economic Documents* (Oxford, 1972), p. 773;
    J. Hanway, *Letters on the Importance of Preserving the Rising Generation of the Labouring Part of Our Fellow Subjects*, 2 vols (London, 1767), II, p. 158; Schwarz, *London in the Age of Industrialisation*, p. 258; Earle, *English Middle Class*, p. 76, n. 187; T. Meldrum, 'Domestic service in London, 1660–1750: gender, life cycle, work and household relations', unpublished University of London PhD thesis (1996).

Table 2.1 Distribution of servants in two City of London parishes, 1690s

Number of staff in household	Number of households		Number of servants		Percentage female
	N	%	Female	Male	
1 servant	100	56.8	96	4	96.0
2 servants	37	21.0	62	12	83.8
3 servants	20	11.4	54	6	90.0
4 servants	7	4.0	16	12	57.1
5 servants	7	4.0	21	14	60.0
6 or more servants	5	2.8	22	17	56.4
Total	176	100.0	271	65	80.7

Source: Earle, *City Full of People*, Table 4.6, p. 125.

thirteenth of London's entire population remains a more plausible metropolitan figure.[6]

Structures of London domestic service

A study of the 1695 Marriage Duties' assessments in two of the few City of London parishes whose records clearly distinguished between domestic and other servants in the household, St Mary le Bow and St Michael Bassishaw, showed that almost 81 per cent of all servants were women (see Table 2.1). As can be seen, over 89 per cent of servant-employing households had one to three servants, and more than 84 per cent of the servants employed within them were women. Clear differences must be acknowledged between upper servants and 'drudges'[7]: most of the former were in households of

---

6   N. Goose, 'Household size and structure in early-Stuart Cambridge', reproduced in J. Barry, ed., *The Tudor and Stuart Town: A Reader in English Urban History 1530–1688* (London, 1990), pp. 106, 107, Table 10; D. Souden, 'Migrants and the population structure of later seventeenth-century provincial cities and market towns', in P. Clark, ed., *The Transformation of English Provincial Towns 1600–1800* (London, 1984), pp. 150, Table 17, 152; R. Wall, 'Regional and temporal variations in English household structure from 1650', in J. Hobcraft and P. Rees, eds, *Regional Demographic Development* (London, 1977), pp. 101 and 107, Table 4.10; S.M. Macfarlane, 'Studies in poverty and poor relief in London at the end of the seventeenth century', unpublished DPhil. thesis, University of Oxford (1982), pp. 64–73, esp. Table 2.11.

7   J.J. Hecht, *The Domestic Servant Class in Eighteenth-Century England* (London, 1956), p. 35; P. Horn, *The Rise and Fall of the Victorian Domestic Servant* (Dublin, 1975), p. 3.

Table 2.2 London servant population, by gender and date of deposition

Gender	Current servants, by period				Ex-servants, all years
	1669–1694	1695–1714	1715–1752	All years	
Female	265	366	293	924	257
Male	64	86	122	272	47
Total	329	452	415	1,196	304
Percentage female	80.5	81.0	70.6	77.3	84.5

$N = 1,500$. Source: church court depositions.

more than three servants and were male; the latter were found in the smallest households and were overwhelmingly female. Wealthy City of London parishes cannot be taken as representative of the whole metropolis, of course, but a ratio of four female to one male is also supported by the church court deposition data, as demonstrated in Table 2.2. Unfortunately, at the London Consistory court in the second quarter of the eighteenth century, a small number of upper gentry and noble divorce cases ensured an over-representation of male servants, resulting in the apparent fall in the proportion of female servants between 1715 and 1752.[8] But it remains appropriate to assume a London-wide ratio of four female servants to every one male.

The servant sex ratio exhibited in Table 2.2 demonstrates that 'feminisation' as a modern process whereby domestic service became increasingly female from the eighteenth into the nineteenth centuries, has limited purchase as far as London is concerned.[9] The decisively gendered nature of London domestic service, highlighted by the data in Tables 2.1 and 2.2, is further reflected in figures for the age structure of servant church court witnesses (Table 2.3). The characteristic bulge in the 15 to 29 cohorts for current female domestic servants (those in service, or only temporarily out of place, when they gave their depositions); the peak at 20–24; the fairly rapid decline after 29; the fact that over three-quarters of current female servants were under 30; all these findings confirm that domestic service

---

8 For example, London Metropolitan Archive (henceforward LMA), DL/C/270 ff. 277 and passim, *Cholmondley* c. *Cholmondley*: 3 male and 4 female servant witnesses in 1736; DL/C/271 ff. 141 and passim, *Savile* c. *Savile*: 12 male and 7 female in 1736–7; DL/C/273 ff. 1 and passim, *Beaufort* c. *Beaufort*: 12 male and 4 female in 1742.

9 A point well made, on a national scale, by L. Schwarz, 'English servants and their employers during the eighteenth and nineteenth centuries', *Economic History Review* **LII** (2) (1999).

Table 2.3 Age structure of London domestic servants, 1660–1750

Age	Female servants		Male servants	
	Current servants	Ex-servants	Current servants	Ex-servants
To 14 years	7	0	1	1
15–19	178	13	17	4
20–4	339	36	80	4
25–9	184	57	53	11
Percentage under 30	*76.6*	*41.2*	*55.5*	*42.6*
30–4	105	60	49	4
35–9	41	31	31	4
40–4	40	19	17	4
45–9	7	11	9	3
50–4	5	13	9	3
55+	6	15	5	7
Unknown	12	2	1	2
Total	924	257	272	47

N (female) = 1,181. N (male) = 319. Source: church court depositions.

was generally a life-cycle occupation, particularly for women. This is re-emphasised by the shift up the age scale among female ex-servants (those who declared in their depositions that they had at some time been domestic servants), over half of whom were 30 years old or more. But a gender differential is apparent: over 40 per cent of male current servants were in service over the age of 30, suggesting that men had far more opportunities for long-term service. A key to this difference lies in domestic servants' marital status.

Unfortunately, male marital status was almost never mentioned in the depositions, and could only be deduced if testimony alluded to it.[10] However, the church courts considered female marital status (Table 2.4) a crucial element of women's 'character', so marriage and widowhood were always noted. When the clerk wrote *famula* or *famula domestica* at the top of the deposition, it incorporated the implication that the deponent was single; on this assumption, 86.1 per cent of current servants were single ('spinster' and 'unknown'). Service might have been a positive choice in place of

---

10 Sixteen current and five former male servants are known to have been married: church court depositions.

Table 2.4 Female domestic servant marital status, by date of deposition

Status	Current servants, by period				Ex-servants, all years (%)
	1669–1694	1695–1714	1715–1752	All years (%)	
Spinster	105	286	227	618 (66.9)	38 (14.8)
Widow	9	32	27	68 (7.4)	45 (17.5)
Wife	12	24	25	61 (6.6)	171 (66.5)
Unknown	139	24	14	177 (19.1)	3 (1.2)
Total	265	366	293	924 (100.0)	257 (100.0)

N = 1,181. Source: church court depositions.

marriage for a few, as Kent has alleged, but most women left service in their late 20s or early 30s: 84.0 per cent of former female servants were or had been married, suggesting that marriage was one of their prime reasons for departure. Any return to service was much more likely to have been motivated by bereavement and/or economic hardship, rather than an exercise of 'relative economic independence'.[11]

In-migration played a vital role in the expansion of London's population, and domestic service was a significant magnet in drawing young people to the metropolis. Overall, both female and male domestic servants exhibited a greater likelihood of having migrated to London than London's population as a whole, including well-known (male) migrant groups like freemen. Domestic service acted as the principal route of induction into the life of the metropolis for adolescent girls and young women, and was possibly just as important as apprenticeship for young men. As Table 2.5 demonstrates, male servants were prepared to travel even further than female: three out of four of the male migrants came from beyond the southern and eastern counties, disproportionately from the western and north-western counties, and from Wales and Ireland.[12]

11 D.A. Kent, 'Ubiquitous but invisible: female domestic servants in mid-eighteenth century London', *History Workshop Journal* **28** (Autumn, 1989), 115.
12 P. Clark and D. Souden, eds, *Migration and Society in Early Modern England* (London, 1987), pp. 35–8; Earle, *City Full of People*, pp. 42, 45, 47, Tables 2.3 and 2.4; D.V. Glass, 'Socio-economic status and occupations in the City of London at the end of the seventeenth century', in A.E.J. Hollaender and W. Kellaway, eds, *Studies in London History* (London, 1969), p. 387, Table 10; M.J. Kitch, 'Capital and kingdom: migration to later Stuart London', in A.L. Beier and R. Finlay, eds, *London 1500–1700: the Making of the Metropolis* (Harlow, 1986), pp. 226, 233, Table 30.

Table 2.5 London domestic servant origins, 1660–1750 (%)

Origins	Female (%)	Male (%)
London-born[a]	26.2	15.9
Non-London S/E[b]	30.8	21.2
Elsewhere	43.0	62.9
Total migrant	*73.8*	*84.1*
Totals	100.0	100.0

N (female) = 500; N (male) = 151. Source: church court depositions.
[a] Cities of London and Westminster, and parts of Middx., Kent and Surrey within the metropolis.
[b] Remainder of Middx., Surrey and Kent, with Herts., Essex, Sussex, Hants., Bucks., Beds., Oxon., Berks., Northants., Cambs., Lincs., Rutland, Hunts., Suffolk, Norfolk.

But the hardest factor to gauge is a migrant's motives for uprooting from one place and settling elsewhere, a perennial problem for anyone concerned with the study of population movement. In the early seventeenth century it seems that the death of a young female migrant's father was a compelling factor in her move to London,[13] but similar evidence for the later period is less forthcoming.

Servant witnesses were rather reticent on their links with people in London, and on whom they relied to smooth their plunge into the great unknown. Inferences can be drawn from the few available cases, and close family members were quoted most often as the vital connection, while other kin came next, and non-kin or 'friends' last, echoing Vivien Brodsky Elliott's findings for the early seventeenth century. These definitions in oral depositions will often be blurred: some 'cousins' may have been wider kin or non-relatives. When contemporaries used the word 'friends' they often elided distant family, godparents, old friends of the family or indeed any other interested party in a category of trusted guardian whose role regarding the young migrant was to act almost *in loco parentis*. Thomas Gregg left Scotland at the age of twenty to begin work in the parish of St James's, Westminster in the household of someone he or his family had known since he was six.[14]

---

13 V. Brodsky Elliott, 'Single women in the London marriage market: age, status and mobility, 1598–1619', in R.B. Outhwaite, ed., *Marriage and Society: Studies in the Social History of Marriage* (London, 1981), p. 90.
14 Brodsky Elliott, 'Single women', pp. 92–4; LMA, DL/C/243 f. 234, Thomas Gregg, 28/1/1691.

Other forms of introduction were evident: for instance, Sarah Jackson (aged sixteen) lodged at the household where her fourteen-year-old sister Elizabeth was servant and was taken on for just three weeks for her bed and board. Mary Moreton had married but she and her butcher husband 'met with misfortune' so they had to separate, and after a year and a half in lodgings someone at her place of abode put her in the way of a place in service. Twenty-three-year-old Thomas Jones was paying a visit to his friend John Gibbons at John's master's house in Holborn; although nothing was explicit in their depositions, both were from Wenvoe in Glamorgan and it seems quite likely that thirty-nine-year-old Gibbons had offered the younger man a welcome friendly face in the metropolis. Once servants had found their first job they were thrust into a network of information and gossip, described by one employer as the 'Intrigues of our Servant-maids', that could have informed them how high a wage they should expect and what sort of perks and tips (or 'vails') they ought to get, as well as helping them to find their next job.[15]

Church court depositions do not include many reasons for leaving home, but they do illustrate the actual process and timing of migration. Servants tended to leave home in their late teens and early twenties, often in 'steps' via jobs *en route*. Edmis Crowe, born in County Carlow in Ireland, left home at the age of sixteen to join the service of a captain in the British army and eventually served a colonel in London; Francesca Squire, born in Warwickshire, served in the household of a Worcestershire knight and an esquire of Bedfordshire, as well as serving a two-year spell in Northamptonshire before entering service in London; Mary Welbeck served in Essex and her home town of Canterbury, Kent, before taking a place in the City of London; and Edinburgh-born Robert Dow followed two of his five siblings to London first by serving as a gardener in Kingston, Surrey, and only then entered London service. As Peter Clark has phrased it, London operated like a set of 'revolving doors': for young people, movement towards the metropolis was not necessarily one-way and servants often returned home between jobs, or even worked elsewhere. Ellen Williams, from Flintshire, Wales, served in that county before coming to London, and between jobs in the metropolis returned home to serve 'amongst her relatives'.[16]

---

15   LMA, DL/C/243 f. 132, Sarah Jackson, 18/7/1690; DL/C/638 f. 281, Mary Moreton, 13/10/1749; DL/C/247 f. 181, Thomas Jones, and f. 182, John Gibbons, both 18/7/1701; Anon., *A Trip from St. James's to the Royal Exchange* (London, 1744).
16   LMA, DL/C/237 f. 102, Edmis Crowe, 20/3/1675; DL/C/242 f. 254, Francesca Squire, 10/2/1688; DL/C/243 f. 428, Mary Welbeck, 9/6/1693; DL/C/638 f. 255, Robert Dow, 30/10/1750; DL/C/249 f. 238, Ellen Williams, 23/12/1706; see also DL/C/250 f. 478, Penelope Barrett, 6/9/1709; Clark, 'Migration in England during the late seventeenth and early eighteenth centuries', in Clark and Souden, eds, *Migration and Society*, p. 232.

The twin alternatives of service in husbandry and textile manufacture must have loomed large for those considering a move to London, and for many would have constituted 'local and "intervening" opportunities', in Kitch's words. Regional and occupational specialisation occurred in industry as the old southern centres of woollen cloth-making declined, but new textiles took their place, while much manufacturing moved out to the north and west. 'Rural industries such as lace and straw-plaiting for hats', as Davison *et al.* have observed, 'were rapidly expanding in southern England during the late seventeenth and early eighteenth centuries, relying almost exclusively on cheap female labour'. Clark and Souden have called the decades after 1660 'the great age of the servant in husbandry', and its decline did not start until 'around 1750' in the south and east. While London itself was 'the greatest manufacturing city in Europe' by our period, female opportunities generally were narrow; work was casual and intermittent, like much male work, but for women it was found at the poorest and least skilled end of the scale.[17]

However, according to Snell, 'there is much evidence on the awareness of single women of their possibilities in London, particularly in domestic service', and it was a well-known fact that 'London and Middlesex money wages were far higher than those of the surrounding counties'. Eleanor Ashwood, after describing her places in London service, added that 'besides which she has lodged at several places in the country within the said time upon haymaking or harvest work': it was presumably only at that time of year that agricultural wages made leaving domestic service in London worthwhile. The evidence of the depositions suggests that the lure of the burgeoning London market for service may well have over-ridden, for part of the life cycle at least, other seemingly less glamorous and less well-paid alternatives, drawing women and men from distant parts. This would tend to reinforce the picture of distinctive post-Restoration female migration patterns painted by Clark and Souden, while at the same time highlighting the historical peculiarities of male domestic service: while male apprentices in this period were coming to London from a shrinking migrationary field, male servants (mostly to elite employers) were prepared to travel very long distances to don the livery.[18]

---

17 Kitch, 'Capital and kingdom', p. 239; C.G.A. Clay, *Economic Expansion and Social Change: England 1500–1700*, 2 vols. (London, 1984), II, pp. 13–22, 98–102; Davison *et al.*, eds, *Grumbling Hive*, xxii; Clark and Souden, eds, *Migration and Society*, p. 33; Earle, *English Middle Class*, p. 18, and his 'Female labour market', p. 342.

18 K.D.M. Snell, *Annals of the Labouring Poor: Social Change and Agrarian England 1660–1900* (Cambridge, 1985), pp. 81, 38; LMA, DL/C/255 f. 268, Eleanor Ashwood, 20/6/1715; Clark and Souden, eds, *Migration and Society*, p. 35; compare Earle, 'Female labour market', p. 333 and Kitch, 'Capital and kingdom', p. 230.

Table 2.6 Occupational status of London domestic servant-employers, 1660–1750

Employer	F	%	M	%	Employer	F	%	M	%
Knight/Noble	69	11.8	93	43.5	Other Building	5	0.9	1	0.5
Gent./Lady/Esq.	117	20.1	43	20.1	Other Manuf.	7	1.2	–	–
Officials	5	0.9	2	0.9	Medical non-prof.	10	1.7	2	0.9
Merchant	26	4.5	3	1.4	'Shop'	37	6.4	4	1.9
Professional	38	6.5	8	3.7	Sexual Services	4	0.7	–	–
Army/Navy	19	3.3	11	5.1	Other Services	11	1.9	4	1.9
Leatherworking	4	0.7	–	–	Distrib./Transport	34	5.8	4	1.9
Metalworking	13	2.2	–	–	Victualling	80	13.7	29	13.6
Textiles/Clothes	32	5.5	2	0.9	Other Food/Drink	18	3.1	2	0.9
Wood/Furniture	15	2.6	–	–	'Widow'	38	6.5	6	2.8

Totals: Female = 582 (100.0%), Male = 214 (100.0%).
Source: church court depositions; categories from Earle, *City Full of People*, Table A.7,
pp. 274–6.

Identifying the occupational status of those who employed servants is a difficult task. Two-thirds of male, but under half of female, servant witnesses described those who employed them at the time of (or immediately before) their deposition. Even fewer described their second, third or successive employers before that (Table 2.6). The gender discrepancy can partly be explained by the data themselves, since as many as 43.5 per cent of male servants worked for knights or the nobility, most likely to be identified by their employees given the great status of the former, and also, perhaps, the latter's vicarious ennoblement by association. But while this factor has its advantages, it does render the overall results somewhat untrustworthy, because it implies that non-elite employers are likely to have been omitted.[19]

Nonetheless, the deposition data offer a striking reminder of the preponderance of elite employers of menservants, which comprised over 63 per cent if the gentry are included (compared to under 32 per cent for female servants). It is further emphasised by the more restricted range of occupational sectors in which the services of male domestics were desired and/or could be afforded relative to female, and by the fact that victuallers and the gentry (largest single employers of women) hired similar proportions of

---

19 Kent's data from settlement examinations in Westminster, on the other hand, seriously underestimate numbers of gentry and noble employers (especially given the location) because 'yearly contracts were losing favour with those wealthy enough to employ [upper] servants': 'Ubiquitous but invisible', 119 and Table iv.

each. It comes as no surprise that large parts of the manufacturing trades and craft sectors employed no male domestic servants, since they were the largest employers of male apprentices. Yet it is interesting to note that middling employers in the merchant, professional and official categories were outweighed as employers of female servants by textile or clothing manufacturers and retailers, keepers of unidentified 'shops' and 'widows' without occupational designation (who may well have had 'shops' too), but also that most of them employed proportionately — and by implication numerically — far more women than men.

How long did servants stay in their 'places' of employment? Male servants appeared even more likely than their female counterparts to engage in what might be termed a 'settlement-achieving strategy' in London. At least a year in a place of service allowed individuals to gain a 'settlement', and therefore entitlement to poor relief, in the parish in which they had served. At least 68.5 per cent of menservants, and well over half of the female servants (a minimum of 57.9 per cent) did so: many of the remainder could not be counted due to a lack of information rather than through firm evidence to the contrary. Of course, servants deposing at the church courts were not necessarily in their first job any longer. Earle found that over half of his sample of female domestic servants had served twelve months or fewer, suggesting that they moved far more frequently than their early seventeenth-century equivalents, only 13.5 per cent of whom stayed for under a year. Even a majority of Kent's mid-eighteenth-century yearly-hired servants only served in one place for a year or less. While many servants were out of place in late seventeenth- and early eighteenth-century London, this change confirms the high level of demand for servants in the later period, and also adds weight to the assumption above that servants deliberately spent more time in their first job for the purposes of future security, in a period of relative stability rather than one representative of the rest of their service careers in London.[20]

Tables 2.7(a) and (b), constructed from the depositions of those servants who declared that they had served in at least three places, confirm the short terms of female servants' jobs but also add complexity. Firstly, comparing female servants' job tenure in the place they occupied when giving testimony

---

20 Earle, *City Full of People*, pp. 128–9, Table 4.7; V. Brodsky Elliott, 'Mobility and marriage in pre-industrial England: a demographic and social structural analysis of geographic and social mobility and aspects of marriage, 1570–1690, with particular reference to London and general reference to Middlesex, Kent, Essex and Hertfordshire', unpublished PhD thesis, University of Cambridge (1978), p. 125; Kent, 'Ubiquitous but invisible', 120–1 and Table v. For the law of settlement in our period, see J.S. Taylor, 'The impact of pauper settlement, 1691–1834', *Past and Present* **73** (1976).

Table 2.7(a) Female domestic servant tenure in place (in reverse order from date of deposition), 1660–1750

	Place one	Place two	Place three
Average stay, months	7.94	9.95	15.30
Standard deviation	10.16	12.55	20.27
N	215	191	186

Source: church court depositions.

Table 2.7(b) Male domestic servant tenure in place (in reverse order from date of deposition), 1660–1750

	Place one	Place two	Place three
Average stay, months	14.06	15.56	14.96
Standard deviation	15.64	14.99	14.42
N	50	47	44

Source: church court depositions.

(or most recently before that date) with the two previous jobs (second and third, in reverse order) demonstrates that the current or most recent tended to be shorter on average. It is not clear whether this was because some female servants had only just begun in that place when deposing or because their memories played tricks with them, causing them to exaggerate or to cite round years rather than irregular months for later places. There is no reason to suspect male servants' memories were any more reliable, and yet the second major complexity observed in these tables is the gender difference: the lengths of male tenures in place remained consistent, and also markedly longer than female servants' first and second jobs (in reverse order). The last point is clearly correlated with the finding above that menservants were far more likely to work for elite employers than women, the sector of servant-employers whose incomes were most stable as well as (usually) the most sizeable and who were therefore able to offer their servants career prospects.

For both genders the variation in tenure (expressed by standard deviation) was apparently extensive, even greater among female than male servants; but the average figures could be distorted by a few individuals remaining in a given place for long periods of time: Grace Egerton stayed in the job before that current when she deposed for ten years, and Catherine Mackernes had

24

been a servant in one place (two before the current) for nine years, while David Foulkes had spent seven years at the place he occupied when he deposed.[21] Once that factor is considered (not to mention the relatively small numbers of men who gave information on a minimum of three places), it is likely that the norm, particularly for women, was a succession of relatively short stays in place after a settlement had been established.

Useful definitions

Service and slavery

At this relatively early stage, it would be useful to establish what is meant by the apparently straightforward term 'domestic service' in its historical context. The ubiquity of the word 'servant' in pre-modern England was acknowledged by contemporaries. William Blackstone, the eighteenth-century lawyer, identified four 'sorts' or 'species of servants': apprentices; labourers; those 'in a superior, a ministerial capacity'; and 'menial servants, so called from being *intra moenia*, or domestics', who form this book's central concern. He began his discourse, 'Of Master and Servant', by distinguishing servants from slaves. Elsewhere masters might have rights to enslave through capture in war, by sale and purchase, or by the particular slave being born to slaves and therefore inheriting bondage. But 'pure and proper slavery does not, nay cannot, subsist in England', so 'the property that every man has in the service of his domestics' was 'acquired by the contract of hiring, and purchased by giving them wages', and while the Elizabethan Statute of Artificers required coercion into service under certain conditions, the relationship between master and servant was contractual.[22]

Somewhat disingenuously, however, Blackstone refused to rule out the possibility that slaves brought from elsewhere onto English soil might be in the 'perpetual service' of their masters, 'the same state of subjection for life which every apprentice submits to for the space of seven years'[23], and it

---

21 LMA, DL/C/638 f. 273, Grace Egerton, 5/10/1749; DL/C/241 f. 48, Catherine Mackernes, 26/5/1684; DL/C/250 f. 200, David Foulkes, 23/11/1708. See also DL/C/242 f. 150, Anne Middleton, 24/11/1687; DL/C/254 f. 260, Mary Apps, 12/6/1714; DL/C/255 f. 137, Elizabeth Cotton, 17/3/1715; Public Record Office (henceforward PRO), PROB 24/39 f. 236, Anne Snell, 16/1/1700; PROB 24/57 f. 275, Eleanor Hillman, 24/7/1719.

22 W. Blackstone, *Commentaries on the Laws of England*, 4 vols (London, 1765–9), I, pp. 411–15, 417; 5 Eliz.c.4. I am grateful to Margaret Hunt for allowing me to see some of her unpublished work on blacks, servitude and free labour in seventeenth- and eighteenth-century England.

23 Blackstone, *Commentaries*, pp. 412–13.

took a series of judgements in the late eighteenth and early nineteenth centuries before the status of slaves in England was clarified. In Somersett's case, a slave brought to England by his merchant owner ran away from his master, who decided to send him back to Virginia to be sold for his insolence. Granted a writ of *Habeas Corpus* Somersett was released from the vessel on which he was being held, and at the King's Bench his barrister, Francis Hargrave, sought to establish Blackstone's principle. Hargrave insisted that Somersett 'left his master's *service*, and that his refusing to return was the occasion of his being carried on board Mr Knowles's ship'. Mobility, a certain freedom of contract and its limited length were some of the criteria distinguishing servitude from slavery; but Lord Chief Justice Mansfield, the presiding judge, still resisted affirming a general principle that would have resulted in the release of all slaves within England.[24]

Slavery and service had long coexisted in Europe, but certainly from Spain's fifteenth-century *Reconquista* of Granada (if not from the earlier Crusades), slavery was becoming associated with heathen, with black peoples or with the exotic more generally, Christendom's 'other'. Medieval sugar-growing slave plantations in Sicily, Crete, Cyprus and the Balearics, followed towards the end of the fifteenth century by the Atlantic islands of the Canaries, were characterised by a western drift which prefigured such plantations in the Americas. But the author of a magisterial new book on New World slavery links his subject to the modern, not the primitive, averring that the scale and scope of slavery in the Americas gave it a 'novelty' that distinguished it from past enslavement because it occurred in new territory. Blackburn writes that 'it is significant that beyond a scattering of servants in Spain and Portugal, there were very few true slaves left in Western Europe by the end of the sixteenth century'.[25] In England, the Tudor attempt to recreate domestic slavery as a tool against vagrants in the Vagrancy Act of 1547 'was the most spectacular failure' and was repealed in 1550. Fifteen years later, Sir Thomas Smith was able to write that the Reformation had moderated slavery, 'finding more civil and gentle means and more equal to have done' what was effected by slaves before: in the minds of ruling elites slavery and service had become, it appears, conceptually distinct.[26]

---

24 F. Hargrave, *An Argument in the Case of James Somersett, a Negro, lately determined by the Court of King's Bench* (London, 1772), p. 4 (my emphasis), p. 46; J. Walvin, *Black Ivory: A History of British Slavery* (London, 1992), pp. 14–15: for Walvin the Somersett case 'signalled the end of slavery in England' (p. 305).

25 R. Blackburn, *The Making of New World Slavery: From the Baroque to the Modern, 1492–1800* (London, 1997), pp. 33, 62, 76–9 and *passim*.

26 1 Edw.VI.c.3, repealed by 3 & 4 Edw.VI.c.16; P. Slack, *Poverty and Policy in Tudor and Stuart England* (Harlow, 1988), p. 122; Blackstone, *Commentaries*, p. 412; Blackburn, *New World Slavery*, p. 57.

However, room for ambiguity existed even beyond our period. The same Lord Mansfield who effectively freed Somersett in 1772 also had the care (in the fullest sense of that word) of his nephew's bastard child by a slave woman. Elizabeth Dido's mother had been captured by an English vessel from the Spanish, and when her mother gave birth to a Mulatto baby, Elizabeth was handed over to Mansfield, who developed a genuine fondness for her. She was in effect employed as a domestic servant within the Lord Chief Justice's household, but was 'on friendly, familiar terms with the household and visitors' in the ambiguous position of many servants engaged in relatives' households. Yet when Mansfield died he left her £500 in his will, together with an annuity of £100, and the injunction that she was to be freed from enslavement. Not only did that document free Dido from the ambiguous position of slave on slave-free soil and ensure that she never needed to occupy any form of subordinate place again, it also exposed the ambivalence Mansfield had held over the blurred meanings of servility.[27]

Domestic and non-domestic service

In English early modern practice, social meanings of 'service' were in general fairly straightforward, but before a definition of specifically 'domestic' forms of service can be made, its other forms must be identified. Fortunately, agricultural service in husbandry has recently been the subject of a thorough body of research, allowing the historian to distinguish the patterns of migration, labour and marriage that marked out farm service by young people in rural England. At least for the period studied here, servants in husbandry were unmarried residents in an agricultural household, and terms of service were for a year at a time, although even here 'no simple distinction was possible' between those who did exclusively domestic work and other servants in these households.[28] Apprenticeship, particularly in urban areas, has long been a subject of historical enquiry, and the parameters of apprentices' service are well known: in London, livery companies organised training for young men formally through the seven-year apprenticeship indenture, by which they were enjoined to follow their masters' moral guidance and, generally, dwell in their masters' households. But it is with this urban group that most ambiguity is found, since in the London records the term 'servant' was often used to apply to domestic, apprentice and even, on occasion, journeyman alike.[29]

---

27   Walvin, *Black Ivory*.
28   A. Kussmaul, *Servants in Husbandry in Early Modern England* (Cambridge, 1981), pp. 5, 133–42.
29   See the discussion in Chapter Five.

Turning to the domestic variety, Marshall declared that 'the domestic servant must be a product of domestic life' with duties 'of a thoroughly domestic character'. She distinguished between households of different status and size, pointing to servant hierarchies in larger, wealthier households but observing that in the seventeenth century, 'most servants were engaged by families of more moderate standing', where 'women had always been more freely employed than men'. Hecht never offered a definition of 'domestic servant' as such, but was sure that collectively they constituted a 'servant class', and he concentrated on the households of the elite, referring to their value as 'a symbol of wealth', and pointing to several potential ambiguities. In families below the rank of the middling sort, 'who kept but a single maid . . . it was often an apprentice who played the role of foot-boy'; and amongst that rank's rural counterparts, 'frequently those who performed the duties of an indoor servant did outdoor work as well'. Earle, refining Hecht's observations, has described the employment of servants in London as if it were an index of comfort: it was one of the middling sort's defining characteristics and virtually anyone counting themselves among their number had servants (which, of course, does not preclude those below this social stratum from employing them).[30]

So far, then, 'domestic servant' would appear to have included full-time, live-in servants dwelling in households of middling status (in the broad use of that term) or higher, engaged (but not necessarily exclusively) in 'domestic' tasks, and usually remunerated at least partly by cash wages. Even in small households, the employment of a servant marked off a significant division of status, and a significant gender division was closely correlated with household size. By turning to the church court depositions, which form the most significant set of sources for this book, it is clear that in London between 1660 and 1750, such households varied greatly in size and complexity. This has important implications both for the gendered structures of service and for servants' working lives: there was a vast gulf between the burden and type of work experienced by, for instance, an employee of Mr Hickey of Richmond in 1709, who kept rooms for lodgers, and the vast 'family' of the Duke and Duchess of Beaufort in the 1740s.

Mary Shrubb served 'as Hickey's maidservant and did sometimes make clean his dishes and clean his rooms and was his only servant'. By contrast, sixteen servants (mostly male) from the Beauforts' family gave testimony at the Bishop of London's Consistory court in 1742, and it is quite likely the divided household of the Duke and Duchess (by then living firmly apart)

---

30 Marshall, *English Domestic Servant*, pp. 3, 5, 7; Hecht, *Domestic Servant Class*, pp. 2, 8–9; Earle, *English Middle Class*, pp. 218–29.

was far larger in total than that. These two examples represent the extremes of the market for service, and a half-way household does make the occasional appearance. Elizabeth Davis was hired in 1708 by a seamstress and her husband, a barber and periwig-maker, for 'household work as washing and dressing [the meat]' in a household which may have had several servants and certainly had a small complement of apprentices, who did not appear to be involved in these tasks. Not uncommonly for a family of this size, a char came in to clean the lodgers' quarters and the laundry was sent out to a laundress or washer-woman.[31]

Ambiguous categories

Despite the apparent clarity of such a tripartite division of household size — small (one servant), medium (several domestic servants, some apprentices and part-time assistance), and large (many servants, both male and female) — the definition of 'domestic servant' in late seventeenth- and early eighteenth-century London demands a consideration of some of the ambiguities on the margins, beginning with a closer look at service as full-time, live-in work. The life-cycle transition that many women in London made from servant to char, scourer and/or washer-woman[32] meant women often changed their residence but not the nature of their labour. Catherine Frankitt, deposing as a witness at the London Consistory court in May 1710, said that 'for these two years last past [she] hath been and now is char-woman to Mr Andrew Gough and his family . . . [and] hath been almost daily . . . to do the offices and business of a servant there'.[33] The difference between Catherine and a domestic servant lay in the fact that she did not live in their household, but travelled in 'almost daily' from a neighbouring parish.

Others, however, did jobs that cannot be so easily distinguished from that of servant. The Inns of Court, located between the City of London and the growing West End, housed many gentlemen largely but by no means exclusively involved in the legal profession; yet while they constituted a concentration of potential and actual servant-employers, the particular conditions that prevailed ensured less formal employment structures. Seventeen-year-old spinster Susannah Colsell of Grays Inn Lane knew John Radford, Esq., counsellor at law, since she 'used to clean his rooms, go on

---

31 LMA, DL/C/251 f. 185, Mary Shrubb, 26/11/1709; DL/C/273 ff. 1 to 65, Beaufort
    c. Beaufort (12 male but only 4 female servant witnesses); DL/C/250 f. 197, Elizabeth
    Davis, 18/11/1708.
32 Earle, *City Full of People*, pp. 118–19.
33 LMA, DL/C/251 f. 396, Catherine Frankitt, 15/5/1710; see also DL/C/249 f. 266,
    Margaret Price, 18/2/1707.

his errands and wait on him'; but during the six years that she undertook those tasks, she had always lived with her father despite her 'services'. Young female lodgers sometimes behaved in the reverse situation, resident and practising 'service' but not necessarily employed as a servant. Sarah Blith was living with her mother in lodgings after leaving a place in service, but she complied when the householder asked her to 'put some sheets on the bed', and she seems to have fetched a lodger a 'pot of drink' and to have cleaned his shoes. There was no mention of remuneration of any kind.[34]

Servants and kin

Relatives and 'friends' played a vital role in assisting young people to a place in the metropolis, thereby acting as a valuable conduit in the difficult and sometimes dangerous process of assimilation. For many of those servants, they also acted as a safe haven when out of place, but at what point did they become these young people's employers? Eighteen-year-old Hannah Bent lodged with distant relatives for the fairly long period of eight months when she found herself out of place in 1750, but she also described herself taking breakfast up to their bedroom. While this could well have been accepted practice for teenage female relatives who were being granted free bed and board, her behaviour is akin to that of working servants and there is no mention of other servants in the household.[35]

Young girls seem to have acquainted themselves with service by accompanying their older sisters at work in their employers' households. Eighteen-year-old Sarah Gamlyn said she was 'maintained by her father', but nine months before making her deposition, her sister's master in Faversham had 'parted with his cookmaid' so Sarah joined the household 'to assist her [elder] sister' Margaret. She 'sometimes went on an errand or did some household business for [her sister's then mistress] at her desire'. Only three months before deposing she went to Richmond 'and lay with her sister' (i.e. shared her bed like another household servant) till Margaret lost her job, when they went to lodgings together in the Strand. However, her sister put a slightly different gloss on Sarah's state of employment when she explained that, 'she and her sister being obliged to go to service for a livelihood', they

---

34 PRO, PROB 24/55 f. 19, Susannah Colsell, 6/4/1716. See also LMA, DL/C/245 f. 233, Honor Fletcher, 7/6/1697; PROB 24/45 f. 7, Tabitha Fellow, 26/1/1706; DL/C/245 f. 160, Sarah Blith, 18/6/1696.

35 LMA, DL/C/638 f. 190, Hannah Bent, 2/1/1750. See also DL/C/272 f. 21, Ann Hopson, 2/2/1738; PRO, PROB 24/42 f. 597, Dorothy Overy, 17/11/1703.

were 'being prevented from so doing' because of the subpoenas forcing them to testify at the London Consistory court.[36]

Casual service

Temporary loss of assistance in the home could be difficult for house-holders, and temporary work to tide those mistresses over was another form of 'casual' service. Hannah Gyles, a former servant since married to a carpenter, came briefly out of retirement to help a grocer: as she was 'destitute of a maid servant, [the grocer] did send to Hannah to come to her and assist her till such time as her maid should come to her', so she stayed two days. Mary Clark 'for six years past used to wash and iron' for a woman in St Bride's, acting 'as her servant when she hath happened to have no other'. Rachel Marlow was lent by her mistress to one of her friends when temporarily without a servant, while Arabella Doell, her former employers 'importuning her to come and live with them, she accordingly at their request went and lived with them as their servant though not hired to be so' and stayed for a whole year.[37] There is an implication here that 'real' service carried the contractual weight of a mutual acknowledgement of employment, a necessary ingredient over and above service work and living-in.

For some London women, there is a sense that service may have been only one among several employments held serially or simultaneously with other metropolitan by-employments or even as a by-employment itself. Sarah Blith, mentioned above, stated that for the twelve years up to making her deposition she 'gets her living by service and winding silk'. The wives of sailors often resorted to service when their husbands were at sea, temporarily leaving their own households for those of their employers: Mary Trevillian (married to a sailor *si inter vivos existit*) was housekeeper to a salesman, and declared that 'when out of service [she] maintained herself by her needle and was partly subsisted by her husband'. Others combined service with needlework, cleaning silks and doing seasonal harvest work. Men also took casual service work, possibly when trade dipped, or perhaps for reasons of honour and status: Christopher Henley was 'by profession a barber surgeon and kept a house and family in Back Lane, Stepney except when out at sea

---

36 LMA, DL/C/266 f. 11, Sarah Gamlyn, 14/6/1729; f. 7, Margaret Gamlyn, 11/6/1729. See also DL/C/243 f. 132, Sarah Jackson; and f. 132ᵛ, Elizabeth Jackson, both 18/7/1690.
37 LMA, DL/C/248 f. 149, Hannah Gyles, 4/5/1704; DL/C/637 f. 604, Mary Clark, 27/11/1747; DL/C/273 f. 436, Rachel Marlow, 7/10/1743; DL/C/257 f. 212, Arabella Doell, 6/6/1718.

and other places with Sir Thomas Hardy, whom he serves in capacity of his gentleman'.[38]

It would be most unwise to assume that any early modern institution, whose origins lay far further back in time, would be defined by clean lines of demarcation, and service is no exception. By beating the bounds of casual service, pre-service and part-time service in London's myriad households, a picture emerges nonetheless of the general determinants of domestic service: subordination to a master and/or a mistress (for whom the collective noun 'employers' will often be used in the book); living-in at the place of work; receiving some form of remuneration for labour in the household; but, unlike the more rigid conventions and legal strictures of service in husbandry or apprenticeship, working for terms of a more flexible length and under more flexible contractual arrangements. The church court depositions demonstrate that the concept of a specifically *domestic* form of servant was well understood in London in 1660, as it had been in 'such major [late-medieval] towns as Nuremberg, Ypres, Reims, Coventry and York' as well as London.[39] This is the briefest of sketches, and in a very real sense 'domestic service' is difficult to define in a vacuum before this book has undertaken a thorough examination of the relations domestic servants had with their employers, and the work they did.

Conclusion

This chapter has sought to demonstrate the social and economic contexts of domestic service in London, and the structures it exhibited during the late seventeenth and early eighteenth centuries. The metropolis was shown to have been the most significant single centre of the employment of domestic servants in pre-modern England. The growth of London in this period was closely related to an expansion in the 'middling sorts' and consequent rises in levels of consumption. An increasing demand for services was one concomitant of that consumption and as the figures discussed above

---

38   LMA, DL/C/245 f. 160; see also DL/C/632 f. 449, Ann Barrow, 10/12/1712; Lambeth Palace Library (henceforward LPL), D.11 f. 320, Sarah Peters, 5/6/1716; DL/C/255 f. 268, Eleanor Ashwood, 20/6/1715; PRO, PROB 24/59 f. 345, Mary Trevillian, 18/9/1721. PROB 24/49 f. 257, Christopher Henley, 20/2/1710; and also DL/C/266 f. 3, Robert Parry, 7/6/1729; DL/C/250 f. 193, James Harris, 18/11/1708.

39   P.J.P. Goldberg, 'Marriage, migration and servanthood: the York cause paper evidence', in Goldberg, ed., *Woman is a Worthy Wight: Women in English Society* c.*1200–1500* (Stroud, 1992), p. 2; and his *Women, Work and Life Cycle in a Medieval Economy: Women in York and Yorkshire* c.*1300–1520* (Oxford, 1992), pp. 186–94.

demonstrated, nearly fifty thousand servants — in a ratio of four women to one man — were likely to have been employed at any given time in this period, most of whom were born outside London. Service was confirmed as a life-cycle occupation for women, undertaken until the mid- or late twenties mostly before marriage (and sometimes after, in widowhood); for men, who tended to work in larger households, longer careers were possible and although data regarding their marital status was elusive, it seems possible that more married men remained in service. The gendered nature of domestic service in the capital was further emphasised by the analysis of servants' employers and their terms in place, as menservants were seen to be far more likely to work for elite employers and to stay (on average) longer in any one employment than their female counterparts.

Yet for such a significant sector of employment within London, defining its members could be frustratingly imprecise. The attention by the law to slavery, particularly in the eighteenth century, helped to clarify the boundaries between service and bondage; and London's lack of agriculture meant that, even if some careers embraced both, domestic service was distinct from service in husbandry. Apprenticeship poses some problems for the historian because, even though the institution was regulated by livery companies (at least for boys), the generic term 'servant' was often used to apply to those with indentures and sometimes those after they had served their term, namely journeymen. By the late seventeenth century it would appear that blood relatives and 'friends' were more important as assistants for migrants in the transition into the London labour market rather than as employers in their own right, although relatives already in service could be useful contacts too. The evidence on rapid turnover of servants in places further emphasises the importance of a casual service sector for those in between places or for those — like sailors' wives — for whom a full-time, live-in place was undesirable. Nevertheless, a serviceable working definition has been established to enable us to analyse the nature of mastery and authority.

CHAPTER THREE

Service, mastery and authority

I mean he never speaks truth at all, — that's all. He will lie like a
chambermaid, or a woman of quality's porter. Now that is a fault.
W. Congreve, *The Way of the World* I, i

Introduction

London teemed with domestic servants in the late seventeenth and early
eighteenth centuries. Ever-present in the paintings both of domestic interiors and of street-scenes, their ubiquity comes down to us most colourfully
in the dramatic literature of the day. Congreve's *The Way of the World* (1700)
or his *Love for Love* (1695), Farquhar's *The Constant Couple* (1699) or his *The
Recruiting Officer* (1706) were not all set in London but were all performed
first on the London stage for theatregoers and the servants who accompanied them. They operated as errand-runners and scene-changers —
'footmen' are rarely enumerated, let alone named, in the published lists of
characters — or as butts for ribaldry: in *The Way of the World*, Mrs Millament's
eponymous waiting woman Mincing is lampooned for her mispronuncia-
tion, while the rough Salopian Sir Wilfull declares of an anonymous manservant, 'Oons, this fellow knows less than a starling; I don't think a' knows
his own name'. They were useful as confidantes and co-conspirators, particularly for the principal female characters: *The Recruiting Officer's* Melinda,
despite recognising that Lucy is 'a servant, and a secret would make you
saucy', simply must confide in her. 'Cause or no cause, I must not lose
the pleasure of chiding when I please', she says: 'women must discharge
their vapours somewhere, and before we get husbands, our servants must

34

expect to bear with 'em' — and so the secret is revealed and the plot advanced.[1]

Servants were as instrumental in the mechanics of the stage as they were in the machinery of the middling or gentry household. Like the subject of Witwoud's complaint cited in the epigraph above, they served to reflect the inconstancy and duplicity of the higher-status characters. Their absence from a character's side, however, helped to denote loss of status, as the disbanded Colonel Standard demonstrated in *The Constant Couple*. 'Tis one of the greatest curses of poverty', he opines when bested in banter by Lady Lurewell's waiting woman, 'to be the jest of chambermaids!' But the significance of service as an early modern social institution is further emphasised by the earnest, ironic or sycophantic use of 'your servant!' in greeting or departing form others — earnestly when directed at firm friends or someone of decisively higher status, ironically at those presumed beneath the speaker, and with cloying sycophancy when addressing those from whom a favour or office is desired. It takes a character without metropolitan guile like the rustic Sir Wilfull, slighted by his half-brother Witwoud, to puncture the insincere airs of the town: 'Your servant! Why, yours, sir. Your servant again, 's'heart, and your friend and servant to that, and a [*puff*] and a flapdragon for your service. Sir; and a hare's foot, and a hare's scut for your service, an' you be so cold and so courtly!'[2]

These exchanges, as much by default as by design, further serve to emphasise domestic servants' presence at the very core of Christian civil society. It was not on the stage but in the household that the skeins of service and mastery were spun into a complex web of power relations within the bounds of the 'family', a term used by contemporaries to include servants and apprentices as well as blood relations. Scripture enjoined masters and mistresses to govern their families and servants to obey their superiors, and a wealth of prescriptive literature written by divines and laymen and women attempted to translate spiritual injunction for their own times. But households, of course, did not function in isolation, and the neighbourhoods and parishes of the metropolis in which they lived influenced the way discipline was exerted over servants. Powers invested at the local level in parish officers and magistrates impacted upon servants and their employers as regulatory authority; gossip and slander within the

---

1 E.S. Rump, ed., *The Comedies of William Congreve* (Harmondsworth, 1985), pp. 348, 366: see also Congreve's *Love for Love* in the same volume; G. Farquhar, *The Recruiting Officer*, Methuen Drama edn (London, 1988), p. 55; also Farquhar, *The Constant Couple*, Swan Theatre Plays edn (London, 1988).
2 Farquhar, *The Constant Couple*, p. 10; Rump, ed., *Comedies of William Congreve*, p. 368.

wider community exposed the vulnerability of an individual or household's reputation to denigration, as Melinda's shared secret did with her maid Lucy. In other words, those in London households interacted with their local social milieux, ensuring that service involved a constant negotiation and renegotiation of authority against which ideal prescription could only fulminate.

Griffiths has recently described the repercussions of early modern authority as the 'politics of place' in which each individual 'had an appointed, divinely-ordained "place" in a subject relationship as governor or governed, according to progress along the life-course'. Links were made by prescriptive writers between 'place', piety, pedagogy and authority, but place also expressed 'a sympathetic sense of unity and mutuality'. 'Place', too, was used to describe not only the social order as a whole, but also the position or job occupied by a servant at any given time. 'Place' was therefore a distillation of the rhetoric of authority which social historians perceive within a wider understanding of politics. Wrightson, who has written extensively and persuasively on early modern social structure, describes politics as 'the manner in which relationships of power and authority, dominance and subordination are established and maintained, refused and modified', or in other words 'the political dimension of everyday life'.[3] The place domestic servants occupied in early modern society was political in Wrightson's sense because the disturbance of household order was perceived by those who profited from the maintenance of patriarchal power as a disruption of good governance. But since patriarchy in ideal, unadulterated form was so rich a draught, the faltering hand gripping the leaden chalice of authority was bound to spill some of that elixir. Households were not merely sites of oppression, paternally benign or otherwise: they were dwelling places whose occupants, differentiated by age, status and customary role, worked out the bounds of their domestic relations on a daily basis within and beyond social and economic parameters which tended to change only slowly.

The complexity of these relations within what was an avowedly hierarchical and stratified society once, under an older historiographical tradition, gave way inexorably to the eighteenth-century emergence of a more sharply-defined class society. But a number of factors recently have prompted, in the words of Barker and Chalus, the quest for a 'new conceptual framework' which moves 'beyond the boundaries of established models'. The dating of the origins of the 'middle class' in London to the late seventeenth century, the lengthening of the period of 'industrial revolution' (and its

---

3 P. Griffiths, *Youth and Authority: Formative Experiences in England, 1560–1640* (Oxford, 1996), pp. 63–71, esp. 66, 69; K. Wrightson, 'The politics of the parish in early modern England', in P. Griffiths, A. Fox and S. Hindle, eds, *The Experience of Authority in Early Modern England* (Basingstoke, 1996), p. 11.

rehabilitation under more complex formulations), and the critical reassessment of gendered 'separate spheres' have all rendered problematic any portrayal of the early modern/modern transition as one simply characterised by sharp social discontinuity.[4] Participating in this mood of reappraisal, the present chapter explores the diversity of modes of authority within London households and neighbourhoods. It will examine ideal forms of patriarchy through the legal, spiritual and prescriptive frameworks utilised and generated by contemporaries, to dissect the roles of masters and mistresses. By interrogating some of the most popular manuals addressed to domestic servants themselves, an account will be given of the expectations they were under and the strictures by which they were bound: their duties to employer and household, the impact of reputation on servants' lives, and the degree to which they might be punished or nurtured both within and beyond the household. The chapter will begin with a discussion of the parameters of patriarchy in servant-employing households.

Household discipline

Mastery

'The householder is called *Pater familias*, that is father of a family', Dod and Cleaver wrote in 1612, 'because he should have a fatherly care over his servants as if they were his children'.[5] This classic formulation of the ideal patriarchal role regarding masters as fathers to the servants in their families was repeated in a plethora of sermons, manuals and tracts throughout the sixteenth, seventeenth and eighteenth centuries, its lack of novelty apparently failing to dim the enthusiasm with which it was restated. Historians have widely acknowledged that early modern England, in Wrightson's words, 'was a patriarchal society in the sense that authority was conventionally vested in adult males generally and male household heads specifically'. Indeed, the patriarchal father, in theory at least, had long held sway over the pre-modern household. Reviewing early modern household and marriage advice manuals, Kathleen Davies has argued that 'what we are seeing

---

4   H. Barker and E. Chalus, eds, *Gender in Eighteenth-Century England: Roles, Representations and Responsibilities* (Harlow, 1997), p. 24; see also R.B. Shoemaker, *Gender in English Society: The Emergence of Separate Spheres?* (Harlow, 1998). For the broader historiographical debates about the 'long' eighteenth century, see the relevant section of the Bibliographical essay at the end of this book.

5   J. Dod and R. Cleaver, *A Godly Forme of Household Governement: for the Ordering of Private Families, According to the Direction of God's Word* (London, 1612).

in the early seventeenth century is a collection of descriptive, rather than prescriptive texts, written by authors who were not advocating new ideals for marriage but were describing the best form of bourgeois marriage as they knew it', and medieval texts had performed similar roles before them. The late fourteenth-century *Le Menagier de Paris*, for instance, advised the wives of burgesses in practical household management, supervising servants and workmen, dealing with tradesmen and so on, but it began with 'a long section on religious observance and the proper behaviour and attitude of a wife towards her husband'.[6]

This is not to suggest that patriarchy remained entirely unchanged. Advocates of the long-term significance of patriarchal social relations such as Judith Bennett acknowledge that 'patriarchy clearly has existed in many forms', calling on historians to 'historicise patriarchy by studying its many varieties'. The Reformation provides one contextual shift in which the switch of emphasis from priestly intercession to personal salvation led to a renewed focus on the strengths and failings of the family, and Patrick Collinson goes as far as asserting that in emerging Protestantism, 'the family as we know it experienced its birth'. Certainly, the combination of doctrinal challenge and print revolution led to an outpouring of advice books which attempted to fashion the godly family, stressing the vital place of its head as spiritual cheerleader as much as supreme governor.[7] In the Protestant family, according to one of its most prominent early seventeenth-century proselytes, all of its younger members were entitled to the instruction, care and protection of the head, and all were equally subject to his correction and guidance.[8]

Commentary on scripture elaborated upon the fifth commandment, to 'honour thy father and thy mother', probably the firmest spiritual validation of mastery. As such, it was central to the catechism, and Baxter gave it concentrated attention in his *Catechising of Families; or, a Teacher of Householders*, where he posed the rhetorical question, 'What is the duty of masters to their servants?' This was his reply: 'To employ them suitably, not unmercifully, in profitable labour and not in sin or vanity; to allow them their due wages and maintenance, keeping them neither in hurtful want nor in

---

6 Wrightson, 'Politics of the parish', p. 13; K.M. Davies, 'Continuity and change in literary advice on marriage', in R.B. Outhwaite, ed., *Marriage and Society: Studies in the Social History of Marriage* (London, 1981), pp. 76–7, 78; E. Power, *Medieval Women*, ed. M.M. Postan (Cambridge, 1975), pp. 50–52.

7 J.M. Bennett, 'Feminism and history', *Gender and History*, **1** (3) (1989), 261; P. Collinson, *The Birthpangs of Protestant England: Religious and Cultural Change in the Sixteenth and Seventeenth Centuries* (Basingstoke, 1988), p. 93; G.J. Schochet, *Patriarchalism in Political Thought: The Authoritarian Family and Political Speculation and Attitudes Especially in Seventeenth-Century England* (Oxford, 1975), pp. 57, 63, 64.

8 W. Gouge, *Of Domesticall Duties: Eight Treatises*, 3rd edn (London, 1634), pp. 579–83.

idleness', and through 'public and family worship . . . further their comfortable passage to heaven'. As for servants' duties towards their masters, they were to 'honour and obey them and faithfully serve them . . . to be trusty to them in word and deed . . . Learning of them thankfully and sincerely'.[9]

'Due correction and punishment' of servants by their masters was sanctioned by scripture, statute, and the teachings of divines and authors of didactic literature. Manuals instructing JPs in their duties throughout the seventeenth and eighteenth centuries, such as that of Richard Burns, had been quite clear that 'the master is allowed by law, with moderation, to chastise his servant'. The term 'moderation' was vital, since *Exodus* xxi, 21, taught that 'if a man smite his servant, or his maid, with a rod, and he die under his hand, he shall surely be punished'. But Burns was none too precise over the grounds for punishing masters for immoderate correctional violence: 'if in his correction he be so barbarous as to exceed all bounds of moderation and thereby occasion the servant's death, it is manslaughter at least; and if he make use of an instrument improper for correction, and apparently endangering the servant's life, it is murder'. There was much room here for flexible interpretation, but no doubt (following the Elizabethan Statute of Artificers) about the penalty for a servant assaulting his master, which was a year's imprisonment with a dose of corporal punishment.[10]

At least rhetorically, 'fatherly care' of servants included (as it did for the master's children) guidance on the moral path of life and correction when the individual recipient of care strayed from that path, since according to Robert Filmer 'the father of the family governs by no other law than his own will'. The earlier household manuals specified that husbands should beat the menservants and wives the maids,[11] although there was some legal disagreement over the latter in the eighteenth century (see below). Nonetheless, it would seem so far that, in the seventeenth-century literature directed at employers, mastery as patriarchal power and obligation within households was not problematised in any significant way (although that for servants was not entirely obeisant, as will be demonstrated).

---

9   R. Baxter, *Works* 4 vols (London, 1707), IV, pp. 115–19: parental duties to their children included servants 'that are at age' (p. 117). For the early modern importance of the catechism, see Griffiths, *Youth and Authority*, pp. 81–96, and I. Green, *The Christian's ABC: Catechisms and Catechising in England c.1530–1740* (Oxford, 1996).

10   R. Burns, *The Justice of the Peace and Parish Officer*, 4 vols, 10th edn (London, 1766), IV, p. 119 (citing Dalton's *Countrey Justice* of 1618); 5 *Eliz.* c. 4 (1563), xiv, repr. in A. Bland, P. Brown and R. Tawney, eds, *English Economic History: Selected Documents* (London, 1920), p. 329.

11   R. Filmer, *Patriarcha, or the Natural Power of Kings*, 2nd edn (London, 1685), pp. 24, 81; Davies, 'Continuity and change', p. 76.

Some of the more explicitly polemical writings of the seventeenth century derided servanthood as base and servile, to be scorned and avoided; others, however, celebrated ideal patriarchal bonds. In his well-known argument for the merits of kingship (written in the turbulent mid-seventeenth century), Filmer declared that 'the scope of master and servant, is preservation . . . of the family', and restated the long-standing perception of a link between family and kingdom in a patriarchal continuum:

> If we compare the natural rights of a father with those of a king, we find
> them all one, without any difference at all, but only in the latitude or
> extent of them: as the father over one family, so the king over many
> families extends his care . . . so that all the duties of a king are summed
> up in an universal fatherly care of his people.

The disdain many members of the propertied elites held for the labouring poor did not evaporate in the eighteenth century, but the Restoration and its aftermath certainly gave Filmer's formulation of the 'natural rights' of the head of the family a new lease of life (notwithstanding Locke's celebrated attack in his *Two Treatises on Government* of 1690). The simile was re-employed in the didactic literature of the early eighteenth century, an improbably-named 'Mr. Zinzano' asserting that 'as a family is a contracted government, a kingdom is an extended family'. It is important to acknowledge, as Wrightson does, that 'both the conventional definitions of familial relations and the actualities of life in households were shot through with ambiguities, if not outright contradictions', something which will become more apparent later in this book.[12] However, the script for patriarchal household mastery was a rhetorical resource available to masters throughout the period, a set of ideal devices that exhibited striking continuity across several centuries.

The mistress

So too did the script for mistresses: they had long been subordinate to their husbands and masters, according to the patriarchal commentators, although evidence for the status of medieval mistresses is even more problematic

---

12 C. Hill, 'Pottage for freeborn Englishmen: attitudes to wage labour in sixteenth and
    seventeenth century England', in his *Change and Continuity in Seventeenth-Century England*,
    revised edn (New Haven, 1991), pp. 219–38 and 291; Filmer, *Patriarcha*, p. 24;
    [Mr. Zinzano], *The Servants Calling; with some Advice to the Apprentice* (London, 1725),
    pp. 7, 11. See S.D. Amussen, *An Ordered Society: Gender and Class in Early Modern
    England* (Oxford, 1988), pp. 36–8; Wrightson, 'Politics of the parish', p. 13.

than that for their early modern counterparts. Power has warned us that 'it might with truth be said that the accepted theory about the nature and sphere of women was the work of the classes least familiar with the great mass of womankind', while Lacey has observed that in London at least, medieval theory was quite removed from women's experience, as far as it can be reconstructed from legal, borough and parochial records. But as Power writes, 'neither the concept of marriage nor the law took note of her as a complete woman', and the established doctrine was one 'of the woman's subjection, a doctrine which was apt to be linked to the notion of her essential inferiority'.[13]

Nevertheless, like the medieval *Le Menagier de Paris* mentioned earlier, the early modern prescriptive literature gave married women whose husbands were heads of households a status of some import within the politics of 'place'. The 'English housewife', wrote Gervase Markham in his popular seventeenth-century tract on housewifery, 'is the mother and mistress of the family, and hath her most general employments within the house'. Some of her 'employments' will be considered in detail in Chapter Five; but the seductive image of the early modern co-operative household has been influentially developed by Alice Clark. In her account, husband and wife worked in separate but complementary spheres of activity within it until the late seventeenth-century growth and triumph of capitalism forced him to work elsewhere, leaving her at home in the enforced semi-idleness of household supervision. More recently, feminist historians of the eighteenth and nineteenth centuries argue that changes forced by accelerating capitalist production in the industrial revolution went hand in hand with the development of an ideology of 'separate spheres'. According to Leonore Davidoff and Catherine Hall, the construction of middle-class identity towards the latter half of the eighteenth century involved a domestic, private distancing: 'the day-to-day management of servants was becoming a central part of middle class women's role'.[14]

Additionally, Bridget Hill has argued that the industrial revolution destroyed the family economy and created a sharper sexual division of labour in which housework became 'more and more exclusively "women's work"

---

13 Power, *Medieval Women*, pp. 9, 10, 19; K. Lacey, 'Women and work in fourteenth and fifteenth century London', in L. Charles and L. Duffin, eds, *Women and Work in Pre-industrial England* (Beckenham, 1985), p. 26.

14 G. Markham, *The English Housewife, Containing the Inward and Outward Virtues which ought to be in a Complete Woman*, 9th edn (London, 1683), pp. 1–2; A. Clark, *Working Life of Women in the Seventeenth Century*, ed. A.L. Erickson (London, 1992): but *cf.* P. Earle, 'The female labour market in London in the late seventeenth and early eighteenth centuries', *Economic History Review*, **42** (3) (1989); L. Davidoff and C. Hall, *Family Fortunes: Men and Women of the English Middle Class, 1780–1850* (London, 1987), pp. 392–4.

... women were left stranded in the home'. This development 'is closely related to the recruitment of domestic servants in the second half of the [eighteenth] century to do the household tasks dictated by a newly acquired affluence'. 'Most of the new tasks associated with "housework" towards the end of the eighteenth century', writes Hill in support of Davidoff and Hall, 'are related to the middle class wife's idea of domestic comfort'. More recently she has asserted that 'what had been a paternalistic relationship with — at least in theory — defined obligations towards, and responsibilities for their servants by masters and mistresses, was in process [sic] of changing into a strictly wage relationship, and with this change the class tensions between masters and servants were increased'.[15] However, the bases of these views have been subject to sustained revision in the 1990s: Vickery has observed that 'it is extremely difficult to sustain . . . the argument that sometime between 1650 and 1850 the public/private distinction was constituted or radically reconstituted in a way that transformed relations between the sexes', let alone led to the creation of separate spheres. Shoemaker, concluding his study of gender in England from the mid-seventeenth to the mid-eighteenth centuries, remarks that 'the concept of separate spheres may be useful if we define it as a loose division of responsibilities between men and women . . . [but] continuities in gender roles across this long period remain striking'.[16]

One area of the early modern housewife's competence will be briefly examined here to demonstrate the longevity of the managerial mistress (at least in rhetorical terms). Hiring servants was considered one of the major tasks the mistress of the household would perform, and a good example of her control can be seen in the hiring of wet-nurses in the eighteenth century, according to Fildes 'perhaps the most significant period' of the occupation's history. The 1729 edition of *The Complete Servant-Maid* stepped briefly out of its role as adviser to servants, and instructed mistresses in detail on choosing a wet-nurse:

> she should not be younger than twenty-four years, nor older than thirty-five; of a fair and ruddy complexion; one who had not been brought to bed or given suck too long. Her breasts should not be either large or small, but of a middle size . . . her temper should be even, not subject to passion, anger, grief or repining; for children generally take after their nurses.

---

15 B. Hill, *Women, Work and Sexual Politics in Eighteenth-Century England* (Oxford, 1989), pp. 123–4, 127; B. Hill, *Servants: English Domestics in the Eighteenth Century* (Oxford, 1996), p. 17.

16 A. Vickery, 'Golden age to separate spheres? A review of the categories and chronology of English women's history', *Historical Journal*, **36** (2) (1993), pp. 411–12; Shoemaker, *Gender in English Society*, p. 318.

As with other facets of these texts, advice on the requisite physical qualities of the best women for breast-feeding has a long and rich history, and this piece mirrors an early Renaissance tract by the German medical writer, Bartholomaeus Metlinger. After making suggestions like those above, he adds that the wet-nurse 'should have a strong thick neck' and 'good praise-worthy habits'. These texts in many respects recycled rather than innovated, their popularity probably having more to do 'with the very familiarity and acceptability of what they contained'. Markham's modern editor has noted that the printer of the first edition of *The English Housewife* suggested 'that Markham had not written or even "collected" the book, but had simply organised it'.[17]

However, our period appears to witness a growth in rates of publication of household advice manuals aimed specifically at women as mistresses or as servants, no doubt in part thanks to the growth of London and in particular to the increasing numbers of domestic servants employed there. The author of one manual from the mid-eighteenth century called *The Accom-plishe'd Housewife* discussed the problems that 'ladies in the capacity of mistresses' might encounter; but also (in an apology for the genre) opined that, since 'most of the sex are too apt to imagine that they lie under no obligation to their servants, it is probable, what we have to advance on that topic may be looked upon either as tedious or impertinent'.[18] But the assumed need to remind 'ladies' that such status entailed burdens as well as benefits, no matter how odious the task might prove, appears more a literary device than evidence of the demise of the patriarchal household.

'Governors of families', stated *The Accomplishe'd Housewife*, 'ought to make a strict inspection into the manners of their servants; and where they find them good, to indulge them with some peculiar mark of their favour'. But 'where they find them to be vicious . . . severely to admonish them, and take the best measures they can to work a thorough reformation in them'. Sometimes, of course, admonition failed to have the desired effect, and mistresses needed recourse to more severe means to cope with servants who had forgotten their duty of obedience to their elders and betters within the household: 'when they despair of that, to dismiss them at once, lest they

---

17 V. Fildes, *Wet Nursing: A History from Antiquity to the Present* (Oxford, 1988), p. 111; anon., *The Complete Servant-Maid; or The Young Maiden's and Family's Daily Companion*, 9th edn (London, 1729), p. 7; B. Metlinger, *Ein Regimen der Junger Kinder* (Augsburg, 1473), cited in Fildes, *Wet Nursing*, p. 70: for ancient continuities in this literature, see pp. 69, 111–13; Davies, 'Continuity and change', p. 78; Markham, *English Housewife* ed. M.R. Best (Kingston and Montreal, 1986), p. xvii.

18 Shoemaker, *Gender in English Society*, p. 21; anon., *The Accomplish'd Housewife; or, the Gentlewoman's Companion* (London, 1745), Dedication, n.p.

infect the whole flock'. It does not seem out of place to read the way the father-as-monarch simile could be drawn on for its implications *vis à vis* household discipline: 'as pride breeds rebellion in kingdoms, it does the same in families, and may be the ruin of both, if not prevented'.[19] House-hold management required a kind of surveillance that led to a tripartite scale of response to servant behaviour: reward, reform or removal.

However, the role of mistresses in physically chastising servants was prob-lematic, according to the legal commentator Blackstone: corporal punish-ment was perfectly permissible for the master, so long as it was moderate, but 'if the master's wife beats him [the servant], it is good cause of depar-ture'. How specifically Blackstone had identified the servant's gender, and whether the law would stand differently were she a maid, is unclear, al-though the distinction (by separate chapters) in his *Commentaries* between servants and apprentices means he is not discussing the latter. The anonym-ous author of *The Accomplishe'd Housewife* recognised that 'the art of govern-ing servants is not so easy as it is necessary', and recommended that 'a mistress should understand how to do everything with propriety and in season'. Divine assistance in this difficult task was advised, and the mistress was encouraged to 'use her utmost endeavours to make all that are hers to be God's servants also'. This had moral implications — 'she will be secure of their truth and fidelity' — and there was more than an element of self-interest involved: 'this likewise will be the best spur to their diligence and industry'. But the really difficult part of her role was 'to employ her servants with so much ease and order, as may make their labour pleasant and their duty desirable', and this meant treading a fine line: 'above all, she must be sure to command that only, which may and ought to be performed; other-wise it will be impossible to preserve in them that respect which is due to her person'.[20]

As the next link in the patriarchal chain of authority within the house-hold, mistresses were expected to exercise power but not tyranny over ser-vants, and affectionate persuasion in at least equal measure with coercion. In a call on classical authority (perhaps suggesting that what might appear to the twentieth-century reader as mawkish and distinctly patronising may have required additional justification even to polite contemporaries), the Marchioness de Lambert asked mistresses to 'use yourself to treat your servants with kindness and humanity. It is a saying of one of the Ancients,

---

19   Anon., *Accomplish'd Housewife*, pp. 427–8; Marchioness de Lambert, *Advice of a Mother to her Son and Daughter* trans. T. Carte (London, 1737), p. 66.

20   W. Blackstone, *Commentaries on the Laws of England*, 4 vols (London, 1765–9), I, p. 416; anon., *Accomplish'd Housewife*, pp. 428, 427.

that we ought to consider them as unhappy friends'. In a typically humbling gesture, the Marchioness asked for kindness while also helping the present or future employer of servants to come to terms with the burden of their superiority, this being noble advice in both senses of the word. 'Remember that the vast difference between you and them is owing merely to chance; never make them uneasy in their state of life, or add weight to the trouble of it: there is nothing so poor and mean as to be haughty to anybody that is in your service'. This analysis was unfortunately not expanded any further, but we can assume the 'chance' to be the accident of birth; and it reminded the mistress that her place was dissimilar to the place of the servant without stressing the divine right of heads of households to govern. It is rhetorical devices like these that allow Langford to describe servants as occupying 'a sensitive position on the line which separated polite from plebeian life'.[21]

Mirroring Markham in his *English Housewife*, who observed 'that evil and uncomely language is deformed, though uttered even to servants', de Lambert commanded mistresses 'never [to] use any harsh language', not because it might be counter-productive, but because 'it should never come out of the mouth of a delicate and polite person'. The duty of care meant that control had to be exercised with kindness, and, employing a secular justification, the author stated: 'Servitude being fettled in opposition to the natural equality of mankind, it behoves us to soften it. What right have we to expect our servants to be without faults, when we are giving them instances every day of our own?' De Lambert's ambivalence was reflected at a later point in her text: 'A mean familiarity with them is indeed ever to be avoided; but you owe them assistance, advice, and bounties suitable to their conditions and wants. One should keep authority in one's family, but it should be a mild authority'. Again, appeals to equality did not mean there was ever any danger that the 'ladies' would lose sight of their status in the relationship, but it did mean treading a tightrope occasionally: 'Never relish or encourage the flattery of servants, and to prevent the impression which their fawning speeches frequently repeated may make on you, consider that they are hirelings paid to serve your weaknesses and pride'.[22]

The same author also pandered to contemporary fears of the influence of servants on young children. 'What would they have them inspire into their children, when from their very infancy they are left themselves in the hands of governantes who as they are taken generally out of the low world, inspire

---

21 De Lambert, *Advice of a Mother*, p. 65; P. Langford, *A Polite and Commercial People: England 1727–1783* (Oxford, 1989), p. 118.

22 Markham, *English Housewife* (1683 edn), p. 3.

them with low sentiments, encourage all the timorous passions, and form them to superstition instead of religion'. In a similar vein, the anonymous author of *The Accomplish'd Housewife* included among seventy 'Instructions for the better regulation of your future conduct', advice to 'suffer no servants to terrify [children] with stories of ghosts and goblins' and 'Let them have no bad examples to converse with, either among servants, or among their companions or play-fellows'.[23]

The manuals directing their instructions to the female managers of households in the late seventeenth and early eighteenth centuries were written by men or women who clearly saw that a market awaited them. Mistresses, among whose 'natural rights' it was to manage servants (as it had been for centuries as far as advice-givers were concerned), needed to be reminded of their obligations towards their servants. These writers also perceived a market for advice on the pitfalls and difficulties of treading the narrow path between effective domestic authority and solicitude. As a consequence, they relied on a well-established patriarchal language of order — of command, obligation and place — shorn of the polemic observed in the seventeenth-century advice on mastery, and (from those translated from the French in the eighteenth century, at least) with a smattering of early Enlightenment rhetoric on equality veiling the demarcation of politeness. But these manuals must be read in the context of this genre of didactic literature over the long term to be understood properly.

Advice to servants

The late seventeenth-century growth of the genre of didactic literature increasingly provided servants with their own manuals of instruction. But the exploitation of this niche did not dispel ambivalence among servant-employers towards their domestic employees. 'Mr. Zinzano' thought conventionally that 'domestic servitude . . . must be undertaken, and exercised upon the same principles and motives that tend to perfect every other office and relation in human life: *viz.* upon those of religion'. Servants could be welcomed within the common fold of humanity without compromising the politics of 'place': 'the office of servant . . . how mean soever it may be reputed, is capable of being adorned with the highest of virtues', because 'not he that has the highest, but he that acts his part best (whatever it is) must be preferable in the true scale of merit'. Seventeenth-century Protestants like George Herbert, as Christopher Hill has observed, 'wrote that

---

23 De Lambert, *Advice of a Mother*, pp. 33–4; anon., *Accomplish'd Housewife*, n.p.; [Zinzano], *Servants Calling*, p. 17.

labour was dignified or degrading according to the spirit in which it was done. "A servant with this clause/Makes drudgery divine . . . ".' In the eighteenth century, Thomas Bouston's sermon acknowledged that the 'greatest inequality found in any relationship among men is that between the master and servant', but he reminded his congregation that 'Christ . . . became a servant for us', citing *Isaiah* xlii, 1 and *Matthew* xii, 18 ('Behold my servant, whom I have chosen . . . ') in support. None of these precepts were intended to undermine the traditional language of order upon which they were based, of course, and the recognition by 'Mr. Zinzano' that 'in some sense we are all servants, as being subject to some powers that are over us' was no concession to levelling.[24]

The author of *A Present for a Servant-Maid* contrived to instil the mixed blessings of servile status in the homely context of the kitchen. Under the head of 'Wasting of victuals', she cautioned the maid against coveting the left-overs: 'I do not deny', she wrote, 'that you have the same appetites as your superiors'. Slightly optimistically she added that 'a good mistress will doubtless allow her servants a taste of everything in season; but then you are not to expect it as often or in as full proportion as she has it herself', because that might lead to an unconscionable equality of mistress and maid. This recognition of undeniable status distinctions might seem conventional, and further comment unnecessary. But in trying to develop a fuller explanation, Eliza Haywood elaborated on the underlying sacrifices that employers made for their servants in a passage that deserves to be quoted at length:

> were you to know the real pinches some endure who keep you, you would find the balance wholly on your side. The exorbitant taxes, and other severities of the times, have for some years past reduced our middling gentry, as well as tradesmen, to very great straits; and the care of providing for you, and paying your wages, is much more than an equivalent for your care of obliging them, and doing your duty by them. It often costs many a biting lip and aching heart to support the rank they have been accustomed to hold in the world while you, entirely free from all encumbrances, all distraction of mind, have only to do your duty quietly in the stations God has placed you. Whatever changes happen in public affairs, your circumstances are unaffected by them. Whether provisions are dear or cheap is the same thing to you. Secure of having all your real necessities supplied, you rise without anxiety, and go to bed without having your

---

24 C. Hill, 'Protestantism and the rise of capitalism', in F.J. Fisher, ed., *Essays in the Economic and Social History of Tudor and Stuart England* (Cambridge, 1961), p. 30; T. Bouston, *The Mystery of Christ in the Form of a Servant* (Edinburgh, 1742); [Zinzano], *Servants Calling*, p. 7.

repose disturbed. And as to your labour, if you consider the difference of education, it is no more to you than those exercises which are prescribed to your superiors for the sake of health.[25]

The self-pitying references to biting lips and aching hearts must have stuck in some of her readers' throats; and the equation of servants' labour with their employers' healthy exertions appears positively comic given many of the experiences of work described in Chapter Five. Yet the respective places of servant and master had doctrinal approval and support that on paper was impervious to ridicule.

Haywood's injunction to servants was not unique: William Fleetwood made similar comments in the early eighteenth century, as did Richard Baxter in the seventeenth, noting that 'most servants may have quieter lives, if it were not for their unthankful, discontented hearts'. But it is fascinating in the way Haywood successfully (in her own terms) managed to reverse the main thrust of duty and obligation that characterised other manuals, or at the very least altered the balance of compassion, while actually offering a further apology for order and 'place'. In outlining this form of live-in labour without responsibility she hit directly upon some of the advantages of service to adolescents and young adults, and inadvertently acknowledged the way a surfeit of demand for servants disturbed traditional vectors of status-obligation and exchange. At the same time, without a hint of irony, she described just the sort of economic fluctuations that frequently threw servants out of their places and into the precarious realm of eked-out savings, makeshift economies and the generosity of friends with which other writers directly threatened servants. According to one, they 'should consider how very dependent they are' on the mercy of employers who could ruin them.[26]

Haywood described with feeling a world where servant plebeians were required to 'do your duty quietly' while their employers, the social amalgam of 'middling gentry' as well as tradesmen, suffered on their behalf in a topsy-turvy reversal of the moral economy of service. Indeed, the very device of a dichotomous 'balance' (whether out of kilter or not) exposed her fear that things could so easily slip the wrong way, one clearly shared by many middling and higher-status employers (see below). Yet even when accepting that upward mobility was not just possible but perfectly understandable as a goal, as some authors did, they still armed themselves with

---

25   E. Haywood, *Present for a Servant-Maid, or the Sure Means of gaining Love & Esteem* (London, 1743), p. 30.

26   Baxter, *Works* I, p. 435; Schochet, *Patriarchalism*, p. 68 citing Fleetwood; [Zinzano], *Servants Calling*, p. 18.

scriptural authority and counselled against pride. 'It is natural for servants to desire advancement, and as difficulties attend servitude, such ambition is most reasonable', wrote one. 'Now certainly they have as good a right to the promise of *He that humbleth himself shall be exalted*, as any other Christian; and therefore the higher they wish to rise, the lower they must abase themselves'.[27]

In the main, Haywood, like other writers, adopted a traditional stance and attempted to instil humility and ingratiation in her servant readers. Under a section entitled 'Studying to give content', she called on servants to adopt a strategy that would satisfy their mistresses almost regardless of their temperament. 'Possessed with a strong desire of pleasing, you will rarely fail of doing it', she wrote: 'because the humours of people are vastly different, it is your interest to study by what sort of behaviour you can most ingratiate yourself, as the scripture says, "The eye of the handmaid looks up to her mistress", so you ought to observe not only what she says, but also how she looks, in order to give content'. Amid words of advice against slothfulness stood a caution against 'being an eye-servant' (i.e. to 'appear diligent in sight and be found neglectful when out of it'). Spiritual authority lay in St Paul's epistles — in *Ephesians* vi, 5–6 and *Colossians* iii, 22 he enjoined servants to obey their masters 'not with eye-service, as men-pleasers, but in singleness of heart, fearing God' — while Richard Baxter linked this both to hypocrisy and, more sternly, to ungodliness.[28] The charge of eye-service, while far from the worst levelled at servants, sums up the ambivalence over their presence as necessary but occasionally problematic members of the family, and encapsulates the fear induced in employers by the inevitable imperfection of surveillance. The ever-possible disjuncture between the visible and the hidden was a frequent theme: masters and mistresses could not control the every action of their servants, nor could they be sure that what they saw was the self-evident truth. Authority and surveillance were desperate to see eye to eye.

Many servants' tasks involved a high degree of trust by their employers, and, not surprisingly, trust was a recurrent issue in these manuals. Just as mistresses were advised to 'have public divine offices . . . daily and regularly' in order to 'secure of their [servants'] truth and fidelity', housekeepers were enjoined to ensure 'that no goods be either spoiled or embezzled'; nursery-maids were advised that, if their young charges hurt themselves, to 'be sure you conceal it not, but acquaint your lord'; cookmaids were told to request higher wages rather than take more perks since that would 'teach you to be a thief'; under cookmaids 'must beware of gossips and charwomen';

27 [Zinzano], *Servants Calling*, p. 17 (emphasis in the original).
28 Haywood, *Present for a Servant Maid*, pp. 4–5, 12; Baxter, *Works* I, pp. 386, 435.

and laundry maids should 'entertain no charwomen unknown to your lady or mistress'. According to *The Servants Calling*, 'The faults of servants are a general theme of complaint. Some families have been ruined; others made uneasy, and great sufferers' by a multitude of sins, including 'frauds and falsehood', and the author enjoined servants, as noted above, to demonstrate 'fidelity to their [masters'] trust' and 'sincerity'.[29]

Haywood's *A Present for a Servant-Maid* provides the best example of this concern, as one of the manuals that most closely resembled a moral tract for servants rather than simply an advice book on the requisite skills for each task or post alone. She was very concerned to rule out lying, 'dishonesty', and telling tales: she stated that 'there is scarce any one thing I would more strenuously recommend to you than speaking the exact truth'; and she wrote that 'to cheat or defraud anyone is base and wicked; but where breach of trust is added, the crime is infinitely enhanced'. Social reputations in London neighbourhoods could be made or lost by gossip about someone's actions (real or imagined), and employers' fears were exhibited in a stiff injunction against 'telling the affairs of the family'. Assuming that many employers felt vulnerable over servant-disseminated gossip, Haywood wrote that 'infinitely worse [than staying out when sent on a errand] is it when you suffer yourselves to be detained in order to discover the affairs of the family where you live'. This was shored up by a statement regarding 'hearing anything said against your master or mistress': 'So far from ever speaking against them yourself, you should never listen to any idle stories to their prejudice, and should always vindicate their reputation from any open aspersions or malicious insinuation'.[30]

If masters and mistresses could appeal to 'natural rights', the anonymous author of *The Servants Calling* thought it his or her task to contrive laws for servants to observe. Servants' 'fundamental duties' were two-fold: firstly, 'humility of mind', and secondly, 'fidelity to their [masters'] trust', including a reminder of the Fifth Commandment. Later on in this tract, these were supplemented by 'some other duties that complete the character of a good servant', namely '1. Singleness of heart, or sincerity. 2. Affection or good will towards a master. 3. Government of the tongue. 4. Sobriety. 5. Diligence.' As observed earlier, the 'natural rights' exercised by patriarchal masters or managerial mistresses were slightly offset by their reciprocal obligations to the family; rules for servants, however, swung over to the

---

29 Anon., *Accomplish'd Housewife*, p. 427; anon., *Complete Servant-Maid* (1677 edn), pp. 35, 110–11, 113, 155, 164; [Zinzano], *Servants Calling*, pp. 9–10, 11, 46–7.

30 Haywood, *Present for a Servant-Maid*, pp. 5–11, 20, 23, 24–5, 29, 31. Reputation: see this chapter and Chapter Four.

realm of 'duties' towards employers, stressing not so much hard work (diligence was the fifth of five) but obeisance. Interestingly, and with uncharacteristic candour, this manual displayed some ambivalence in their representation of ideal relations between master and maid: 'In servitude, which is a subjection to the will of another, difficulties may be expected by those that must be subjected not only to the good and gentle, but (as it may happen) even to the froward [perverse or untoward] masters, who will sometimes punish them (though it be a hard case) even for doing well'. But the solution to the problem was better on hope than redress: 'it more generally happens that a servant who is careful to discharge a good conscience, will be valued even by bad masters'.[31]

Character and employment

Reputation

J.A. Sharpe has written that 'considerations of honour, good name, and reputation were of central importance' to early modern English society, and recent work on defamation, slander and insult in the period has outlined the popularity of suits in the ecclesiastical and secular courts for offences that were deemed to have damaged reputation by words. In her study of women and the ecclesiastical courts in London during the late sixteenth and early seventeenth centuries, Gowing has stressed that 'words ... were crucially linked with reputation; and the concept of reputation held considerable sway both legally and socially'. Although the regulation of slander through the London church courts was on the wane from the Civil War if not earlier, defamation disputes initiated independently by one private party against another constituted some 60 per cent of the London Consistory court's business in the early eighteenth century. More importantly, actions for slander at the Middlesex and Westminster quarter sessions and before justices summarily were increasingly numerous.[32]

It is not, therefore, surprising that an obsession in the advice literature over appearances and the 'realities' they masked went hand in hand with a

---

31 [Zinzano], *Servants Calling*, pp. 11, 46–7; 'froward', *OED*. For a similar list, see anon., *The Complete Servant-Maid; or The Young Maiden's Tutor* (London, 1677), pp. 1–2.

32 J.A. Sharpe, *Defamation and Sexual Slander in Early Modern England: The Church Courts at York*, Borthwick Papers 58 (York, 1980), p. 1; L. Gowing, *Domestic Dangers: Women, Words and Sex in Early Modern London* (Oxford, 1996), p. 111; T. Meldrum, 'A women's court in London: defamation at the Bishop of London's Consistory court, 1700–1745', *London Journal* **19** (1) (1994), 2–6; R. Shoemaker, *Prosecution and Punishment: Petty Crime and the Law in London and Rural Middlesex, c.1660–1725* (Cambridge, 1991), pp. 55–9.

concern for the reputation of the household, and particularly that of the employers. But a servant's reputation, his and especially her vulnerability to gossip or adverse opinion among employers and those who lived in the households or neighbourhoods in which they worked, also resulted in the need for servants to guard against its damage or loss. Servants were enjoined by Haywood to look for an 'honest service' and the first task was to 'make some enquiries into the place before you suffer yourself to be hired. There are some houses which appear well by day, that it would be little safe for a modest person to sleep in at night', and not just Covent Garden brothels, bagnios and coffee houses, 'but houses which have no public show of business, are richly furnished, and where the mistress has an air of the strictest modesty'. If due care was not taken, a servant might end up 'ensnared into the service of the devil'.[33]

'Great regard is therefore to be had', Haywood warned servants, 'to the character of the persons who recommend you, and the manner in which you heard the place'. But servants' own reputations were not always in their own hands even if they chose a worthy household. Of course, lying and dishonesty were deemed to be 'crimes' in their own right, and they could have real repercussions for the servants themselves. After outlining how dependent servants were on their employers' mercy, *The Servants Calling* warned: 'They should consider likewise how soon a just or unjust accusation may deprive them of all credit, and exclude them from every family, and how much harder it is for them to recover it, or live without it'.[34] The discovery of 'eye-service' and other faults would lay bare the real nature of a servant's character, and the reputation that character acquired might do them real harm amongst fellow servants and would-be employers.

The term 'character' came to denote what would now be termed a reference, in other words a statement (preferably but by no means always written) by a servant's former employer detailing how trustworthy, honest and diligent he or she had been. Samuel Pepys for one approved of the 'French habit of requiring testimonials' from previous employers, although 'he did not insist that the recommendations should be in writing'. He did write at least one himself, for his coachman, which survives in the Bodleian. Great store had been set in controlling such certificates of reference throughout the early modern period: the Elizabethan Statute of Artificers had sought to involve the local authorities not just in the setting of wages, but also by preventing servants leaving their town of employ without a 'testimonial [which] shall be delivered unto the said servant and also registered by

---

33 Haywood, *Present for a Servant-Maid*, pp. 2, 3.
34 Haywood, *Present for a Servant-Maid*, p. 2; [Zinzano], *Servants Calling*, p. 18.

the parson, vicar or curate of the parish where such master [etc.] shall dwell'.[35]

Proposals for regulation in the late seventeenth and early eighteenth centuries inevitably focused on a servant's reputation as a necessary indicator to employers of his or her reliability and employability. Private initiative burgeoned from the 1680s with varying degrees of success: for instance, the Office for Servants in Fleet Street published the weekly 'Servants' Guide' from 1698. John Beattie has observed that 'there had been at least twelve attempts in the reigns of William and Anne to get legislation that would have regulated servants in some way', mainly by enforced registration and the carrying of testimonials, and at least one from 1704 'was to control theft'. Noting that 'servants are now become a general grievance', a broadside entitled *The Usefulness of, and Reasons for a Publick Office, for Registering of Servants* (published in 1700) complained that, since the regulations of the Statute of Artificers had fallen into disuse, 'the present liberty allowed . . . extravagant servants to remove at pleasure, rather than be subject to the government of well-regulated families'. This 'puts many out of service, and exposes them to a vicious life, increases the number of thieves and vagabonds . . . and consequently follows all manner of wickedness and debauchery'.[36]

The author of *The Usefulness of . . . a Publick Office* considered the proposal for a public registry office advantageous on several fronts: for society at large, since they 'will prevent the increase of, if not wholly suppress vagabonds, and much lessen the number of all sorts of thieves, keep many from Tyburn, discover idle disorderly persons, and consequently in great measure quiet the minds of the people'; for employers, because 'servants are thus obliged to demean themselves well in order to obtain a certificate at their departure'; and for servants themselves, who, with their characters, 'will be qualified for, and immediately received into service, without the expense of time for enquiries about them, or the expense of charge at the Intelligence Office to find out a service, or friends to engage for their fidelity'. Needless to say, this scheme never made it on to the statute book.[37]

One private initiative for regulating characters and controlling servant reputations that came to fruition in the mid-eighteenth century was that

---

35 S. Pepys, *The Diary of Samuel Pepys*, 11 vols, eds R. Latham and N. Matthews (London, 1971), III, p. 196; 5 *Eliz. c.* 4, 1563, vii.

36 M.D. George, 'The early history of registry offices', *Economic Journal* Supplement 1 (1926–9), 570–90; anon., *The Usefulness of, and Reasons for a Publick Office, for Registering of Servants, and the more easie discovering of Idle and Disorderly Persons* (London, 1700); J. Beattie, 'London crime and the making of the "Bloody Code", 1689–1718', in L. Davison, T. Hitchcock, T. Keirn and R.B. Shoemaker, eds, *Stilling the Grumbling Hive: The Response to Social and Economic Problems in England, 1689–1750* (Stroud, 1992), p. 69.

37 Anon., *Usefulness of . . . a Publick Office*, n.p.

proposed by the Fielding brothers: at the end of London magistrate Henry Fielding's *Enquiry into the Causes of the Late Increase of Robbers* of 1751, the author printed a full-page advertisement for his Universal Register Office (URO) which dwelt on the 'rude behaviour and insolence of servants'. He and his half-brother (later Sir) John Fielding had opened the URO in the Strand in 1750, 'the design of which is to bring the world as it were together into one place. Here . . . the master and the scholar, the master and the apprentice, and the master and servant are sure to meet'. In a broadside of 1751 entitled *A Plan of the Universal Register Office* and published almost exactly a year after the URO had opened, Henry Fielding outlined the ten forms of business that were facilitated by this central point of information and exchange: together with the registration of estates, advertising of lodgings to let and so forth was a section on 'servants of all kinds'. He claimed the URO would keep a register of servants' personal and past employment details

> with every particular of their characters, and by whom given. And the public may be assured that the utmost care will be taken to prevent any imposition; and that none will be registered in this office who give the least suspicious account of themselves and who have lived in any disreputable places . . . We, however, take this opportunity to desire all gentlemen and ladies who turn away servants for any gross fault, to put themselves to the expense of a penny-post letter to the office, and we will faithfully promise that no such servant shall be registered here.

The modern editor of the *Plan* has remarked that in advertisements and letters to newspapers, Henry Fielding 'harped on that the URO is conducted by *gentlemen*', and the scheme certainly relied on polite self-regulation for its effectiveness. Before competition in the 1750s undermined its dominance of the market and forced its closure in 1761, the Fieldings' URO appears to have been somewhat successful. Whether it lessened the burden on Albion's fatal tree at Tyburn is open to doubt, and even its more limited aims were insufficiently met to persuade Sir John Fielding himself to call (ineffectually) for a statutory registry office in 1768, while others later in the eighteenth century promoted further schemes, finally getting an Act passed in 1791.[38] These projects seemed to have been driven almost as much by an exasperation with those employers who were prepared to give false testimony

---

38 H. Fielding, *Enquiry into the Causes of the Late Increase of Robbers* (London, 1751); H. Fielding, *The Covent Garden Journal and A Plan of the Universal Register Office* ed. B.A. Goldgar (Oxford, 1988), pp. xviii–xxiii, 6; J.J. Hecht, *The Domestic Servant Class in Eighteenth-Century England* (London, 1956), pp. 83–5, 92–5.

of former servants as with servants manufacturing characters. At least before 1750 (and probably thereafter too), repeated attempts to define individual domestic servants by employer-drawn 'characters', and to police the entire servant labour market by formally-disseminated reputations, failed miserably.

Dress

Attempts to regulate domestic servant dress were equally hopeless in our period. Sumptuary legislation (laws designed to demarcate social status by regulating apparel) had long been ineffectual in England, but like the concern over 'eye-service', clothing was central to the issue of appearance and reality. Female servants' dress provided a vehicle for many of the arguments linking attire and social station to be rehearsed within a social and economic context in which divisions between social orders were in some ways becoming less rigid, and where consumption patterns were widening the possibility of many to express status in a more heightened, visible manner. The issue was firmly on the agenda in the late seventeenth- and eighteenth-century debate on luxury.[39]

Chapter Four will demonstrate how important clothing was as part of many servants' remuneration; yet contemporaries perceived that this form of payment in kind created tensions between the employers' desire to profit from reflected glory by having the best-dressed servants around, and the subsequent blurring of the divisions between the social orders. Defoe famously warned that female servants dressed so well that sometimes they could not be distinguished from their mistresses, so that wives dressed even more expensively 'to go further than their maids', and he proposed that maidservants wore a uniform or livery like menservants; for his pains he was satirised by the footman-poet Robert Dodsley for his inability to tell superior from subordinate. Queen Caroline's attempt to force female domestic servants to wear insignia 'to distinguish them from their mistresses' was, according to Harte, more an example of her vanity rather than a socially significant modernisation of dress regulation.[40]

---

39 N.B. Harte, 'State control of dress and social change in pre-industrial England', in D.C. Coleman and A.H. John, eds, *Trade, Government and Economy in Pre-industrial England* (London, 1976), pp. 132–65.

40 D. Defoe, *Everybody's Business is Nobody's Business; or, Private Abuses, Public Grievances* (London, 1725), pp. 15, 19–20; R. Dodsley, *Servitude: a Poem* (London, 1729), p. 29; N.B. Harte, 'Silk and sumptuary legislation in England', in *La Seta in Europa, Secc. XIII–XX* (Prato, 1993), p. 816.

A servant's 'modesty in dress' may have been a recommended method for preventing their overweening pride, but this created tensions of which writers were quite aware: 'some persons thinking themselves honoured by the habit of their domestics, expect that they should dress up as much as possible', one wrote, 'and are most pleased when they are superfine, assisting them with materials which are often the rich clothes that they themselves have worn'. Less aware of the ironies and contradictions, Haywood warned in mild disapproval (under the title 'Aping the fashion') that one of two 'errors or failings, for I think neither of them simply in themselves can be called a vice, is the ambition of imitating your betters in point of dress'. Generally, girls wishing to become domestic servants had to 'be neat, cleanly, and housewifely, in your clothes'; cookmaids were advised, 'Lay not all your wages on your back . . . for you may assure yourself it is more commendable, for one in your employment to go decent and clean, than gaudishly fine'; and even 'waiting gentlewomen' were advised to 'learn to dress well' in order to be 'neat in your habit'.[41]

Yet in fact the hierarchy of service was more than implicit: it was made visible in the rewards of dutiful labour, particularly in the 'esteem and fortune' of upper female service as waiting woman or housekeeper. 'Ladies will much covet and desire your company', wrote the anonymous author of *The Complete Servant-Maid*: 'you will gain respect from the rest of the servants, you will wear good clothes, and have a considerable salary'. This less formal sumptuary code pushed the vast majority of servants in the opposite direction: given that the manual writers' perception of the ultimate goal for servants, to 'gain the title of a complete servant-maid, which may be the means of making you a good mistress', its achievement relied on a different conjunction of dress and reputation. There was, apparently, 'no sober, honest, and discrete man, but will make a choice of one, that hath gained the reputation of a good and complete servant for his wife, rather than one who can trick herself up fine, and like a Bartholomew baby, is fit for nothing else but to be looked upon'.[42]

The account above has focused primarily on female servants since they were the object of the literature under consideration, but this appeal to plain sobriety re-emphasises just how the discussion of servant reputation was a gendered one. The most exalted of upper male servants were dressed as gentlemen, while the wealthiest employers aimed, according to Hecht, 'to dress their lower menservants in the richest manner possible', and he

---

41 [Zinzano], *Servants Calling*, pp. 21, 22; Haywood, *Present for a Servant-Maid*, p. 22; anon., *Complete Servant-Maid* (1677 edn), pp. 2, 4, 114.
42 Anon., *Complete Servant-Maid* (1677 edn), pp. 59–60, Epistle, f. A3.

has argued for the importance of livery as a public reflection of their masters' status. Employers 'fully appreciated the importance of the livery suit as part of the equipment of display', and were 'conscious of the prestige derived from being served by men and women who dressed like members of the upper classes'.[43]

Fairchilds, a historian of eighteenth-century French domestic service, has employed E.P. Thompson's theory of elite cultural hegemony to explain the importance of male servant uniforms. Thompson wrote that 'ruling class control in the eighteenth century was located primarily in a cultural hegemony, and only secondarily in an expression of economic or physical (military) power'; in particular, the use of law as an ideological tool involved the development of a calculated theatricality in the exercise of power. According to Fairchilds, 'one major function of domestic servants [in livery] was to provide a public demonstration of the nobility's right to rule', or in other words provide a component of the theatre through which the elites manufactured their legitimacy. The widespread popularity of such display at the Restoration led Charles II to 'prohibit all pages, footmen and lackeys from carrying or using swords or other weapons within the cities of London and Westminster, or the Liberties thereof', but the proclamation was widely flouted. Certainly, Pepys only two years later had his boy wear a sword as part of a new livery in a bid to upstage his more exalted colleagues at the Naval Office; he noted that his patron the Earl of Sandwich's pages and footmen dressed in livery that was 'handsome, though not gaudy', while the Duchess of Newcastle's coachmen and footmen were liveried in velvet, one of her aristocratic 'extravagances'.[44]

However, the significance of this symbol of power must not be overstressed, since some contemporaries perceived it not as legitimising pomp but as nauseating excess. In the early years of the eighteenth century John Evelyn, stung by hearing a sermon 'concerning the pride and luxury of apparel', remarked defensively on 'the sobriety and regularity of my own domestics'; he thought the cleric's condemnation would have been more appropriate in St James's, Piccadilly, or even aimed at the clergy themselves. Steele railed against 'equipages' (horse-drawn coaches and those that attended on them):

---

43   Hecht, *Servant Class*, pp. 119–21.
44   E.P. Thompson, 'The patricians and the plebs', in his *Customs in Common* (London, 1991), esp. p. 36: see also D. Hay, 'Property, authority and the criminal law', in D. Hay, P. Linebaugh, J. Rule and E.P. Thompson, eds, *Albion's Fatal Tree: Crime and Society in Eighteenth-Century England* (Harmondsworth, 1977); C. Fairchilds, *Domestic Enemies: Servants and their Masters in Old Regime France* (Baltimore, 1984), p. 13; *By the King A Proclamation . . . forbidding Footmen to wear Swords, or other Weapons, within London, Westminster, and their Liberties*, 29/9/1660, Goldsmiths Coll. 1538; Pepys, *Diary* II, p. 79, III, p. 77, VIII, p. 186.

'the horses and slaves of the rich take up the whole street', he protested in *The Tatler*, and suggested the removal of 'the horses and servants of all such as do not become or deserve such distinctions'. Defoe's proposal to force maids to wear livery as well as the menservants was intended to emphasise the wearer's servile status, not to raise that of all employers.[45] Male domestic servants of the gentry and nobility when resident in London, of course, were only one set of cast-members in the ever-evolving show of power, and the aggrandisement often worked in reverse: footmen themselves were to a large extent reliant on the afterglow of their masters' status to establish their own standing vicariously. Fairchilds has a gentry-made perspective on livery which by default is instructive about liveried menservants themselves: a signal component of their reputations was governed, unlike that of most female servants, by an intense publicity of role where attachment to the household was as much symbolic as it was functional. But the mutual re-inforcement of social display described above, together with public ambi-valence and the widespread use of livery, even by servants of lesser state officials, makes such symbolism more resistant to a single interpretation than Fairchilds permits.

Chastity

It is apparent that this aspect of the politics of 'place' is one dynamically fractured by gender, and it should come as no surprise to find that the aspect of female servants' characters that excited most prurient concern among these commentators, and therefore received substantial attention, was their sexual reputations. 'Cleanliness', according to *The Servants Calling*, was one of the 'chiefly ornamental' duties of the servant, but Haywood played on that theme when admonishing servants to avoid 'sluttishness' in order to draw a direct parallel between their work and their reputations:

> The constant attendant on sloth is sluttishness: she who gives her mind to idleness can neither be thoroughly clean in her own person or the house; and though her pride may force herself to prink herself up when she goes abroad, or her fear of being turned away make her keep those rooms in order in which her neglect, if otherwise, would be most conspicuous; yet all her neatness will be outside; there will always be some dirty thing about this one, and some unswept corners in the other . . . everything infallibly

---

45   J. Evelyn, *The Diary of John Evelyn* ed. J. Bowle (Oxford, 1985), p. 423; R. Steele, *The Tatler* ed. A.C. Ewald (London, 1888), no. 144 (11/3/1710), pp. 256–9; Defoe, *Everybody's Business*, p. 16.

shows a slut, than which there cannot be a more scandalous character or that will more effectually disqualify you for any good service.

It remains to be seen whether domestic servants themselves identified so closely with their labour, even if they were prepared to accept that their bodies were temples behind whose facade might lurk 'unswept corners'. But the simile restates the constant dichotomous theme of appearance and reality, and the message could not be clearer: gaining a reputation as a 'slut' would seriously damage a female servant's chances of finding a well-paid place in an agreeable household, and female servants at all levels of the hierarchy were vulnerable.[46]

'Waiting Gentlewomen' were advised to 'remember to be courteous and modest in your behaviour, to all persons according to their degree', and 'sober in your countenance and discourse, not using any wanton gesture, which may give any gentlemen an occasion to suspect you of levity; and so court you to debauchery, and by that means lose a reputation irrecoverable'. Chambermaids were told not to be 'giggling or idling out your time or wantoning in the society of men'; and even under cookmaids should 'take heed of the solicitations of the flesh for they will undo you, and though you may have mean thoughts of yourself, and think none will meddle with such as you, it is a mistake, for sometimes brave gallants will fall foul upon the wench in the scullery'.[47] No female servant was judged too low to have a reputation that was at risk of ruin, although various strategies existed to avoid losing it, restore it if threatened, or at least contest attempts to denigrate it. These included informal negotiation and argument, recognizance or summary hearing before a magistrate, a defamation suit at the church courts, or simply departure from their places (see the discussion of defamation disputes in Chapter Four). Servants quitted households where the behaviour of its occupants, especially the master and mistress, threatened to tarnish the reputations of those who worked in it by reflection.

Misbehaviour

From the opposite standpoint, the didactic literature of the late seventeenth and early eighteenth century suggested that the ultimate sanction for misbehaviour was termination of a servant's employment, and Samuel Pepys and his wife, his colleagues and acquaintances certainly availed themselves of it; but this appears to have been the expedient used by both employer and

---

46 [Zinzano], *Servants Calling*, p. 61; Haywood, *Present for a Servant-Maid*, p. 7.
47 Anon., *Complete Servant* (1677 edn), pp. 4, 62, 156.

employee albeit for different reasons. 'By far the single most effective means' servants had in bargaining terms, according to Ben-Amos, 'was to leave and find another master'.[48] Why did servants in such circumstances resort to departure, or employers to dismissal? A servant's indiscipline or drunkenness, 'differences' or arguments between servant and employer, and the violence used by employers in corporal punishment or sexual assault form a significant minority of the reasons given by servants for their departure from particular jobs; sexually-motivated violence can be seen as a form of punishment, at least in the minds of some masters.[49]

Departure, the rather drastic expedient of complete withdrawal of labour, was a real option for a servant since finding another place was relatively unproblematic in the metropolis during our period. For the employer, the withdrawal of employment in sacking a servant had to be retained as the ultimate economic sanction, but it was not without its attendant costs, since difficulties might be had in finding a replacement. When Pepys and his wife sacked Ashwell, Elizabeth Pepys's companion, and the cookmaid Hannah decided to leave before she was dismissed for theft, all within a day of each other, the diarist noted: 'my wife and I being left for an hour, till my brother came in, alone in the house, I grew very melancholy'. Returning home later, he found 'a sad distracted house, which troubles me . . . till my house is settled, I do not see I can mind my business of the office, which grieves me to the heart'. Temporary help had to be brought in (a former servant, and a Naval employee's wife), but the family's plight was exacerbated when its next intended member, a parish girl called Jinny, ran away on her first day with the clothes Pepys had her dressed in.[50]

In early seventeenth-century Norwich, second city of England, magistrates 'naturally related service to tranquillity and good order' and offered the idle and out of place the choice of punishment or going into service. A century later, Defoe rued 'the insolence and unsufferable behaviour of servants in England', where 'the poor govern and the rich submit', and urged a closer regulation of servants' manners by masters.[51] Does the Restoration mark a watershed in the concerns or efficiency of local governance? Or could there have been a vacuum of control between the informal enforcement

---

48 Pepys, *Diary* I, pp. 233–4 and 240, III, p. 57, IV, pp. 13, 92, 154, 279, 280–1, VIII, pp. 212, 375–6, and so on; I.K. Ben-Amos, *Adolescence and Youth in Early Modern England* (New Haven, 1994), p. 213.
49 See Chapter Four, this volume.
50 Pepys, *Diary* IV, pp. 279–82.
51 Griffiths, *Youth and Authority*, p. 354; D. Defoe, *The Great Law of Subordination considered; or, the Insolence and Unsufferable Behaviour of Servants in England duly enquired into* (London, 1724), p. 105.

of order in the household and the formal authority of the magistracy which late seventeenth- and early eighteenth-century servants were exploiting? Ann Kussmaul, writing in regard of service in husbandry, found few presentments to rural quarter sessions of disorderly servants, and concluded that 'the good order of servants was effected by their masters and not by the larger state'.[52] But the evidence from the secular courts and jurisdictions points to real differences in practice between the metropolis and the provinces.

Perennial difficulties in enforcing household order — the 'servant problem' that bedevilled the historian Dorothy Marshall and her readership in the mid-1920s and alluded to in her first published work on eighteenth-century service — were far from novel even in 1660. The original Statute of Labourers (25 *Ed.* III *c.* 2, 1351) governing compulsory service arose in response to labour shortages in the aftermath of the Black Death, and the social and economic crises at the end of the sixteenth century also stimulated attempts to control the young and mobile. Michael Roberts has discussed the implications of rising urban migration of young women in that period and the perceived threat of relatively independent unmarried women as service became casualised, short term and harder to regulate. Griffiths finds that during the late sixteenth and early seventeenth centuries in Norwich 'the generalised concern with fetching young people within the regulatory reach of service . . . became more narrowly focused on issues of gender as investigations turned up a greater number of women living independently', and that this development was clearly linked to increasing numbers of female migrants.[53]

In London, concern over the behaviour of servants and other adolescents manifested itself in a series of initiatives from the mid-sixteenth century onwards. 'The laws of the trade, town and state all contained provisions for regulating disordered households', writes Griffiths again, and Archer observes that the 'dense network of highly developed regulatory institutions' in the capital ensured wide access to punitive sanction: in particular, Bridewell received its charter in 1552, giving its governors sweeping discretionary powers of punishment in practice aimed at (among others) disorderly apprentices and servants. Of course, the livery companies that governed apprenticeship and the Mayor's court in the City of London were formally empowered and represented a far clearer structure of regulation than

---

52 A. Kussmaul, *Servants in Husbandry in Early Modern England* (Cambridge, 1981), p. 33.
53 D. Marshall, 'The domestic servants of the eighteenth century', *Economica* **9** (25) (1929), 16; M. Roberts, 'Women and work in sixteenth-century English towns', in P. Corfield and D. Keene, eds, *Work in Towns 850–1850* (Leicester, 1990), pp. 91–3; Griffiths, *Youth and Authority*, pp. 377–8.

anything available to domestic servants and their employers: 'in the case of servants who were not formally apprenticed', writes Griffiths, borough courts and quarter sessions 'were often courts of first resort' if household or neighbourhood mediation failed.[54]

JPs had traditionally spent much of their regulatory time mediating matters of vital importance to servants, in particular their role in wage and labour regulation through powers granted in the Statute of Artificers (5 *Eliz. c.* 4, 1563), their supervisory role in respect of the overseers of the poor granted by the poor laws, with their frequent direct participation in enforcing the settlement and bastardy laws. Magistrate and parish collaborated to govern the activities of the labouring poor, which usually embraced most servants for a large part of their lives. More particularly as Dalton and other writers of advice to JPs pointed out, magistrates had a key part to play in punishing servants for wrong-doing or indiscipline, and for instance took powers of summary conviction under statutes establishing and regulating houses of correction (especially 7 *Jac.* I *c.* 4) to commit them there: they had to be deemed 'idle and disorderly', or according to Dalton a 'vagabond that will abide in no service or place', a reading of the statute which criminalised unemployed youth.[55]

Accelerated female in-migration into towns in the late seventeenth century and heightened fears of uncontrolled or disobedient young women gave renewed impetus to concerned members of the elite. Magistrates and parish authorities had a central role in the concerted attempt to regulate the movement of labour through the settlement laws, and certainly by the second half of the eighteenth century Rogers finds that women, especially domestic servants out of place, formed the 'great majority' of those passed out of metropolitan London without a settlement to give them the right to stay (as discussed in the Introduction). Likewise, the attempt to control the burden on parishes of bastard children born to young women in the metropolis, usually female domestic servants whose babies were often enough fathered by their male counterparts, absorbed much parochial energy. It is important to note at this stage that the operation of the poor laws in London in particular have been reassessed in a much more favourable light: in a recent volume Boulton has suggested that 'most London parishes [in the seventeenth and early eighteenth centuries] failed, in practice, to use parish poor relief to discipline the poor', while Hitchcock has commented

---

54 Griffiths, *Youth and Authority*, pp. 303, 308; I.W. Archer, *The Pursuit of Stability: Social Relations in Elizabethan London* (Cambridge, 1991), p. 218.

55 A. Fletcher, *Reform in the Provinces: The Government of Stuart England* (New Haven, 1986), Chapter 7; Dalton, *Countrey Justice*, pp. 119, 150, 170, 514.

that the mid-eighteenth century provisions for bearers of bastard children in suburban London supplied a 'remarkably open and available social service'. There is also evidence that the poor were able to play off JP against overseer to gain what they increasingly perceived to be their entitlement to relief. The poor laws and their administration can no longer be portrayed as an oppressive monolithic whole, but must be seen as a locally-negotiated 'balance of communal identification and social differentiation' in which the rhetoric of exclusion might mask compassion and generosity as often as punishment and discipline.[56]

The political climate in late seventeenth- and early eighteenth-century London could, however, prove uncomfortable to large numbers of domestic servants. According to Shoemaker, members of societies for the reformation of manners (resurgent from the 1690s) thought that discipline and hierarchy had been undermined and servants threatened morality more widely than just within the household. Female servants, especially when unemployed, were seen to be major providers of sexual services in the West End and were frequently prosecuted for prostitution by the societies, women being more than twice as likely as men to be committed to houses of correction (including Bridewell). Many of the inmates of these institutions were young people of service age since 'impatient masters often committed their charges to houses of correction for a quick spell of corporal punishment', but most of them were 'out of place' at the time they allegedly committed their crimes. Defoe decried the 'amphibious life' of female domestic servants who, 'if they are out of place . . . must prostitute their bodies' such that 'many of them rove from place to place from bawdy-house to service . . . nothing being more common to find these creatures one week in a good family and the next in a brothel'.[57]

Shoemaker writes that 'during the 1690s, 1710s and 1720s it was commonly thought that London was experiencing a "crime wave"', and the

---

56 N. Rogers, 'Vagrancy, impressment and the regulation of labour in eighteenth-century Britain', *Slavery and Abolition* **15** (2) (1994), 106; J. Boulton, 'Going on the parish: the parish pension and its meaning in the London suburbs, 1640–1724', and T. Hitchcock, ' "Unlawfully begotten on her body": illegitimacy and the parish poor rate in St. Luke's Chelsea', both in T. Hitchcock, P. King and P. Sharpe, eds, *Chronicling Poverty: The Voices and Strategies of the English Poor, 1640–1840* (Basingstoke, 1997), pp. 30–1, 37, and 76 respectively; R. Connors, 'Poor women, the parish and the politics of poverty', in Barker and Chalus, eds, *Gender in Eighteenth-Century England*, p. 139; K. Wrightson, *English Society, 1580–1680* (London, 1982), p. 181. See Chapter Four, this volume.

57 R. Shoemaker, 'Reforming the City: the reformation of manners campaign in London, 1690–1738', in L. Davison, T. Hitchcock, T. Keirn and R.B. Shoemaker, eds, *Stilling the Grumbling Hive*, pp. 104–7, 110; R. Shoemaker, *Prosecution and Punishment*, pp. 184–6, 297; Defoe, *Everybody's Business*, p. 8.

elites indulged in further collective fears of a growing unruliness or, in Defoe's words, the 'unsufferable liberty' of London servants. Defoe offered the most insistent and coherent expression of these concerns, and he warned ominously of the result should servants ever forget their place: 'The poor will be rulers over the rich and the servants be governors of their masters'. Indeed, a new and increasingly repressive rhetoric of control developed between 1689 and 1750, exemplified by the passing of an 'act for the preventing and punishing robberies that shall be committed in houses' (12 *Anne c.* 7, 1713) which, according to John Beattie, was specifically aimed at servants in London. Whether a product of such legislation or despite it, Defoe could observe in 1725 that 'our [Old Bailey] sessions papers of late are crowded of instances of servant maids robbing their places', and he succeeded in articulating the fears of middling employers of the potential enemy within doors.[58]

It is important to remember that disputes between master and servant 'occurred between individuals who were acquainted with each other', as the historian of late seventeenth- and early eighteenth-century London petty crime has remarked, and therefore they 'were often informally mediated'. For those where no agreement was found, JPs had powers to deal with them. Section xxx of the Statute of Artificers required magistrates to make at least an annual 'special and diligent inquiry' into master–servant relations as regulated by the statute, and any breaches of its stipulations were to be 'severely corrected and punished' by them. They had several regulatory tools at their disposal before recourse to the relative severity of Bridewell, and 'numerous masters, servants and apprentices were bound over [by recognizance]', according to Shoemaker, 'for failing to fulfil the terms of their contract of service or indenture' by Westminster and Middlesex magistrates in the late seventeenth and early eighteenth centuries.[59]

There is, therefore, some sense here of London's regulation of disordered households embodying what John Styles and John Brewer have called 'a multiple-use right', in which tribunals and legal authorities were available to both superior and subordinate. One case serves to reinforce the point that this was a resource potentially available to servants as well as to employers: in the second decade of the eighteenth century, Justice William Booth at the Middlesex quarter sessions bound over gentleman Richard

---

58 Shoemaker, *Prosecution and Punishment*, p. 182; Defoe, *Great Law*, pp. 13, 17; J. Beattie, 'London crime and the making of the "Bloody Code", 1689–1718', in Davison *et al.*, eds, *Grumbling Hive*, p. 68; Defoe, *Everybody's Business*, p. 8. For servant theft in the late eighteenth century, see Peter King, 'Female offenders, work and life-cycle change in late eighteenth-century London', *Continuity and Change* **11** (1) (1996), 75–8.

59 Shoemaker, *Prosecution and Punishment*, pp. 55, 99, 207–12; 5 *Eliz. c.* 4, 1563.

Manley, lodging in Clerkenwell, for allegedly beating his servant. The particular popularity of this prosecutorial tool with single women suggests that some mistresses and female servants in the metropolis used this route. It would seem that domestic servants, like their apprentice counterparts, had modes of redress for household grievances and JPs were prepared to find in their favour on occasion. The differences between the institutions of livery company and City corporation and those which governed domestic servants have been emphasised, but nonetheless the evidence concurs with Griffiths's remarks that 'respect for justice and equity seems to have been a regular aspect of proceedings . . . it is clear that legal standards were introduced into disordered households'.[60]

There is a proviso: 'multiple-use right' in terms of process risks exaggeration when disciplinary outcomes are examined, since the social imbalance between master and servant was expressed most clearly in the way punishment for masters often damaged their wallets or pride, whereas for servants it could mean imprisonment. The royal pardon of Colonel Charteris for the rape of a servant maid (widely believed by contemporaries to be the result of 'Skreenmaster' Walpole's shielding of members of the social elites) reminded all that discretion within the courts frequently favoured the strong. Shoemaker's study of petty crime in London between 1660 and 1725 confirms that the selection of prosecutorial option, and therefore the likely severity of punishment, was greatly influenced by social status.[61] But further than this, a tribunal-centred perspective risks underestimating something the exponents of patriarchal authority repeatedly emphasised, that much power was exercised within the household: while family members and neighbours may have observed its operation, its immediacy always offered the chance for employers to be not just the primary but the only source of justice.

Conclusion

Exchanging the social currency of mutually-reinforcing reputation — the 'characters' of individual servants and the common fame of the households in which they worked — helped to weave the web which bound together

---

60   J. Brewer and J. Styles, eds, *An Ungovernable People: The English and their Law in the Seventeenth and Eighteenth Centuries* (London, 1980), p. 20; Shoemaker, *Prosecution and Punishment*, pp. 118–19, 208–10; Griffiths, *Youth and Authority*, p. 308.

61   Langford, *Polite and Commercial People*, p. 22: Charteris was satirised in Hogarth's *A Harlot's Progress* (plate 1) and Fielding's play *Rape upon Rape*; Shoemaker, *Prosecution and Punishment*, pp. 201–7.

patriarchal social relations: servants to employers, and the household to parish, neighbourhood and metropolis. Reputation was regulated by gossip, slander, taunts, reports of character and the visual indicators of place, dress and appearance. Whether masters and mistresses liked it or not, and frequent injunctions against 'eye-service' in the prescriptive literature suggests that they did not, their servants took an active role in creating and maintaining their employers' social personae. The reverse was also true, and gender was an inescapable element, as female servants defended their sexual credit while male servants tried to maintain their pride and dignity. But the account above has suggested that the very publicity of this interaction of patriarchal forces ensured vociferous disagreement amongst those driven to debate the issues (in terms of the printed discourse mostly servant-employers), as irritations and fears over servant dress illustrate.

Nevertheless, ideals expressed in prescriptive, spiritual or legal injunctions delineated clearly the perimeters of patriarchal authority which continued to be summarised most succinctly in the father-monarch simile: as the king to his subjects, so the father to his family. Moreover, the inclusiveness of the early modern use of the term 'family' was not merely semantic, as this and following chapters demonstrate. The patriarchal master and mistress of the household exercised authority over their servants within ideologies and structures that permitted at least moderate chastisement and also facilitated external intervention, yet which in Griffiths's words 'were sufficiently flexible to contain most disputes'.[62] The household embedded in the community was ideally in contemporary eyes a vital, if not the key, site of enforcement of the social order, and nursery of the norms by which that order would be preserved for posterity; but in an age sensitive to the imposition of authority, it was not perceived necessarily as a locus of tyranny.

The rhetoric of patriarchy seemed most persistent in its exposition of firm mastery within the household, but it must be this that has tricked some historians into describing the alleged novelty of the managerial mistress from the late eighteenth century. When prescriptive and other related texts are examined, it is clear that in terms of the quotidian regulation of the London household in which servants were employed, mistresses were deemed to have significant authority. The chronological limitations of this present study do not allow conclusive statements regarding change from the mid-eighteenth century; but a model of 'separate spheres' predicated upon a transition after that point, in which an increasingly distant mistress assumed command over her (female) domestic servants, will now have to establish why the English metropolis was exceptional in this regard. Here, it is much

---

62   Griffiths, *Youth and Authority*, p. 298.

more plausible to acknowledge long-term continuity in the validation of these forms of household relations, components of patriarchy which do not dispense with the gendered nature of that paradigm.

Of course, while the politics of 'place' between 1660 and 1750 looked very much like that of the period before (and probably that which came after too), social and cultural change conspired to vary its impact and scope. The years before and after the turn of the eighteenth century witnessed another perceived 'crime wave' and felt the chill blast of a further concerted attempt to reform manners, in which out-of-place female servants were particularly vulnerable. It is not unreasonable to assume that some employers in sympathy with the Jeremiahs of reform exercised a more oppressive vigilance as a result. Yet the very forces which may have fostered these middling and elite fears also served to lessen their impact: despite attempts by employers as householders or magistrates to put the control of servant reputation on a more institutional footing in the late seventeenth and early eighteenth centuries, the sheer scale and vigour of the market for domestic service in London ensured limited success for dress codes and register offices before 1750. The growing demand for servants meant that a major weapon in the master or mistress's armoury, the option of summary dismissal, was far less effective. It is possible that late eighteenth-century economic and demographic shifts resulted in the initiative returning to employers, but in the period under consideration here, 'place' was as political in its negotiations and compromises as it was in the attempts to impose patriarchal authority. The next chapter will attempt to put some flesh on the ideal framework discussed above, by exploring the testimonies of servants themselves to get under the skin of day-to-day relations within servant-employing metropolitan households.

CHAPTER FOUR

Household relations

. . . you must beware of gossips and charwomen, for they will misadvise you.[1]

Introduction

Relations within the household between masters, mistresses and servants have been central to contemporary conceptions of order and divinely-ordained authority, as the previous chapter demonstrated. The impact of the politics of 'place' always varied from household to household, but its over-all framework differed little at the turn of the eighteenth century from that at the turn of the seventeenth. An ideal of patriarchal relations developed in which masters and mistresses tried to govern their domestic servants within the household through a variety of persuasive and coercive mechanisms, while attempting to preserve order more widely via the negotiation and regulation of reputation. This was assisted by extra-household institutions, including spiritual and secular courts, but these were seen to operate to some extent as a 'multiple-use right' for all parties in domestic disputes. The idea that the eighteenth century witnessed a new managerial mistress was challenged, and while the potential for household tyranny existed, patri-archal ideals encouraged more mutually-supportive relations. The present chapter will attempt the difficult task of reconstructing the complex inter-action between servants and their masters and mistresses in the daily lives of households in late seventeenth- and early eighteenth-century London.

---

1 Anon., *The Complete Servant-Maid; or The Young Maiden's and Family's Daily Companion* (London, 1677), p. 156.

However, since there has been only one major text on the subject for most of the post-war era, Jean Hecht's *The Domestic Servant Class in Eighteenth-Century England* of 1956, we have been saddled with a slightly jaundiced view for too long. Hecht painted a picture of a formal hierarchy of increasingly insolent lower orders in which gender differences were taken for granted rather than explained.[2] Such a limited characterisation is insufficient today. But given the wider range of materials available to the historian of service now, how are we to conceptualise relations in servant-employing households? Some years ago, Sarah Maza developed a model of eighteenth-century service as mediation at the 'threshold' of the master's house that left servants in a liminal position, on the cusp between their employers and the rest of society. 'The stigma that derived from servility, imitation, and social ambiguity', particularly for menservants, and the vulnerability of female servants to 'accusations of prostitution and loose living' meant they 'often protected themselves by retreating to the territory that was really their own: the doorsteps of their masters' houses'.[3] This is an imaginative response to the way work might structure life in such a way as to exclude groups of servants from both the privileged lives of their masters and the social milieux of other members of the labouring classes around them. Under certain circumstances, they were consciously putting their servants between themselves and the rest of the world (for instance, when servants ran important errands for them), and this could leave servants in social limbo. This model may well have some resonance for the liveried servants of the *haute-bourgeoisie* and nobility of both France and England.

However, the 'threshold' model is predicated on spatial as well as psychological exclusion, and given the extensive range of household type and size which employed servants in London, its purchase is limited. It may well be restricted to some of the servants of the wealthy whose living and working conditions (in terms of the size and nature of the premises, and the degree of formality of dress, comportment and employer–employee relations) fostered such distance from London life. Within the small minority of London households in which these factors prevailed at any time between 1660 and 1750, certain compensations existed: even hierarchical 'families' engendered camaraderie and friendship. But in fact, the intercession of errand-running or controlling entry or exit across the threshold could have resulted in the opposite of the isolation of Maza's model: servants for those

---

2 J.J. Hecht, *The Domestic Servant Class in Eighteenth-Century England* (London, 1956); Hill's defence of Hecht is bewildering: B. Hill, *Servants: English Domestics in the Eighteenth Century* (Oxford, 1996), p. 9.

3 S. Maza, *Servants and Masters in Eighteenth-Century France: the Uses of Loyalty* (Princeton, 1983), Chapter 3, esp. pp. 109–10, 131, 134.

employers who relied on their employees to act as their eyes, ears and hands will have found themselves even more *of* the world, and not (as the threshold model suggests) in a social limbo *between* worlds. To take a well-known example, Pepys's second footboy Wayneman (brother of his maid Jane) was beaten 'for his staying of errands and other faults', suggesting that there was life beyond the confines of his master's household and commands.[4] This chapter demonstrates how servants were able to create their own spaces within households and even sometimes outside them.

Perhaps more important than the threshold thesis, there are a number of arguments made by historians for increasing privacy within the household which depend upon a growing distance between employers and servants. There are several related strands to these arguments. The first is a conceptual one that revolves around the breach of the link between 'household' and 'family'; the second asserts that a new gendered 'domesticity' or 'domestic ideology' was born in the emergence of the middling (or middle class) managerial mistress in the eighteenth century; and the third argues that the servant–employer relationship gradually became contractual in this period as patriarchy dissolved in the onslaught of modernity. The fortunes of patriarchy have been addressed in the previous chapter, and the remunerative aspects of servant contracts will be discussed in more detail in Chapter Six (although some aspects of the contractual argument will be dealt with here). As for the first and second strands, these appear to exhibit disturbing traits of theses stretched beyond the parameters within which they were originally bound.

This chapter will employ a variety of approaches. Firstly, inclusive notions of 'family' will be examined alongside the idea of privacy within the household, to demonstrate the need for a sensitive reading of social relations that sees the period in its own terms rather than imposes an anachronistic conceptual straight-jacket on the past. Then, a picture will be portrayed of day-to-day interaction between employer and employee, examining in particular the implications for the servant of illness while in place, and the extent to which employers acted *in loco parentis*. Thirdly, the chapter considers the nature and significance of sexual relations within the household between servants and other occupants, together with the risks and dangers attendant upon servant pregnancy. Finally, the chapter ends by analysing why servants left households. The subject of service relations is certainly not served by descriptions tinged with the rosy glow of retrospective romance, but nor is the varied evidence of servant histories forced into awkward patterns

---

4   S. Pepys, *The Diary of Samuel Pepys*, 11 vols, eds R. Latham and W. Matthews (London, 1971), III, p. 66.

or misshapen moulds: the goal is as authentic a portrayal of domestic relations within servant-employing households as the evidence permits, and an assessment of the significance of these results for our appreciation of the broader canvas of social relations in London during the long eighteenth century.

Privacy and the family

The private realm, the conceptual links made or assumed by historians between it and oncoming modernity, and the supposed 'growth of privacy' in the eighteenth century were all the subject of renewed debate in the 1990s. Before this bout of revision, the private was defined in reflected terms thanks to the 'powerful dichotomy' it forms with the notion of the public, and to some extent that was an omission mirrored by the sources: according to John Brewer, the term 'private' in the eighteenth-century printed literature has a 'residual character', where privacy is often defined by default as everything not deemed 'public'. But even where the private sphere has been the focus of extensive debate, amongst feminist historians of the nineteenth century for instance, it is circumscribed by the way the public/private dichotomy has been naturalised. 'Until recently', writes Davidoff, 'debates about the public and private have taken the domestic for granted as well as being unaware of a gender dimension'.[5] These influential constraints have consequently had an impact on our understanding of domestic service, and servant–employer interaction in the long eighteenth century can only be fully understood by problematising historians' usage of 'household' and 'family', which is where the present analysis will begin.

Chapter Three established that contemporaries located service, as a form of social relationship as much as a mode of employment, firmly in a domestic arena within the early modern household. The term 'household' was certainly current in the period and several definitions were in use from medieval times, including 'the inmates of a house collectively; an organised family including servants or attendants, dwelling in a house; a domestic establishment' (and, of course, 'the royal or imperial household'). In other words, 'household' described a group of individuals in a discrete domestic location, organised or at least in coherent form within a 'family' in the early

5   D. Castiglione and L. Sharpe, eds, *Shifting the Boundaries: Transformation of the Languages of Public and Private in the Eighteenth Century* (Exeter, 1995), p. ix; J. Brewer, 'This, that and the other: public, social and private in the seventeenth and eighteenth centuries', in the same volume, p. 8; L. Davidoff, 'Regarding some "old husbands' tales": the public and the private in feminist history', in her *Worlds Between: Historical Perspectives on Gender and Class* (Cambridge, 1995), p. 228.

modern, inclusive sense of that term. Tadmor has recently reminded us of what she calls 'the concept of the household-family', declaring that usually when writers in the seventeenth and eighteenth centuries used the word 'family', 'it was not the nuclear family they had in mind' but 'a household, including its diverse dependants, such as servants, apprentices and co-resident relatives'. She cites the definition Johnson gave for 'family' in his mid-eighteenth-century *Dictionary of the English Language* as 'those who live in the same house'. This would have been somewhat problematic in the sub-divided, multi-occupancy London dwelling, but otherwise coincided with 'household'. It is precisely the elision between these related concepts that has troubled historians and muddied the waters lapping between servant and employer.[6]

The idea of a new 'domesticity' in which employers withdrew from their servants has acquired most force in the hands of feminist historians who have sought the origins of what they term 'domestic ideology'. When Hill asserts that servants were 'often virtually cut off from contact with the world outside' with little eighteenth-century evidence to support so bleak a portrait, she appears to have adopted an aspect of late nineteenth-century historiography and dragged it, mute and pliant, backwards one hundred years. Leonore Davidoff influentially described Victorian middle-class households in 'isolated settings' that 'made English domestic service extremely confining', and with Hall posited an ideology of domesticity in which the household was the locus of middle-class construction in the late eighteenth and early nineteenth centuries. Here, 'the day-to-day management of servants was becoming a central part of middle class women's role', who without them 'would have become exhausted drudges, incapable of much cultural or religious activity'. Servants may have 'fitted the familial model', but when dealing with them, mistresses 'experienced the contradictions of operating across class lines in a family setting'. In further support, Hill also attributes changes 'to the middle class wife's idea of domestic comfort' near the end of the eighteenth century.[7]

6 *OED*, entry for 'household'; N. Tadmor, 'The concept of the household-family in eighteenth-century England', *Past and Present* **151** (1996), 112. For an extended discussion of historians' confusion over the family/household elision see T. Meldrum, 'Domestic service in London, 1660–1750: gender, life cycle, work and household relations', unpublished University of London Ph.D. thesis (1996), Chapter 6.
7 Hill, *Servants*, p. 19; L. Davidoff, 'Mastered for life: servant and wife in Victorian England', *Journal of Social History* 7 (1974), 408–9; *cf.* P. Horn, *The Rise and Fall of the Victorian Servant* (Dublin, 1975), p. 122; L. Davidoff and C. Hall, *Family Fortunes: Men and Women of the English Middle Class, 1780–1850* (London, 1987), pp. 392, 394; B. Hill, *Women, Work and Sexual Politics in Eighteenth Century England* (Oxford, 1989), p. 127. 'Exhausted drudges' are examined in Chapter Five.

How might these ideas apply to households in the English metropolis in our period? Seleski argues strongly that the sub-genre of advice literature aimed at women either as mistresses or as servants was vital in the construction of middle-class domestic ideology, 'and as the concept of household management evolved in the course of the eighteenth century, the duties of a mistress became part of women's natural role'. She alleges that 'the creation of middle-class domestic ideology and the re-creation of the household as the natural and exclusive domain of women involved domestic servants from the very beginning'. So the thesis depends on, firstly, the novelty of the managerial mistress in the latter part of the eighteenth century; secondly, the 'ideological' quality of such housewifery in its links with class formation; and thirdly, the coherence of something called the 'middle class' in more than just ideological terms.[8]

These are very large issues, but even at this early stage several factors appear to render Davidoff's, Hall's and Seleski's assumptions uncertain. Chapter Three demonstrated that a literature has existed from at least as early as the fourteenth century exhorting mistresses to be better managers of their servants: there was nothing new about mistresses managing servants in the 1750s, let alone their being advised to do so. In Vickery's words, 'The effective government of servants had long been seen as an essential duty'. And if the post-Restoration period (certainly well before the mid-eighteenth century) marks a growth in advice literature to mistresses and female servants, it is far from clear how such recycled texts exhibit a new raising of middle-class consciousness in ideological form in the late eighteenth century, particularly if (following Earle) the 'making of the English middle class' began in London after the Restoration.[9]

Further than this, the 'domestic ideology' thesis exhibits a marked tendency to render the middle classes (or 'middling sorts of people', for the period covered by this book) homogeneous to a degree that stifles the variety of experience found in servant-employing households of different sizes and types. According to Earle, an author cited approvingly by Seleski several times in her chapter, around the turn of the eighteenth century an annual income of £50 'would allow a family to eat well, employ a servant and live comfortably', and his middle class includes families with incomes far larger than that, tending to employ more servants as they got richer.

8 P. Seleski, 'Women, work and cultural change in eighteenth and early nineteenth-century London', in T. Harris, ed., *Popular Culture in England, c.1500–1850* (Basingstoke, 1995), pp. 146, 156. For the managerial mistress at work, see Chapter Five, this volume.

9 A. Vickery, *The Gentleman's Daughter: Women's Lives in Georgian England* (New Haven, 1998), p. 127; P. Earle, *The Making of the English Middle Class: Business, Society and Family Life in London, 1660–1730* (London, 1989), Chapter 8.

Edward Higgs's dissection of the nineteenth-century censuses, it is hoped, will encourage a rethinking of domestic service in that period given his finding that 'the largest occupational group amongst the heads of servant-employing households was retailers of some sort' in mid-Victorian Rochdale. Is it not likely that the social breadth of nineteenth-century servant-employing middle classes precludes the application of a universal character of domestic relations?[10]

There is another strand linking the alleged increasing centrality of middle-class employment of servants to increasing distance between employer and servant, the process of domestic service 'feminisation' in the eighteenth and nineteenth centuries. Fairchilds, one of the more widely-read historians of domestic service in *ancien régime* France, has declared that domestic service in France 'ceased to be public and it ceased to be patriarchal' by the end of the eighteenth century, in contrast to England where privacy had rendered servant and employer distant by the early part of that century. In France, 'servant disloyalty' was avoided by hiring only 'docile and devoted' servants; in other words, by employing 'women and boys' the growing number of *bourgeois* masters and mistresses guaranteed their own privacy (in the twentieth-century sense) and ensured their servants would be of the kind to obey them.[11]

How that shift ensured a diminution of patriarchy is difficult to envisage, and Maza has countered Fairchilds and the French historian Gutton by doubting 'that the shift to a more nakedly "contractual" relationship occurred as early or as decisively as these writers suggest'. She did not deny that 'the relationship between master and servant was fundamentally transformed between the seventeenth and the nineteenth century', but 'framing the problem around the "decline of paternalism" [presumably, the reciprocal qualities of patriarchy] in the eighteenth century amounts to hitching up the proverbial cart before its horses. What is at first most intriguing' about paternalist values, wrote Maza, 'is not that they eventually became obsolete, as indeed they did, but that they endured for so long'. And Seleski, writing on late eighteenth-century London service, rightly seeks to undermine the 'feminisation' thesis by dismissing the 'facile equating of women's numerical dominance among the ranks of domestic service and the radical reduction of servants' independence', since it 'ignores

---

10   Earle, *English Middle Class*, p. 14; E. Higgs, 'Domestic service and household production', in A.V. John, *Unequal Opportunities: Women's Employment in England 1800–1918* (Oxford, 1986), p. 135.

11   C. Fairchilds, *Domestic Enemies: Servants and their Masters in Old Regime France* (Baltimore, 1984), pp. 16–17, 38–40, 158 — for her debt to Lawrence Stone, see p. xiv, n. 6.

the other factors involved in circumscribing women's economic and behavioural options'.[12]

The impact of post-structuralism has assisted in encouraging further revision, and symptomatic of recent historiographical shifts was the publication in the 1980s of *L'Histoire de la vie Privée*. In a section entitled 'The Urban Family', Farge observed (in a comment echoed by another writer in the collection) that in eighteenth-century Paris 'the life of the family was not withdrawn or self-centred . . . The typical family was permeated, if not in fact constituted, by a network of external dependencies'. The contingency of modern notions of privacy was reinforced by Castan: 'doorways, streets, and even public squares were taken over by women . . . During the seventeenth and eighteenth centuries this is where the shifting boundary between public and private was located'; the *bourgeoise* mistress 'not only supervised the work of her household staff but also lived with them on terms of familiarity, not to say complicity'. She ends her piece somewhat ambiguously with the following words: 'Private life did exist but it was inseparable from the indispensable community'.[13] Volume three of *L'Histoire de la vie Privée* avoids schematic formulations of 'family' and 'household', although in doing so perhaps betrays a lack of precision. Yet it constitutes a valuable contribution to the comparative history of urban *mentalités*: imprecision is inevitable in the description of the blurred categories at the household–family elision, and this recent French work has highlighted how overdrawn were some of the conceptual boundaries of earlier orthodox accounts.

While the overlap between notions of household and family has led some historians to get bogged down in definition, the lived reality of this domestic conflation for many contemporaries in London means that the elision retains conceptual utility, but certainly need not imply a single form of institution or way of life. The recognition in the Introduction of the importance of the life cycle applies to all members of the household-family: membership may have been stable for long periods of time or subject to unceasing change, and narrowing historical models down to a single interpretation is misleading. So models describing a relatively homogeneous 'middle class' risk missing the variety of arrangements in servant-employing households throughout the long eighteenth century. The applicability of a notion of

---

12 Maza, *Servants and Masters*, p. 15; P. Seleski, 'The women of the labouring poor: love, work and poverty in London, 1750–1820', unpublished Ph.D. thesis, Stanford University (1989), pp. 27, 115.

13 A. Farge, 'The honour and secrecy of families', p. 574; M. Aymard, 'Friends and neighbours', pp. 447–8; N. Castan, 'The public and the private', pp. 414, 411, 445: all in R. Chartier, ed., *A History of Private Life*, vol. III, *Passions of the Renaissance*, trans. A. Goldhammer (Cambridge, Mass., 1989).

isolated servants to urban domestic service in Britain appears *prima facie* to be inadequate: some large country houses may have controlled servant space in such a way, but the utility of universal models based on elite evidence of growing 'privacy', or the novelty of managerial mistresses, appears at this early stage to be doubtful. As the above account has tried to show, some of the problems that exist in the most influential theses about privacy and the household–family elision revolve around historical timing. It is perfectly possible that a significant ideological shift occurred in the late eighteenth and early nineteenth centuries, a period not covered here; but this chapter suggests that servant–employer relations, if they are to be recruited to explain growing 'domesticity' and increasing privacy, need to be examined more sensitively and among a wider range of servant-employing households before a definitive conclusion can be reached. These themes will be tested further in this chapter by an examination of day-to-day domestic friendship and violence in contemporary London households, and sexual relations in servants' as well as employers' words. But the work of *L'Histoire de la vie Privée* team demonstrates the value of an examination of the spatial aspects of life in the metropolitan household, and the next section will focus on the potential physical manifestations of privacy secluding employer from domestic employee.

Servants and spatial segregation[14]

Early modern researchers have dug up a variety of evidence in attempts to map room use and the changing nature of domestic space. Recently, probate inventories have been extensively mined to answer a range of historical problems, and this section begins by examining findings from urban communities which deal with domestic space in (or just after) use. Brown employed probate inventories in conjunction with house plans to analyse room use in seventeenth-century London. Brown's key finding relates to the parlour: he believes it remained a withdrawing space throughout the seventeenth century, but in the first few decades it became situated towards the rear of the house, 'a place to which members of the family could retire for greater privacy'. Priestly and Corfield used inventories to examine changes in room use in early modern Norwich, England's second city for most of the early modern period. Their inventories came overwhelmingly from

---

14 This section is a summary of my 'Domestic service, privacy and the eighteenth-century metropolitan household', *Urban History* **26** (1) (1999).

middling trades and craft households, most if not all of whom would have employed servants of some nature. They noted an overall decrease in the number of truckle or trundle-beds in these Norwich houses together with a tendency for the chambers over the parlour to be used as a bedroom, 'following', they allege, 'the trend to greater convenience allied to greater privacy. The custom of having servants and children sleeping in the same room as the master of the house, on the easily-moveable "truckle" or "trundle" beds, apparently died out'.[15]

These are all important findings, but as far as broader cultural change is concerned, the authors give too much weight to long-term changes in room layout. Brown fails to specify whether the 'families' who withdrew to the rear parlour included their servants, and so does not discuss the implications that inclusion or exclusion of domestics might have for an understanding of seventeenth-century metropolitan privacy. Priestly and Corfield do not provide corroborative evidence to reinforce that of their inventories, and in its absence we might speculate that numbers (or even the heights) of servants, apprentices or children shrank in Norwich households between 1580 and 1730: the authors later observe that the fall in the numbers of truckle beds may have occurred due to a change in fashion with 'larger bedsteads replacing them', making 'increased bed-sharing feasible'.[16] This must beg the question of how privacy has been enhanced if bed-time intimacy has grown; both papers require answers to questions of whose privacy is being discussed at any given point, and the meanings of privacy in these contexts.

For the period under scrutiny in this chapter, the late seventeenth and early eighteenth centuries, it is the work of Lawrence and Jean Fawtier Stone which has had the greatest impact as far as domestic space and cultural change is concerned. Lawrence Stone wrote that 'it was not until the *late* eighteenth century that the growing desire for privacy and improved technology led to the removal of all the servants' bedrooms to a separate attic floor, linked to those of their employers merely by a bell and a bell-wire'; indeed, this 'must have been one of the most important innovations in the creation of private space for the owner and his family'. The Stones' researches have led them to construct a two-pronged thesis. Firstly, they outline a chronological shift in domestic architecture over the eighteenth century which, by the end of that century, marks a growing demand for

---

15 F.E. Brown, 'Continuity and change in the urban house: developments in domestic space organisation in seventeenth-century London', *Comparative Studies in Society and History* **28** (3) (1986), 588; U. Priestly and P. Corfield, 'Rooms and room use in Norwich housing, 1580–1730', *Post-Medieval Archaeology* **16** (1982), 115.

16 Priestly and Corfield, 'Rooms and room use', 116.

'privacy'. For this they evince the alleged novelty of corridors, the servants' hall, servants' separate bedrooms, bells, and back stairs — a device that meant, as Girouard has delicately put it, that 'the gentry walking up the stairs no longer met their last night's faeces coming down them'.[17]

Secondly, they suggest a trickle-down theory of the sociology of privacy and a trend from rural to urban housing. In earlier writing, Stone insisted that 'the first protests against the invasion of privacy came from the middle classes', yet also that 'trends to architectural privacy mainly affected the wealthy, but in the seventeenth and eighteenth centuries the housing of all classes down to that of yeomen and tradesmen became more varied, more subdivided and more specialised in function, and thus afforded greater privacy'. In later work on the aristocracy, however, the Stones chart the emergence of such novelties listed earlier in the large elite country house in stages from the end of the seventeenth century, while in Stones' books on divorce, the spatial layout of London houses (aristocratic and middling) appears to militate against privacy throughout much of the eighteenth.[18] The implication, it is reasonable to infer, is that the propertied elites began the shift to built-in seclusion at the beginning of our period which most of the middling sort could only aspire to, rather than afford, until its end.

However, it will be argued here that there is a tendency towards architectural determinism in these writings which should be resisted. Evidence of matters as complex as the conscious distancing of relations between employers and their servants, or the emergence of key cultural components of modernity like 'privacy', cannot be read straight from the fabric of contemporary buildings. If such transformations occurred, they were the product of — among other phenomena — the nature of relations between servants and their masters and mistresses and need to be observed within such a context. The present critique begins with an analysis of the thesis's chronology of change. Girouard and the Stones have provided ample evidence for the increasing interest by the nobility and upper gentry in these architectural innovations for their country estates, and have also shown how the wealthiest resident gentry in large London households invested in devices that apparently encouraged servants to become, in Girouard's words, 'if not

---

17 L. Stone, *Road to Divorce: England 1530–1987* (Oxford, 1990), pp. 212 (my emphasis), 229; his *Family, Sex and Marriage in England 1500–1800* (London, 1977), pp. 254–5; L. Stone and J.C. Fawtier Stone, *An Open Elite? England 1540–1880* (Oxford, 1984), pp. 347, 348; M. Girouard, *Life in the English Country House* (Harmondsworth, 1980), pp. 136–40 (esp. 138), 219, 264–5; M. Waterson, *The Servants' Hall: A Domestic History of Erdigg* (London, 1980), p. 8, plate 9.

18 Stone, *Family, Sex and Marriage*, pp. 254–5; Stone and Stone, *Open Elite?*, pp. 343–7; Stone, *Road to Divorce*, pp. 213–14.

invisible, very much less visible'. This thesis has recently received support from Port in his work on aristocratic town-houses in the eighteenth-century metropolis.[19] But the London church court depositions given by servant and other witnesses reveal that the pace of this change appears in some respects to have been faster than the Stones have claimed, and in others much more complex.

Mrs Anderson's case offers insights into the spatial ambit of servants' lives within the early eighteenth-century London house. It concerned illicit events that took place on the premises of the well-to-do uncle of the principal witness in the case, a young unmarried woman who had come out of the country to lodge with her uncle in London. Mrs Anderson, apparently separated from her husband, was the uncle's servant, and his niece possibly worked alongside Mrs Anderson in the completion of some household chores. This 'family' also housed exalted lodgers, Lord Murray and his footman, while Parliament sat. Following the contemporary convention that supposedly guaranteed female chastity as well as segregation by sex of servants' sleeping quarters, the niece and Mrs Anderson both slept in the same bed up three flights of stairs in the house's garret. But despite this, Anderson and Lord Murray's footman John McGlashan still managed to conduct an affair in the garret, in a room next to that in which Anderson and her master's niece normally lay. McGlashan's vindictive testimony against the woman with whom he had had sex — he claimed she had given him the pox — did not make clear whether the affair took place in his room. It is more likely (given gender sensitivities illustrated below) that he either lodged on the same floor with his master, probably the first floor, or, as did footman Francis Hughes and other menservants in the metropolis, boarded out in premises nearby. Hughes found lodgings of his own when his mistress's lodgings had no room for him in 1728.[20]

Anderson was unlucky to be one of the few targets of the London Consistory court's waning regulatory powers against spiritual offences during the eighteenth century. Her case demonstrates, however, that once the issue of servants in separate rooms is examined more closely, the Stones' model fails to fit the chronology observed here. Anderson and her master's niece resided in the garret in 1714, years before they should have done if the Stones are to be believed. But they were not unique: in 1684, a maidservant named Elizabeth Melchior slept in a common bedroom with all the female

19   Girouard, *English Country House*, p. 138; M.H. Port, 'West end palaces: the aristocratic town house in London 1730–1830', *London Journal* **20**, 1 (1995), 30–33.
20   LMA, DL/C/254 ff. 67–71, *Office c. Anderson*, March 1714; DL/C/254 f. 71, John McGlashan, 12/3/1714; Francis Hughes, DL/C/265 f. 82, 5/12/1728.

servants to families within the same building, including her household and those of the lodgers; in Elizabeth Cram's master's house in 1720, the servant of people lodging on the first floor slept in the garret. In 1744, maids to a gunsmith in the parish of St Bride's slept in a second-floor room while the apprentices lived in an outbuilding, demonstrating clear gender segregation; in the same year, in a household that was seemingly without lodgers or apprentices, the cookmaid and chambermaid shared the garret room. These findings are supported by Earle, most of whose inventories from the same period showed servants living in garrets. By contrast, Martha Gordon shared a series of lodgings with her mistress where sometimes she had a bed in a separate room, but at other times she shared the only bed with her mistress.[21]

Other architectural innovations identified by the Stones as marking a later eighteenth-century arrival of privacy can be found far earlier in London. The house of John Dormer, Esquire, in Albemarle Street had both a servants' hall and back stairs in the 1710s, and one of his servants seemed quite aware of the latter's stated architectural purpose at least. One of Dormers' footmen commented that a former fellow-servant 'went up the great stairs more like a master than a servant and not up the back stairs as the rest of the servants generally did'. As for servant bells, summons from a distance by bell-wire would certainly have been a 'considerable advance in sophistication' on Pepys's bell to summon servants in the 1660s, which simply hung outside his bedchamber. But if the aim of bells was to facilitate 'the segregation of the family from the servants', as the Stones have put it, Pepys in his town-house had surely achieved as much in 1663: he could send the servants away to enjoy his 'seclusion', and still summon them when required.[22] It is apparent that the first (chronological) part of the Stones' thesis, the emergence of a material culture of privacy in the eighteenth century which gained momentum towards 1800, is undermined as soon as scrutiny has broadened out from architectural evidence to the testimony of individuals who lived in contemporary housing.

The second aspect of the Stones' thesis to be considered is the alleged cultural trickle-down of privacy, and the trend from rural to urban housing.

---

21   T. Meldrum, 'A women's court in London: defamation at the Bishop of London's Consistory Court, 1700–1745', *London Journal* **19** (1) (1994), 2, Table 1; LMA, DL/C/241 f. 31, Elizabeth Melchior, and f. 14, Martha Amar, both on 7/4/1684; DL/C/259 f. 181, Elizabeth Cram, 19/11/1720; DL/C/273 f. 248, Elizabeth Cole, 2/2/1744; f. 305, Martha Taylor, 7/2/1744; DL/C/250 f. 54, Martha Gordon, 13/2/1708; Earle, *English Middle Class*, pp. 207, 210.

22   LMA, DL/C/255 f. 133, Robert White, 17/3/1715; Girouard, *English Country House*, p. 264; Stone and Stone, *Open Elite?*, p. 347; Pepys, *Diary* IV, p. 325, and V, p. 322.

But the characteristics of service in the metropolis — the largest labour market for domestic servants in Europe by the early eighteenth century thanks largely to middling demand, where most servant-employing house-holds kept one or two female servants — mean we must consider the implications that arise. Firstly, few individual households would have had the headache of accommodating large collectives of domestic servants. Indeed, the evidence cited above suggests that houses of multi-occupation appear to have already developed means of coping with several households' servants: rendering armies of flunkies 'invisible' was not a problem for most servant-employers. Secondly, the spatial complication of gender segrega-tion was far more likely to involve female domestic servants and male apprentices, as it did in the gunsmith's household in St Bride's, than housemaids, cookmaids, nurserymaids and the livery. In other words, the complexity of membership within most servant-employing households in London was different in nature from that suggested by the Stones: there is no sense in their writings that the diverse nature of service work may have had differing impacts on employer–servant relations or their spatial manifestations.

The evidence suggests that London middling houses already utilised some of the Stones' architectural devices at a time when, according to their model, they should only have been available to the rural elites. Further, it is clear that up-market architectural evidence should be treated warily. Many of the Stones' architectural innovations were beyond the reach of some of England's wealthiest even in the late eighteenth century. Port has demon-strated that in eighteenth-century London, most aristocratic house-builders opted to rent or lease terraced houses rather than build 'insulated man-sions', in which innovation might be indulged, usually because of the sharp differences in relative cost.[23] But the range of possible motives explored by Port for selection of residence by the nobility, and Lord Murray's lodgings in a middling household (see Anderson's case above), suggests that multiple interpretations of their use of domestic space are possible.

How precocious was eighteenth-century London in this matter? The parameters of the physical spaces in which servants worked were necessarily affected by the particular nature of housing in the metropolis. While much of London remained socially heterogeneous in the eighteenth century, the regulations governing the rebuilding of the City after the fire in 1666 and the growth of London's new squares in the seventeenth and eighteenth centuries introduced a degree of social zoning, ensuring that servants'

---

23   Port, 'West end palaces', pp. 30–3 and *passim*.

experience varied according to the wealth of their employers.[24] More than that, in Summerson's phrase the 'insistent verticality of the London house' in this period allowed domestic functions to be segregated, and differentials in rent also led to degrees of social stratification within houses if the house was occupied (as so many were) by several families and lodgers: the first floor tended to be the most expensive in subdivided houses, with rents falling as tenants rose or descended the staircases.[25]

It is this lack of correspondence between the clean lines of design and the blurred shades of habitation that undermines the utility of architectural evidence for judgements upon those who employed most servants, that great swathe of middling Londoners. Historians wishing to employ such evidence must recognise that 'the houses [that vast numbers of inhabitants of the great cities] occupied were often rambling pre-Georgian buildings, but it is clear that the terrace house, with its two or three rooms per floor, was commonly occupied by several independent tenants'. Indeed, tenement-style letting meant that 'the vertical divisions of the terrace house were often breached to meet the contingencies of multiple occupation': if a family needed more space along the horizontal plane, and a room was available in a neighbouring house, with the next-door landlord's consent a door would simply be knocked into the wall. As for identifying the application to which rooms in such houses might be put even when architecture and usage coincided, 'there are indications that servants were parcelled around the house in a most *ad hoc* manner to suit the convenience of the family'.[26] Under such circumstances, the language of architectural intent is a distinctly problematic indicator of the way lives were lived long after architect and speculative builder had gone.

However, the question we are left with is this: can any necessary relationship between architecture and sentiment reasonably be constructed at all? Is it not possible, for instance, to entertain the possibility that the advent of bells to summon servants may have simply originated with a fashionable distaste for shouting rather than a desire on behalf of employers to distance themselves from their domestic employees? It cannot be denied that the Stones' argument for the growth of privacy and affective relations is a complex one, although architectural evidence is central to both their

---

24 M.J. Power, 'The social topography of Restoration London', in A.L. Beier and R. Finlay, eds, *London 1500–1700: the Making of the Metropolis* (Harlow, 1986), p. 221 and *passim*; Port, 'West end palaces', pp. 26–7; T.F. Reddaway, *The Rebuilding of London after the Great Fire* (London, 1940); J. Summerson, *Georgian London* (London, 1988), Chapter 4, esp. p. 35.

25 Summerson, *Georgian London*, pp. 31, 45; D. Cruickshank and N. Burton, *Life in the Georgian City* (London, 1990), pp. 52–63; Earle, *English Middle Class*, pp. 206–12.

26 Cruickshank and Burton, *Georgian City*, pp. 58, 60.

chronology and sociology of change as far as servant–employer relations are concerned. But even conceding that contemporaries indulged in the contradictory desire for both pampering and privacy, spatial innovation was no guarantor of seclusion: for instance, the eighteenth-century Anglo-French novelty of building servants' anti-chambers adjacent to employers' bedchambers actually assured loss of privacy for both parties. Indeed, Stone himself has noted that, especially in London houses, bedrooms were open to prying eyes, as an example from the London Consistory court demonstrates: Elizabeth Carrick, for instance, mopping the passage 'where the door of a room where [her mistress] generally lay, her mop hit against the door, upon which it not being double locked immediately flew open' and she saw her mistress with her lover.[27] If the goings-on were blatant enough or the servants were sufficiently curious, privacy as seclusion was impossible, as the rest of this chapter will demonstrate — evidence discussed here gives the Stones' thesis the appearance of a faulty rigidity.

Social withdrawal or seclusion may, of course, have been possible for some employers and some servants part or much of the time regardless of architectural innovation, as suggested in the discussion of evidence on servant sexuality below. At the very least, these records point to the possible existence of multiple realms of activity within the spaces created by life and work in eighteenth-century metropolitan households. The Stones' model is history through the eyes of employers, and it erroneously plays down servant agency:[28] the footman who spurned the back stairs and waltzed down John Dormer's main staircase voted against an employer's attempts to control the domestic arena with his feet. Evidence presented here of the impact of seventeenth-century changes in room use or eighteenth-century architectural novelty is mixed and inconclusive, suggesting cultural continuities and far more complexity than certainly the Stones are prepared to allow, and refusing to offer firm support for either the chronological or cultural theses they advance. Meanwhile, the work on probate inventories shows that historians must ask whose privacy is changing and what privacy meant in any particular historical context. The remaining sections of this chapter will further explore the church court depositions, words spoken by servants themselves, to chart their lives alongside employers and fellow-servants, observing the extent to which notions of privacy have explanatory value for servant-employing households in late seventeenth- and early eighteenth-century London.

---

27 Waterson, *Servants' Hall*, p. 28; Maza, *Servants and Masters*, p. 186; Stone, *Road to Divorce*, pp. 213–14 and *passim*; LMA, DL/C/250 f. 439, Elizabeth Carrick, 4/6/1709.

28 Elsewhere Stone concedes that they could be 'self-confidant & ambitious human beings': *Road to Divorce*, p. 228.

Proximity to the person

Large households

The politics of 'place' was first and foremost a domestic politics, a point established in Chapter One, and the household–family elision described a network of relationships as much as a location that was governed by patriarchal constraints. If the 'growth of privacy' is to be advanced as a plausible thesis for the long eighteenth century, in other words a growing distance in the interaction between servants and their employers and therefore a shift within patriarchy from paternalism to managerialism, it seems that architectural innovation fails to offer it confirmation. The servant–employer relationship in thousands of households in late seventeenth- and early eighteenth-century London necessitated a degree of face-to-face contact and physical proximity which might seem intolerable to the overwhelming majority of people who do not employ servants today. The fact that domestic service was widespread within living memory, and an experience that many grandparents had in the early twentieth century, does not necessarily make it any easier to visualise for their grandchildren. The socio-economic forces encouraging today a minor renaissance of live-in domestic assistance (usually for childcare) touch few of the readers of this book, even if Palmer can introduce her study of twentieth-century American domestic service with what resembles an apology for the present-day employment of illegal immigrants as maids by white, middle-class professional women like herself.[29] A leap of the historical imagination is therefore required to understand what it meant to be servant, master or mistress living cheek-by-jowl in contemporary London. The depositions in the London church courts allow glimpses of day-to-day relations, and the largest households will be discussed first.

The testimony of servants from the households of the Calverts in the first years of the eighteenth century, and the Duke and Duchess of Beaufort in the 1730s, provides an indication of the proximity of employer–servant relations within large families at the top of the social scale. In the Beauforts' household, the duchess confessed to Martha Owers, her waiting woman, how often she made love adulterously, and consulted her over the contents of a revealing letter to her husband; but still excluded her with the other

---

29 P. Palmer, *Domesticity and Dirt: Housewives and Domestic Servants in the United States, 1920–1989* (Philadelphia, 1989).

servants from the room when her lover was present.[30] Most unusually, it was a footman who appears to have had the greatest access to his mistress at this time. William Dibble was 'ordered to be the only servant to attend her both at Grosvenor Square' and at the Beauforts' country residence at Woodcot: he ran errands and delivered letters to his mistress's lover and was instructed to keep everyone else at bay — but even he was told 'never to come into the room unless the bell was rung', and was never party directly to his mistress's confessions of adultery. His trustworthiness may have been assured by the debt he felt for his rapid elevation after five years as stable-helper, but a manservant may have been used because the noble lover 'always came in a private manner attended by a common servant only, with hackney horses', i.e. not one driven by his own servants.[31]

More conventionally, in the Calvert family cookmaid Penelope Barrett explained that she 'had not any business in the lady's bedchamber, dining rooms or withdrawing rooms'; as for the parlour, she had 'no other business' there except to clean the floors and fireplace 'in the morning before the said lady or her family was up', or 'of an evening after the lady and her family were gone to bed'. In fact, she received most of her orders from the butler, who had secured her initial hiring, paid her wages, and eventually dismissed her, although she 'had several times the honour to speak with [her mistress] . . . about dressing of anything extraordinary'. On the other hand, Mary Cockrill believed her intimacy with her mistress gave her testimony extra weight, despite its contradicting that of the other servants deposing in the matrimonial dispute, because she was the woman who 'did make or help to make her bed' and 'much attend upon her person in her chamber'.[32]

The apparent polarity of experience in the Calvert household is encapsulated in the rarity of one servant's face-to-face dealings with her mistress and the regularity of another's. Hierarchies of servants in the larger households, and hence distance in relations between those separated by rank, were central to Hecht's study, but his emphasis was slightly different. 'The

---

30 LMA, DL/C/272 f. 188, Martha Owers, 9/7/1740. For other intimate confidences from mistresses to maids, see DL/C/243 f. 310, Ann Marshal, 12/5/1691; DL/C/244 f. 92, Mary Bowers, 11/11/1693; DL/C/247 f. 338, Martha Daugherty, 4/2/1702; DL/C/248 f. 140, Margaret Denton, 1/2/1704; DL/C/262 f. 323, Elizabeth Benfield, 4/5/1725; DL/C/264 f. 9, Mary Waltho, 22/2/1727.

31 LMA, DL/C/272 f. 192, William Dibble, 23/7/1740; for the Duke and Duchess's separation case, see L. Stone, *Broken Lives: Separation and Divorce in England, 1660–1857* (Oxford, 1993), pp. 117–38.

32 LMA, DL/C/250 f. 478, Penelope Barrett, 6/9/1709; DL/C/250 f. 453, Mary Cockrill, 2/7/1709; for the Calverts' separation case, see Stone, *Broken Lives*, pp. 49–78.

principal line of cleavage', he wrote, 'was that which divided upper and lower servants', but for him the key determinants of the former were 'executive and supervisory' work, and the possession of 'special skills'. Lower servants were those 'whose activities were controlled and directed, and whose work was of a relatively unskilled, manual variety'. Yet service work and its management must be observed in the context of household relations and not just in terms of office or skill. Chapter Six will demonstrate that differentials in nominal wages between upper and lower servants of the order of ten to one were by no means impossible (the largest households sometimes had young retainers receiving no wage at all), and served starkly to highlight the status gap. Servants conducting housewifery and drudgery in larger households were fully appraised of their relatively lower status by the fact that they were not 'immediately about the person' of their employers; those engaged in the 'idle luxury' of upper service exhibited role-demarcation most clearly, particularly among female servants such as Mary Cockrill and their relative access to the mistress; in taverns and inns, the humble drawer took orders from the chamberlain, who on occasion could behave like a close personal servant towards the establishment's paying guests.[33]

Hecht's point about supervision is, of course, important and is expressed most concretely in contemporary writings like the *Plan of a Person of Quality's family*, a remarkable hand-written schema of the servant hierarchy in the largest English households, dating from around 1690 and found in the Earl of Uxbridge's manuscripts. On the male side, *valets de chambre* were 'under the direction of the gentlemen of the bedchamber'; 'postillions and [stable] helpers are under the direction of the coachmen, who are all, as also the grooms are, under the direction of the master of the horse' if there was one; footmen were 'under the directions of such chief domestics attending the lord and lady', in other words explicitly to be commanded by male and female upper servants. In large households less elaborately staffed than those of the nobility, like that of the Calverts, the butler played an orchestrating role over both male and female lower servants. The housekeeper 'has the direction of the laundry maids and housemaids [and] sees they do their work', and chambermaids were 'under the direction of the gentlewomen of the bed chamber'.[34] These ideal hierarchies were usually affirmed by gradients of age and/or experience within the household, and

---

33 Hecht, *Domestic Servant Class*, p. 35; LMA, DL/C/250 ff. 453 and 478; for these categories of service work, see Chapter Five in this volume.

34 Hecht, *Domestic Servant Class*, pp. 48, 63–5; anon., *Plan of a Person of Quality's family* (1690?), LMA Acc. 2079/A2/4/1–2.

this will have enhanced the distance between those at different ends of the chain of authority as the giving of orders and even hiring and firing were delegated down from employer to upper servant.

The domesticity of the politics of 'place' left ample room for variation in relations within individual households, and ideal prescriptions could be undermined by whim and fancy: the Beaufort case illustrates how exceptions to this order could occur in unusual circumstances, but it could be usurped on a more day-to-day basis by an employer's favouritism. One particular mistress's over-attentiveness towards one of her footmen and the jealousy it caused was so palpable that the master's gentleman, Thomas Lewin, could date the time and place from which that affection commenced. During the proceedings of another case, maid Elizabeth Padwick testified in 1718 that John Oakley 'appeared or seemed . . . to be rather a play fellow or companion' of her mistress's daughters than just footman to their brother. Joanna New demonstrated that the value of favouritism was such that it could be competed over by close personal servants: she claimed in 1712 to have known her employer's family for over a decade and was 'more intimately acquainted and conversant' with her mistress's daughter 'than any other witnesses except her fellow servant Rose Jones', and New believed the daughter had 'communicated to her the most material business of her life'.[35]

Particular affection and its denial was a constant part of many servants' dealings with their employers, and often resulted in differential treatment which frequently took on a distinct gender dimension. In an example of a stark contrast in relations between one mistress and her servants, Ralph Stockton 'was informed by Ellen Monk, their mistress's servant, who seemed her favourite, that he should sit up' that night. When he attended his mistress in a hackney coach after midnight, she left as soon as her lover rapped on the coach door, telling him to meet her at Covent Garden; but he 'never saw her since and therefore he believes she never returned home'. In households in which relations between mistress and master had soured, familiarity and affection could be twisted to one of the parties' advantage: one master had his wife constantly 'watched and followed by Sophia Cook . . . [she] went under the name of her lady's woman though in reality she was made rather her mistress'. Favouritism, or at least particular attention, could be earned, as Benjamin Habberley found when he collected nuts in his hat for his employers, and was then asked by his mistress to sleep

---

35 LMA, DL/C/255 f. 129, Thomas Lewin, 16/3/1715; DL/C/257 f. 155, Elizabeth Padwick, 27/3/1718 (see also DL/C/265 f. 55, Mary Gould, 29/6/1728); DL/C/632 f. 380, Rose Jones, 24/11/1712, and f. 405, Joanna New, 9/12/1712.

in an adjacent chamber to ensure she was not abused by her husband.[36] Indeed, the evidence assembled here has shown how an employer's favouritism could strengthen or undermine the distance between them and particular employees in larger households where, ideally, hierarchies were fixed.

Wealthier employers engaged enough servants to foster a recognisable hierarchy within their households, although in particular circumstances that hierarchy could become fluid. Relations within small households could exhibit stratification with as few as two servants present, and favouritism might take on a serial quality with one servant compared to past employees when there were no others simultaneously in place. But they also generated the sort of intimacy associated with close personal servants to the nobility. In the depositions (a source more likely to report the breakdown of household relations, given the nature of the cases before church courts), servants in less exalted places can be seen enjoying the company of their employers. They describe themselves happily sitting round the fire with their mistresses or their employers' children, drawing for Valentine sweethearts on February 14th, leaning over the shop-door hatch together, or chatting with mistress and fellow servants at the front door late one August evening. One cookmaid, Dorothy Walker, who had lived with her mistress for over a year, declared in 1701 that she liked it well enough she could live there another seven years.[37] Even if this was an overstatement for the purposes of positive testimony, contractual companionship not unnaturally blossomed into genuine friendship in some cases. The happy household, in which contentment for moments, months or even years was experienced between servant and employer, was not solely the province of myth.

Illness

Margaret Pelling's work has expanded greatly the current state of knowledge on the treatment of young people when ill in early modern England. In particular, she has focused on the way masters and mistresses responded to apprentices' ill health, and the disputes that arose at the Mayor's court in London between those parties over these and other issues in the later seventeenth century. Both domestic servants and apprentices received the

---

36 LMA, DL/C/270 f. 277, Ralph Stockton, 14/7/1736, and f. 281, Ellen Monk, 16/7/1736; DL/C/637 f. 570, Joseph Clark, 26/2/1748; DL/C/273 f. 365, Benjamin Habberley, 24/5/1744.

37 LMA, DL/C/247 f. 27, Dorothy Walker, 25/6/1701; DL/C/236 f. 2, Mary Speed, 11/10/1669; DL/C/244 f. 287, Mary Stiles, 18/4/1695; DL/C/269 f. 75, Hannah Humphries, 10/3/1732; DL/C/242 f. 136, Isabella Stevens, 1/6/1688; DL/C/243 f. 369, Margaret Robinson, 29/11/1683; DL/C/241 f. 252, Elizabeth Bennett, 23/11/1685.

'necessaries' of bed and board, i.e. the basic components for keeping body and soul together; but a key difference in the binding of apprentices was the legal obligation of masters to supply medical care, should it be required, during the period of the apprentice's indenture (though this obligation may have been falling into disuse by the eighteenth century).[38]

The extent to which masters and mistresses acted *in loco parentis* has been an issue since Dunlop and Denman's classic work established this familial precept as central to the institution of apprenticeship. While Ben-Amos notes that the later age of going into service meant that 'the description of the childlike apprentice does not quite fit' her increasingly independent subjects, she finds in seventeenth-century Bristol, Norwich and London that there was a 'lack of clear boundaries between the contractual and the moral aspects' of service because it 'was, in addition to being an interaction based on contract, something akin to the special obligations associated with kin and even parents'. So support 'could be expected when an apprentice became ill', and that to send him away in that condition 'was considered a violation of the norm'. Griffiths is less optimistic and warns that neglect 'was not uncommon', apprentices sometimes being turned away or otherwise mistreated when ill and unfit for work. 'Much depended', he writes, 'upon how a master viewed his servant; as cheap labour, a nuisance, an employee, a colleague, or friend'.[39]

The emphasis on variation in the quality of employer–servant interaction and the way that might affect this litmus test of household relations is important, but it is vital to note that much of the information on the treatment of sick apprentices is culled from records of regulatory institutions. Perhaps this is the difference that highlights most clearly the respective positions of apprentice and domestic servant: while indentured apprentices had a legal document guaranteeing (at least on paper) their treatment and care when ill to something approaching the standards they would receive from their own parents, a guarantee enforceable in the Mayor's courts, domestic servants had no such guarantee, and were far more at the mercy of their employers' whims or affections. Illness in domestic servants in London seems much more likely to have led to the termination of their contracts,

38 M. Pelling, 'Child health as a social value in early modern England', reprinted in her *The Common Lot: Sickness, Medical Occupations and the Urban Poor in Early Modern England* (Harlow, 1998), pp. 119–31; her 'Apprenticeship, health and social cohesion in early modern London', *History Workshop Journal* **37** (1994), 45–7.
39 O.J. Dunlop and R.D. Denman, *English Apprenticeship and Child Labour: A History* (New York, 1912); I.K. Ben-Amos, *Adolescence and Youth in Early Modern England* (New Haven, 1994), pp. 85, 171, 172; P. Griffiths, *Youth and Authority: Formative Experiences in England, 1560–1640* (Oxford, 1996), p. 320.

without any sign that employers considered themselves responsible for their care. The evidence establishes quite clearly that servants' illnesses formed one of the several reasons for departure from any particular place (see the Conclusion to this chapter): for instance, Mary Thompson was sacked when she developed toothache, while Margaret Cook left her service because she was 'sick and lame'. Like Ralph Josselin's daughter Anne and his two apprenticed sons Thomas and John when sent to London, Elizabeth Cotton contracted the classic migrant's disease of smallpox which forced her to leave her employment, but after four months in lodgings to recover, she was well enough to take up another place.[40]

The unfortunate Mary Nicholls left two consecutive jobs on account of illness, staying at her father's for six months after the first bout, and when she became ill at her next employer's, she went into lodgings to recover. Mary Horne left her service to a Dutch gentleman for 'want of health', while John Faulkner 'was obliged to leave [his place] by reason of being afflicted with the rheumatism', and 'does not now follow any employment except going upon errands'. On the other hand, Winifred Carter had an epileptic fit after a scare one night, and her mistress slept most of the night with her to comfort her; Francis Smith left when sick, but her employers let her return when she had recovered five weeks later. Illness among members of the servant's own family and friends might also lead to departure, as it did for Elizabeth Bennett, who left her job 'upon being sent for to an uncle that was sick'. On one occasion, a servant stayed on at her post despite having a serious contagious disease: Dorothy More accompanied her mistress's daughter and her suitor upon their elopement even though she had smallpox, and her position as trusted confidante notwithstanding, it must be assumed that daughter and suitor had already survived the disease and were therefore immune. The favourite footman of another mistress was taken ill with smallpox, so she 'ordered that they should remove him out of the stables where he usually lay and put him to bed in the room next to where her daughter lay', observed Richard Haynes, 'notwithstanding [her husband] and their daughter had never had the smallpox': an attachment that led to exceptional and dangerous treatment.[41]

---

40 LMA, DL/C/250 f. 150, Mary Thompson, 15/12/1681; DL/C/246 f. 62, Margaret Cook, 11/5/1698; DL/C/255 f. 137, Elizabeth Cotton, 17/3/1715; A. Macfarlane, *Family Life of Ralph Josselin, a Seventeenth-Century Clergyman: An Essay in Historical Anthropology* (Cambridge, 1970), pp. 112, 120.

41 LMA, DL/C/255 f. 174, Mary Nicholls, 17/5/1715; DL/C/251 f. 116, Mary Horne, 14/3/1715; PRO, PROB 24/58 f. 24, John Faulkner, 3/2/1720; LMA, DL/C/250 f. 474, Winifred Carter, 11/8/1709; DL/C/251 f. 367, Francis Smith, 28/6/1710; DL/C/241 f. 252, Elizabeth Bennett, 23/11/1685; DL/C/252 f. 10, Dorothy More, 19/6/1710; DL/C/255 f. 178, Richard Haynes, 17/5/1715.

However, in some cases even workplace injuries failed to merit special consideration. Edward Hughes was coachman to one Mrs Brampton and was shot in the hand by an intruder; at the time of deposing he 'does not follow any employment, he being disabled by the shot', and there was nothing to suggest his former mistress had assisted him in any way after his departure. But there appears to have been a philanthropic tradition amongst some of the largest aristocratic households to offer some care for long-standing servants: forty-nine-year-old Elizabeth Hayfield, 'thick of hearing', was living off the Earl of Effingham's charity since she had been in and out of his family's service for years. As the examples above suggest, lodgings or parental homes seem to be favoured places for recuperation: the former might be expensive if the illness was long term, but even if parents were alive and willing to have a child home again, distances could make this option difficult. Elizabeth Taylor availed herself of both, moving out of her employers' household into lodgings in London first and only then returning to her mother's in distant Herefordshire.[42]

Pelling has noted that in eighteenth-century voluntary hospitals, 'where admissions policies were explicit on excluding servants, as many of them were, it seems to be *domestic* servants that are meant'. The only two occasions in the church court depositions where servants made reference to availing themselves of institutional care were both to the City Corporation's ancient hospitals of St Bartholomew's and St Thomas's: James Dunn lay in the former for six months to cure his eyes, while twenty-four-year-old Mary Bourne spent thirteen weeks in the latter to recover from lameness.[43] These records suggest that, in the main, domestic servants were left to their own devices, and rather than there being any change in the eighteenth century, since at least as early as 1660 they failed to receive the benefits many apprentices could expect. There were always exceptions, but this marked difference between forms of metropolitan service exhibits all the signs of long-term continuity.

Correction and violence

Chapter Three established that masters had the legal right, ordained by scripture, to exercise 'due correction and punishment' over their servants.

---

42 LPL, Eee 12 f. 154, Edward Hughes, 31/10/1722; LMA, DL/C/638 f. 49, Elizabeth Hayfield, 27/11/1749; DL/C/255 f. 318, Elizabeth Taylor, 8/7/1715.
43 Pelling, 'Apprenticeship, health and social cohesion', p. 45 (emphasis in the original); her 'Child health', p. 156; LMA, DL/C/632 f. 335, James Dunn 14/7/1712; PRO, PROB 24/52 f. 69ᵛ, Mary Bourne, 14/10/1713.

The evidence in the late seventeenth- and early eighteenth-century depositions for physical chastisement of either male or female servants within the household (i.e. their corporal punishment by master or mistress for perceived misdemeanours) is as sparse as were calls for its use in the advice manuals from the same period. The little there is shows men being treated more harshly than maids. Thomas Churchill pulled his master from assaulting his mistress several times, once taking the full force of a flying candlestick for his pains, and one evening he cut Churchill in the face with his sword for not collecting him from the drinking club.[44]

Thomas Pugh was suspected by his master of having an affair with his wife, and one evening he challenged Pugh to a wrestling match; Pugh refused but his master hit him a few times and goaded him into a fight, after which his master called the watch to have him arrested. Pugh left his place as a result of the violence. Pepys and his wife certainly had no compunction in beating many of their servants, particularly the footboys, one of whom was beaten at least eight times in two years. The boy Wayneman received a flogging from his master for letting gunpowder off in the yard, a punishment meted out despite the self-inflicted burns he received, and for lying about some whey he drank in the kitchen; on several occasions Pepys beat him for accumulated misdemeanours until his own arm ached.[45] It seems that the younger the male servant, the more likely it was that he would be physically punished by his employers.

The meagre depositional evidence of employers exerting discipline over maids suggests widespread compliance with manual-writers' insistence on caution. Dorothy Catherell declared that she 'has seen her [mistress] sometimes angry with her servants, and more with her than any other person', but denied she had ever been violent or vexatious. Eleanor Morgan described her mistress as 'quiet', and when she tried to hit her, Eleanor simply stopped her; Susannah Redfern did get beaten, but by her master's cane, and when she hid from him under the bed her mistress tried to force him to desist. Catherine Atkinson was repeatedly hit by her mistress, who also threw an iron poker at her; but she ended up leaving that household not, surprisingly enough, for the violence but 'on account of her [mistress] often calling her scurrilous names'. The chastisement meted out by Samuel and Elizabeth Pepys to their female servants occurred less frequently than it did for their male servants, but one was 'basted' by Samuel with a broom until

---

44 LMA, DL/C/264 f. 167, Thomas Churchill, 2/5/1727; and f. 163, Dorothy Evans, 28/4/1727.
45 LMA, DL/C/269 f. 77, Thomas Pugh, 20/3/1732; Pepys, *Diary* II, pp. 206–7, III, pp. 37–8, 66, 116, and IV, pp. 7–8, 12–13, 109, 193, although *cf.* IV, p. 220.

she cried for misplacing some things, and the 'little girl' was beaten by Elizabeth for gossiping. Elizabeth returned home one day and found her maid Barker 'to have been abroad, and telling her so many lies about it that she struck her, and the wench said she would not stay with her'.[46]

Those victims of abuse or correction notwithstanding, many servant witnesses complained of living in families where violence between their master and mistress was, if not the norm, then far from rare. Of course, the representativeness of London servant-employing households in church court cases is coloured by the demands of litigation. Under spiritual jurisdiction, Stone observes, separation from bed and board could be granted 'on three grounds only: adultery, life-threatening cruelty, or a combination of both', and at the London Consistory court between 1670 and 1755, 153 of 303 separation cases were brought on charges of cruelty or cruelty with adultery. Margaret Hunt has rightly observed that in these cases, 'the level of abuse was probably on the upper end of the spectrum of severity', yet servants certainly lived with some extremely violent masters. They 'maimed' their wives with fire-tongs, or called servants to bring up beer deliberately to throw in their wives' faces; locked them in at home to confine them, or to beat them unhindered; kicked them to induce miscarriages, raped them when they themselves had venereal disease, or dashed them against the wainscot; threatened them with swords, or beat them up for having two pairs of gloves cleaned for sixpence. Eleanor Watson declared that six months in her employers' family seemed a year 'because she never saw contentment in the house'.[47]

Servants themselves frequently got caught up in the violence as their masters threatened them, and deliberately or by mistake caught them with blows, usually (but not always) when they came to their mistresses' aid. Female servants often helped their mistresses out in difficult times, sometimes at risk to themselves: Mary Hill was threatened by her master when she

---

46   LMA, DL/C/258 f. 88, Dorothy Catherell, 21/2/1719; DL/C/239 f. 166, Eleanor Morgan, 29/11/1680; DL/C/240 f. 405, Susannah Redfern, 24/7/1682; DL/C/248 f. 161, Catherine Atkinson, 24/5/1704; Pepys, *Diary* I, p. 307, V, p. 13, VIII, p. 212, and see also VI, p. 39, and VIII, p. 164.

47   Stone, *Road to Divorce*, p. 192, and p. 428, Table 1.8; M. Hunt, 'Wife beating, domesticity and women's independence in eighteenth-century London', *Gender and History* 4 (1) (1992), 13; LMA, DL/C/238 f. 1, 13/2/1679, Sarah Arnold; DL/C/254 f. 420, 20/1/1714, Mary Beckley; DL/C/244 f. 228, Mary Hubbard, 17/10/1694, and f. 300, Mary Curry, 3/5/1695; DL/C/244 f. 383, Susannah Winton, 9/12/1695; f. 343, Ann Atkin, 4/7/1695; DL/C/636 f. 37, Mary Husbands, 11/2/1740; DL/C/637 f. 590, Ann Stevens, 17/3/1748 (one of nine servant-witnesses to violence in the eponymous *Wallop c. Wallop*, DL/C/637, ff. 566–592); DL/C/244 f. 48, Elizabeth Williams, 14/5/1703; DL/C/264 f. 163, Dorothy Evans, 28/4/1727; DL/C/263 f. 65, Elizabeth Daniel, 26/2/1726; DL/C/638 f. 311, Eleanor Watson, 3/11/1749. *Murray c. Murray*, DL/C/636, ff. 31–55 saw ten servant-witnesses testify to their master's violence.

tried to prevent him from hurting his wife, and was not allowed to bring her food. Ann Ellis heard a noise in her mistress's bedchamber so went upstairs, finding her mistress holding off her master, who held a sword in his hand. Thinking he might 'do her some mischief, Ann caught hold of his arm and by force wrenched the sword' away from him, so he left shouting (without any visible sign of irony) 'Damn you and all your fraternity!'[48]

That female 'fraternity' in the household was often expressed through a simple intimacy. Female servants slept with their mistresses while their masters were absent from the house 'for [her mistress's] warmth, as a protection against possible rape, and as proof of her innocence' (as they did with other lone women or girls within the household, including fellow servants).[49] But servants' own beds could act as mistresses' refuges from husbandly pig-headedness, venereal disease or violence. Jane Child let her pregnant mistress sleep in her bed while she 'and the other two maids sat up to prevent their master from murdering her'. Her mistress complained to Jane 'that her master had punched her on the loins with his knee and put her to great pain, and the next morning Jane rubbed her loins with some spirits of wine'; this gesture of caring intimacy was to no avail, for a little later her mistress miscarried. Sometimes, though, even masters admitted that servants' interventions saved their mistresses' lives, as did that of Mary Pergiter in 1705. These expressions of care, support and intimacy may have only come to light at times of crisis, but it is more than likely that they represented one aspect of the friendship and respect that could grow between mistress and maid.[50]

Domestic allegiance

Some female servants were prepared to support their masters against their mistresses, for instance when the master 'kept and maintained his wife

---

48 LMA, DL/C/242 f. 61, Ann Stanley, 17/6/1687; DL/C/244 f. 298, Elizabeth Ross, 3/5/1695; DL/C/268 f. 35, Elizabeth Turner, 22/10/1731; DL/C/635 f. 51, Ann Matthews, 29/6/1732; DL/C/242 f. 59, Dorothy Holden, 17/6/1687; DL/C/244 f. 330, Elizabeth Lind, 25/6/1695; DL/C/632 f. 130, Elizabeth Thomas, 4/12/1711; DL/C/252 f. 272, Francisca Baldwin, 27/2/1711; DL/C/264 f. 167, Thomas Churchill, 2/5/1727; DL/C/269 f. 77, Thomas Pugh, 20/3/1732; DL/C/246 f. 166, Mary Hill, 3/12/1698; DL/C/258 f. 213, Ann Ellis, 10/6/1719.
49 Stone, *Road to Divorce*, p. 213: see LMA, DL/C/264 f. 9, Mary Waltho, 22/2/1727; DL/C/265 f. 47, Ellen Slater, 27/6/1728; DL/C/272 f. 188, Martha Owers, 9/7/1740; for France, see Maza, *Servants and Masters*, pp. 185–6.
50 LMA, DL/C/636 f. 49, Jane Child, 19/2/1740 (see also DL/C/244 f. 343, Ann Atkin, 4/7/1695; DL/C/247 f. 259, Elizabeth Wrangell, 8/12/1701; DL/C/244 f. 328, Elizabeth Fletcher, 25/6/1695, and f. 342, Mary Underwood, 4/7/1695); DL/C/248 f. 315, Mary Pergiter, 26/1/1705.

handsomely and according as she desired': Elizabeth Hill and Lucy Camden, servants in the same household, both chorused that if married to him, they could live with their master 'if his treatment towards [them] was the same as [they] had observed towards [their] mistress'. If the co-ordination of testimony is suspect, the sentiment is still interesting; and there were other circumstances in which maidservants were prepared to express disapproval of their mistresses. One was extravagance, a sin that contradicted the precepts of housewifely economy and smacked of luxurious over-consumption, and which could have direct repercussions for the servants as well: Mary Tillshead felt she had to lend her mistress money, which she 'wasted and foolishly and extravagantly spent'. Another was adultery, which could alienate maidservant from mistress. Sarah Vane's mistress purported to spend the night in Vane's bed rather than that of her husband (a man Vane described as always kind and tender) because 'he was very fat and it was warm weather and she could not bear to live with him'. In fact, she was having an affair with their male servant, something almost guaranteed to disrupt household loyalties.[51]

Disapproval could clearly be heard when adultery and extravagance, or even theft, were combined: Elizabeth Stephens's adulterous mistress walked out with the family silver, plate, jewellery and lottery tickets, and Stephens sided with her master even though he owed her £10 in back wages. Of course, it is not clear how much of the haul was her mistress's own property, and Stephens may have been threatened with loss of her wages, but in her testimony her disapproval is plain. A sense of justice may have motivated Eleanor Davis, who defended her master in 1687 because (as she claimed) her mistress wanted to ruin him and burned the house down to force their family to move. Other female servants were prepared to testify to their mistresses' attempts to poison their husbands via the food that the servants themselves had made or to charm them with occult brews.[52]

Menservants' relations with their mistresses never achieved the levels of intimacy of their female counterparts, except in very rare cases of sexual relations (see the following section). Close female servants, protective of their mistresses' reputations, might actively prevent menservants from witnessing

51   LMA, DL/C/249 f. 167, Elizabeth Hill, 29/8/1706; f. 167ᵛ, Lucy Camden, 13/11/1706
     (see also DL/C/238 f. 8, Edith Hix, 27/5/1679; DL/C/636 f. 45, Mary Child,
     18/2/1740); DL/C/245 f. 284, Mary Tillshead, 4/5/1697; DL/C/249 f. 153,
     Mary Tyley, 16/4/1706; DL/C/637 f. 74, Sarah Vane, 26/4/1746.
52   LMA, DL/C/249 f. 166, Elizabeth Stephens, 26/8/1706; DL/C/242 f. 113, Eleanor
     Davis, 24/6/1687; DL/C/242 f. 305, Mary Williams, 19/6/1688; DL/C/632 f. 172,
     Mary Nuby, 29/1/1712.

arguments or conflict within the household between their employers, as Jane Temple did in 1734. But they frequently came to their mistresses' aid when confronted by violent husbands, often demonstrating courage and protective affection towards them: Benjamin Habberley, who tried to protect his mistress from her husband's violence in the coach as he drove them to Bristol, was both angered and ashamed at his master's behaviour. As evidence above demonstrated, however, menservants might be trusted but still held at arm's length. Francis Hughes had been told to keep himself and other servants out of his mistress's room when she had company, but 'she was very jealous and fearful' that he and the other servants 'should listen at the door', forcing him to swear an oath in front of the landlady that he would not do so himself.[53]

Menservants tended to work in households where the social distance between them and their employers was made plain by their wearing of the livery, and relations had a more formal character. Edward Higgins, coachman, said that he and his master's other servants 'were respectful to [their master's adulterous lover] as they would or ought to have been to any other person of quality'. Relations between master and manservant could be warm, particularly when the master was relatively young: James Ottey spoke indulgently of his late master, a 'handsome young gentleman of a very good family' who 'always kept company with persons of worth and good esteem'. His master had been a 'man of pleasure, of late hours, apt to swear', and Ottey had accompanied him to Newmarket to watch his horse race; finally, he was with him until he died. Menservants were prepared to defend their masters in court as 'mild and peaceable' men who treated their wives 'lovingly and kindly', and Thomas Aldridge's master thought him loyal enough to intercept his mistress's mail to her lover.[54]

Chapter Three demonstrated the importance of individual and household reputation, and just as violent behaviour by masters and mistresses towards their servants or each other could induce feelings of shame, reputations

---

53 LMA, DL/C/635 f. 35, Jane Temple, 22/3/1734; DL/C/258 f. 84, Benjamin Romaine, 20/2/1719; DL/C/264 f. 174, Cornelius Garland, 19/7/1727; DL/C/636 f. 33, James Burnell, 10/2/1740; DL/C/637 f. 98, Euphan Thomson, 27/12/1744; f. 104, Rebecca Born, 4/1/1745; DL/C/273 f. 365, Benjamin Habberley, 24/5/1744; DL/C/265 f. 82, Francis Hughes, 5/12/1728 (see also DL/C/250 f. 435, James Shortell, 4/6/1709; DL/C/265 f. 96, Thomas Long, 13/12/1728; DL/C/270 f. 277, Ralph Stockton, 14/7/1736).

54 LMA, DL/C/251 f. 230, Edward Higgins, 28/1/1710; DL/C/250 f. 435, James Shortell, 4/6/1709; DL/C/248 f. 300, James Ottey, 21/5/1705; DL/C/248 f. 138, Timothy Hills, 20/1/1704; DL/C/249 f. 152, Folk Middleton, 16/4/1706; DL/C/272 f. 198, Thomas Aldridge, 24/7/1740.

could be threatened in other ways. Lucy Young gave her mistress 'warning to quit her service on account of [her mistress's lover] coming to her there, at the same time telling her that her reputation would be injured if she continued in her service any longer'. Mary Horne left the Dormers' household 'being offended at her mistress's scandalous keeping company with her footman and not thinking it reputable to live in such a family where it was so notorious'.[55] Unlike the female parties in defamation disputes (see below), these women were not necessarily of middling origins, or even working in upper service; but like those disputes, servants leaving on this pretext were overwhelmingly female.

A rare example of a male servant departing on the basis of possibly becoming tarnished by his master and mistress's reputation was that of Samuel Foster, when he discovered that his employers were not actually married: 'that was the reason none of the gentry or people of fashion or credit never came to visit them', a factor which would also have limited his access to lucrative tips. Mirroring the advice manuals' dire warnings, these servants felt that their own reputations — and therefore their chances for worthwhile future employment — would be adversely affected. The maintenance of household reputation even meant that servants were often used as proxies: Ann Very and her mistress were both called 'whores' when Ann went alone to collect money from her mistress's debtors; and Mary Fenton was called 'a whore' by a neighbour at the kitchen door, who then told her she actually meant to slander her mistress.[56]

In defamation suits at London ecclesiastical courts around the turn of the eighteenth century, like those observed by Gowing a century earlier, 'the words of insult were understood to be related only opaquely to actual sex', but litigation was 'based on the principle that slander damaged a person's reputation'. No doubt because of this, and in the face of the advice books' injunctions 'never [to] use any harsh language', employers were not averse to using slanderous words against their own servants. Some of them knew only too well that 'the art of governing servants is not so easy as it is necessary', and slander when used deliberately was one weapon in the armoury of household government. Susannah Eles had to put up with her mistress calling her 'coachman's whore . . . several times and almost

55 LMA, DL/C/271 f. 63, Lucy Young, 15/12/1737; DL/C/255 f. 116, Mary Horne, 14/3/1715.
56 LMA, DL/C/637 f. 178, Samuel Foster, 30/4/1746; DL/C/238 f. 203, Ann Very, 10/11/1677; DL/C/254 f. 58, Mary Fenton, 25/2/1714; see also DL/C/242 f. 123, Susannah Maine, 28/11/1687; DL/C/240 f. 262, Gertrude Nicholson, 14/11/1682, and f. 269, Mary Serjeant, 4/12/1682; and DL/C/243 f. 83, Thomas Jennings, 23/12/1689.

daily', insinuating that Susannah was having an affair with the resident coachman.[57]

Most cases of defamation at the London Consistory court in this period were pursued between middling women as intent on affirming status distinctions as reasserting their 'credit', but there were a number of cases brought by servants against other servants that give us some insights into the tensions that could arise within households. In one dispute between a female cook and a coachman in the middle-sized household of a widow, the servants were divided on strict gender lines. The footman, Humphrey Cook, described the coachman as 'a very quiet, civil, honest fellow no ways addicted to quarrelling and one who behaves himself civilly and courteously to all people', whereas the cook 'was very quarrelsome and troublesome, and much addicted to give foul language and to scold with himself and others of her fellow servants'. But female servant Eliza Scafe 'esteems the cook to be a modest woman and never heard otherwise', and Martha Lambert 'never saw any immodesty in the [female cook] nor hear any person speak any immodesty of her'. These commendations put the footman's statement that he and 'his then fellow servants rejoiced and were very glad at her removal' in quite a different light.[58]

Reputation-threatening gossip could also lead to defamation cases, and two of the Earl of Effingham's footmen testified to an allegation of bastard-bearing in their 'family' in 1749: a 'brother-coachman' had told one of them that the Earl's housekeeper had given birth to a child fathered by one of the grooms which was being kept in the mews round the corner from the Earl's house in Upper Grosvenor Street. Smaller households were more likely to see employers getting involved: in one family of three female servants and one clerk to the master (a scrivener), the cook's accusation in the basement kitchen that the chambermaid had slept with the clerk was met with the mistress's bellow down the stairs, 'Why then, I kept a whore in my house!' But after hearing the cook's allegation she interrogated both of the parties, defending the chambermaid as 'honest'.[59]

---

57 Meldrum, 'Women's court in London', esp. 14–15; L. Gowing, *Domestic Dangers: Women, Words and Sex in Early Modern London* (Oxford, 1996), pp. 59, 112; Marchioness de Lambert, *Advice of a Mother to her Son and Daughter* trans. T. Carte (London, 1737), p. 66; anon., *The Accomplish'd Housewife; or the Gentlewoman's Companion* (London, 1745), p. 428; LMA, DL/C/265 f. 139, Susannah Eles, 24/6/1728, and DL/C/248 f. 161, Catherine Atkinson, 24/5/1704.

58 Meldrum, 'Women's court in London', 5–8; LMA, DL/C/633 f. 94, Humphrey Cook; f. 95, Eliza Scafe; f. 96, Martha Lambert: all dated 16/2/1716; see also the case of *Griffiths c. Payne*, discussed in Meldrum, 'Women's court in London', 1, 12.

59 LMA, DL/C/638 f. 45, John David, and f. 47, John Pidgen: both dated 10/11/1749; DL/C/248 f. 167, Sarah Baldock, 24/6/1704: the mistress's deposition is at f. 170.

It was far less likely for disputes between men in this period to revolve around 'spiritual' topics (i.e. those dealt with at the church courts) alone, so this evidence may be overstressing the importance of gender-based quarrels. Yet the London Consistory court evidence demonstrates that for some servants an expensive and drawn-out process, costing typically between £7 and £10 and usually taking several months, could prove desirable in order to preserve or rescue reputation. This must be set against the cheaper, more flexible and far more accessible process of binding over defamers by recognizance in the quarter sessions. Shoemaker cites a common figure for costs of 4s 4d and adds that 'in a few cases the fees were reduced or eliminated entirely for the poor', presenting a viable route for redress (or prolongation of an abusive exchange in a relatively formal arena). The figures speak for themselves: Shoemaker's projected annual figure for non-indicted recognizances against 'common disturbers and defamers', 1720–22, was 156 cases (disregarding offences under the blanket category of 'keeping the peace'), when by the early eighteenth century the London Consistory court was hearing only 237 to 346 cases *per decade*. Cases such as the one between Alice Joell and Mary Cole were typical — in 1664 Cole called Joell a 'pocky whore and common whore to footmen' — but perhaps less typical was Cole's repetition of the insult even after being fined 16d by the magistrate. It is unfortunate that no depositions of the quality of church court testimonies are available for the sessions, but the opportunity for disputes over character and reputation between or among servants and employers is evident.[60]

Two impressions emerge from the evidence cited in this section. The first is that members of the largest families cannot stand as a model for servant–employer relations in total. The sometimes rigid stratification present in households where many servants were employed, and if large enough where hierarchies governed male and female servants separately, created distinct forms of interaction and generated particular tensions not found in the majority of servant-employing households. 'Attending upon the person' of a socially-exalted master or mistress could lead to mutual affection and the exchanging of confidences, and was markedly different from working out of his or her sight; but even proximity did not guarantee intimacy or friendship if the relationship was bound by formality, and favouritism disrupted, even usurped hierarchical or gender norms. Smaller households were likely to be much better nurseries of master–servant, and especially mistress–servant affection, although it might be argued that co-residence in small spaces also fostered petty and not-so-petty grievances.

---

60 Meldrum, 'Women's court in London', 2–5, 6, 10; R. Shoemaker, *Prosecution and Punishment: Petty Crime and the Law in London and Rural Middlesex, c. 1660–1725* (Cambridge, 1991), pp. 58–9, 66, 86–7.

Secondly, it would be misleading to paint an unremittingly pessimistic picture about the day-to-day relations in servant-employing households. Court depositions tend to emphasise the negative, and those arising from cases of matrimonial violence or defamation are especially likely to portray dysfunctional households riven by dispute. But even in such sources a diverse set of experiences are described, hardly surprising when servants might have been viewed 'as cheap labour, a nuisance, an employee, a colleague, or friend'; or when masters and mistresses might have been viewed as simply a temporary provider of bed and board, a daily irritant, an employer, an associate in the household, or even a friend.[61]

Sexual relations between household members[62]

Maids and masters

A rare regulatory 'office' case before the London Consistory court in 1716 illustrates the behaviour of one London master towards his female domestic servants. Spinster Elizabeth Wade served at the house of a widower and salesman, a 'substantial man' who, according to other witnesses, was 'of good credit and reputation', and an overseer of the poor in the parish of St Giles in the Fields (Wade had to be presented with a subpoena to give evidence against him). She alleged that he had 'several times attempted her chastity'. On one occasion, finding Wade to be in the kitchen alone, 'he there told her he would give her a crown if she would permit him to put his hands up her coats, upon which Elizabeth in a passion [rage] went out of the kitchen and left him, asking him if he took her to be a common whore'.[63]

Martha Vose, another of his servants, was rumoured to have 'threatened to be revenged on him for his turning her away at an hour's warning'. However, her own account of her experience gives us a harrowing picture of the servant as victim of a predatory master. Repeating a pattern made

---

61 Griffiths, *Youth and Authority*, p. 320; obviously, in this context the word 'friend' is being used in the twentieth-century sense of pal or mate rather than guardian or even relative, as in early modern usage.

62 Preliminary observations on this subject were offered in my 'London domestic servants from depositional evidence, 1660–1750: servant-employer sexuality in the patriarchal household', in T. Hitchcock, P. King and P. Sharpe, eds, *Chronicling Poverty: The Voices and Strategies of the English Poor, 1660–1840* (London, 1997), pp. 47–69; a more thorough account superseded this in my thesis, Chapter 6, section vi, and Chapter 8.

63 LMA, DL/C/633 f. 220, Elizabeth Wade, 15/6/1716; for the rarity of regulatory cases in this period, see my 'Women's court in London', 2–3.

familiar by Wade's account, Vose had been in his house for only three or
four days when her master, 'both by words and actions several times attempted her chastity, and she opposed his unlawful desires'. After a week,
in 'his lodging room behind his shop in the house', her master 'prevailed on
Martha to drink some strong waters and thereby intoxicated her brains,
and then taking advantage' he raped her. Thereafter she appears to have
had sex with him by consent several times, and in June 1715 she gave birth
to a baby boy in St Giles, and she 'constantly owned and acknowledged
such child to be begotten on her body by her master'. She stressed that it
was only after she left her service that she found out he was reputed to be 'a
lewd and debauched man'. It is crucial to the accounts of both these servants that there was no mistress at home, enhancing Wade's vulnerability
to attacks in the kitchen and especially the bedchamber, and permitting the
master to have sex with Vose 'sometimes on her bed in the kitchen and
sometimes on a bed up two pairs of stairs'.[64]

What remained of her reputation was central to Vose's testimony in
terms of its content (i.e. her experience as a servant) and also in the manner
in which she gave it. She stated,

> as she has nothing else to maintain herself by but by going to service, and
> services are only to be had by a good character and reputation, and she
> having already lost two or three places by means of the knowledge and
> report of her having had a child by her former master, and being now in a
> very good service, she hopes that the court will not oblige her to set forth
> or discover the particular places she hath lived in within the time [asked]
> or where she now lives.

She had already 'performed a penance [probably asking forgiveness at the
church altar] for the incontinence in the parish church of St Giles . . . and
performed the same to avoid being under the lash of her former master and
being put in prison by him for incontinency with him and upon no other
consideration . . . in order to prevent further harm befalling herself'. When
he offered to do nothing except give her £10 to lay the child's paternity to
someone else ('which she refused to do'), she said that if he 'would allow her
£15 she would lie in the country in private without bringing any disgrace
upon him, and if the child would die she would refund him £5'. He refused, and as he still 'took no care of her', the overseers and parish churchwardens of St James, Westminster (presumably the parish with which she
had her original settlement) 'took away her child from her when it was

---

64   LMA, DL/C/633 f. 220; DL/C/633 f. 226, Martha Vose, 17/8/1716.

three days old and provided for it, and the parish of St Giles supported her in her lying in', probably after coercing a lump sum from her master.[65]

Vose was a tailor's widow who had spent the previous three years in service, 'but for about four months happening within the time when she was very big with child' by this former master, when 'she maintained herself as privately as she could to avoid disgrace by working at her needle'. Whatever her motives, Vose's behaviour after her master had had 'the carnal knowledge of her body', allowing him to have repeated access to sexual favours, mirrors that of spinster women who claimed to have given in after being given promises of marriage.[66] But these apparent ambiguities and complexities have not prevented historians of service or of women more broadly from characterising sexual relations between female servants and masters or other male members of the household in terms central to Vose and Wade's narratives, as ones of servant vulnerability and victimhood.

The accounts of French domestic service in the eighteenth century, so influential on historians of early modern Britain, have painted a bleak picture. 'The most abiding threat that a female servant faced was sexual', writes Maza: according to records of illegitimacy, 'the women most likely to be sexually abused and exploited' were servants. 'Masters', she adds, 'could easily get their way by means of extravagant promises, small gifts, threats of dismissal, or brute force'. Fairchilds, too, has observed that most female servants 'accepted their master's advances because they had no choice', and she believes that the French perceived master–servant sexual relations to be 'socially acceptable . . . part of the privileges of a patriarch', but is unclear about her employers' social strata; Stone is more sociologically precise about the British when he states that 'elite opinion on the whole was tolerant of adultery by the male, especially with women of inferior social status such as maidservants, kept mistresses or prostitutes'. Hill would doubtless accept that accounts like those of Wade and Vose were representative: 'The very characteristics which distinguished female domestic servants made them particularly prone to sexual exploitation', she has written. 'The fact that by far the overwhelming majority of them were young, single girls, away from their family, their friends, and relations meant that just when they needed

65 LMA, DL/C/633 f. 226 and *passim*. For ecclesiastical penance, see M. Ingram, *Church Courts, Sex and Marriage in England, 1570–1640* (Oxford, 1987), pp. 3, 53–4; for lump sums, see M.D. George, *London Life in the Eighteenth Century* (London, 1966), p. 214; N. Rogers, 'Carnal knowledge: illegitimacy in eighteenth-century Westminster', *Journal of Social History* **23** (2) (1989), 360. Another example can be found at DL/C/258 f. 88, Dorothy Catherell, 21/2/1719; f. 106 and *passim*.

66 LMA, DL/C/633 f. 226 and *passim*; Maza, *Servants and Masters*, pp. 92–3; Rogers, 'Carnal knowledge', 363.

protection from such exploitation they were taken away from those best able to give it'.[67]

Current models of pre-modern sexual behaviour are more sophisticated. Hitchcock has developed a thesis which attempts to reconcile the findings of demographers and those of historians of the family and marriage, arriving at a cultural explanation for the eighteenth-century population explosion. Demographers have established that there were high rates of pre-nuptial pregnancy in seventeenth-century London and rising rates nationally from the early eighteenth century onwards; that the proportion of the population never marrying fell considerably in the eighteenth century; and that in the same period, the bastardy rate — the proportion of babies born outside wedlock — rose significantly.[68] Perceiving an inability on behalf of economic and social historians on the one hand, and cultural historians on the other, to explain these phenomena convincingly, Hitchcock offers his answer: 'there was indeed a "sexual revolution" in the eighteenth century' in which people equated sex 'more firmly with activities that could lead to pregnancy', particularly heterosexual penetrative sex. Following Wilson's research on abandoned infants taken to the Foundling Hospital in London from the 1740s, he argues further that there was a 'metropolitan fashion for penetrative sex' that only later in the century spread to the rest of the country.[69]

Can vulnerability, then, stand as the byword, the principal *leitmotif* for servant sexuality? There is no doubt that servants living under certain circumstances suffered sexual harassment or rape in our period, and that, as in Wade and Vose's case, service to an unmarried man — bachelor or widower — must have been particular risky on occasion. We also need to accept that many, even most cases of violent or other forms of coercive sex went unreported and are therefore without historical record. But if the demographers are right about the nature of population growth, and

---

67 Maza, *Servants and Masters*, pp. 68, 89, 90, 91; C. Fairchilds, 'Female sexual attitudes and the rise of illegitimacy: a case study', repr. in R.I. Rotberg and T.K. Rabb, eds, *Marriage and Fertility: Studies in Interdisciplinary History* (Princeton, 1980), p. 175, and her *Domestic Enemies*, pp. 88, 167; L. Stone, *Broken Lives*, p. 242; Hill, *Servants*, Chapter 3, esp. p. 44.

68 R.A.P. Finlay, *Population and Metropolis: the Demography of London, 1580–1650* (Cambridge, 1981), p. 150; E.A. Wrigley and R.S. Schofield, *The Population History of England 1541–1871: A Reconstruction* (Cambridge, 1981), p. 254, n. 96 and *passim*; E.A. Wrigley, 'The growth of population in eighteenth-century England: a conundrum resolved', *Past and Present* **98** (1983); P. Laslett, 'Introduction: comparing illegitimacy over time and between cultures', in P. Laslett, K. Oosterveen and R.M. Smith, eds, *Bastardy and its Comparative History* (London, 1980).

69 T. Hitchcock, *English Sexualities, 1700–1800* (Basingstoke, 1997), pp. 40, 41, 39; A. Wilson, 'Illegitimacy and its implications in mid-eighteenth century London: the evidence of the Foundling Hospital', *Continuity and Change* **4** (1) (1989).

Hitchcock's cultural explanation has some purchase, we must be careful not to deny young men and women in service a degree of control over their own bodies, and over their own words in encounters with the authorities — illegitimacy or bastardy proceedings before magistrates, rape trials or dealings with overseers of the poor — in which they constructed narratives of their experiences. To subsume servant sexuality under categories of experience defined by vulnerability and oppression alone is to distort the historical record and to circumscribe too tightly the variation, opportunity and pleasure possible in these lives. Acknowledging that some servants experienced the worst forms of sexual violence and abuse is to recognise the outer limits of sexual interaction, not to elevate them to the norm.[70]

The writings of Porter and Hall, among others, have demonstrated that at least by our period, there was an active public culture of sex in which a relatively high degree of knowledge about procreative heterosexuality was widespread. It is fair to assume that servants in their various guises formed a large proportion of the young people for whom acquisition of such knowledge was increasingly important.[71] Yet the advice manuals that deal with the subject convey the impression of constant threat and female servant vulnerability, and only a very limited form of servant autonomy. Wade and Vose might have been forewarned by Eliza Haywood's *Present for a Servant-Maid*, which advised caution to the servant of the single man because he was 'under less restraint . . . opportunities will not be wanting to prosecute his aim': the author may have had bachelors in mind, but she could well have been writing about widowers. In a section on 'Chastity', the main danger was attempted sexual conquest by masters, 'pert and saucy' male servants, gentlemen lodgers and apprentices, trying to equip young women with strategies of self-defence or at least to warn them of the dangers within households.[72]

With apprentices, even though 'they are servants only to become masters', 'overtures of love' should be scotched immediately, and servants should 'not think, as some of you have done, to draw him into marriage by encouraging his addresses . . . young men of that age are incapable of knowing their own minds'. Gentlemen lodgers were also likely to have been from a

---

70   For narratives of rape, see G. Walker, 'Rereading rape and sexual violence in early modern England', *Gender and History* **10** (1) (1998); for the construction of testimonial narratives generally, see N.Z. Davis, *Fiction in the Archives: Pardon Tales and their Tellers in Sixteenth-Century France* (Stanford, 1987).

71   R. Porter and L. Hall, *The Facts of Life: The Creation of Sexual Knowledge in Britain, 1650–1950* (New Haven and London, 1995), Chapter 1; Hitchcock, *English Sexualities*, pp. 28–38.

72   [Haywood], *Present for a Servant-Maid*, 1743 edn, pp. 44, 35; 1771 edn, pp. 16–17.

different social class, but some of them 'do not keep servants of their own to sit up for them'; as a consequence, 'you may be subjected to some inconvenience when they stay out till after the family are gone to bed'. The differences in the attitude female servants were likely to adopt were presented in distilled form under the heading of 'Temptations from your master's son'. If he 'happens to take a fancy to you', his seductive armoury may include 'even a promise to marry you as soon as he shall be at his own disposal. This last bait has seduced some who have been proof against all the others', as the lure of making the fabled transition from maid to mistress was so attractive. But the author advised servants not to 'flatter yourselves that because such matches have sometimes happened, it will be your fortune'. These cases were 'rare and seldom happy', since 'such a disparity of birth, of circumstances and education can produce no lasting harmony'.[73]

Historians will never be able to ascertain how many female domestic servants travelled hopefully to London with the dream of an upwardly-mobile marriage to the master's son in the back of their minds. But such liaisons were not beyond the bounds of possibility, even at the highest social echelons: Mary Bacchus testified that she had been a servant to Wortley Montague, Esq., when his son and heir married one of his father's other servants in a public house, not surprisingly against his parents' wishes.[74] Certainly, below the exalted level of 'the quality', such matches were not entirely out of the question, and may have been quite successful. At the age of 23, Dulcibel Mason was servant to a merchant in Newington Green, just beyond the northern suburbs. At some point soon after that she married his son, and far from being abandoned by her husband or ostracised by his family, when she gave her deposition at the age of 30 she said 'she hath been maintained by her husband as she now is, and her husband is main-tained by his father'. The relatively wide range of servants' social origins meant that the distance in status between a merchant's son and his father's servant may have been quite close: Ralph Josselin, the Essex clergyman, sent two of his daughters into service in London in the late seventeenth century.[75] Affection between master's son and servant, and its sexual ex-pression, clearly flourished in some households, and may even have won the approval of parents-cum-employers.

---

73 [Haywood], *Present for a Servant-Maid*, 1743 edn, pp. 35–6, 47–8, 49.

74 LMA, DL/C/273 f. 145, Mary Bacchus, 23/6/1740; see also the 1696 case of *Belton or Chambers* c. *Chambers*, DL/C/245 f. 58 and *passim*, discussed in my thesis, pp. 204–5.

75 LMA, DL/C/633 f. 66, Dulcibel Mason, 25/1/1716; A. Macfarlane, *The Family Life of Ralph Josselin, a Seventeenth-Century Clergyman: An Essay in Historical Anthropology* (Cambridge, 1970), pp. 49, 93, 112.

Haywood's manual was most strikingly candid about the threats to a servant's chastity that contemporaries found so alarming, 'temptations from your master'. Pamela's fictional father bemoaned her position: 'what a sad hazard a poor maiden . . . stands against the temptations of this world, and a designing young gentleman . . . who has so much *power* to oblige, and has a kind of *authority* to command as your master'. Haywood echoed that dilemma succinctly: 'Being so much under his command, and obliged to attend him at any hour . . . will lay you under difficulties to avoid his importunities, which it must be confessed, are not easy to surmount', and the author's prescriptions for repelling his advances cannot have inspired too much confidence since she conceded that 'a vigorous resistance is less to be expected in your station'. She advised servants 'to keep as much as possible out of [the single master's] way', and employ a 'steady resolution' which, by 'persevering, may perhaps, in time, oblige him to desist'; she had enough sympathy for her readership to add, 'it is a duty, however, owing to yourself, to endeavour it'. Imitating the style in which Richardson wrote *Pamela* (whose subtitle was, of course, *Virtue Rewarded*) she gushed: 'How great will be your glory if, by your behaviour, you convert [the single master's] base design he had upon you, into an esteem for your virtue!' But, failing miracles, 'it is much better you should lose a month's wages, than continue a moment longer in the power of such a one'.[76]

'Greater caution is still to be observed if he is a married man': the lascivious attentions of married masters had particular ways of disrupting household order by overturning the strict division of household labour characterised by Filmer as, on the one hand, the housewife's 'generation', and on the other, the servant's 'preservation'. If avoidance failed, 'you must remonstrate the way he would do his wife, and how much he demeans both himself and her by making such an offer to his own servant'; again, if these measures proved ineffective, 'your only way is to give warning' to leave the job. Potentially inconsistent with a manual which characterised mistress–servant relations with the aphorism, 'the eye of the handmaid looks up to her mistress', another route of redress was explicitly closed:

> be very careful not to let your mistress know the motive of [your departure].
> That is a point too tender to be touched upon even in the most distant
> manner, much less plainly told: such a discovery would not only give her
> an infinite uneasiness (for in such cases the innocent suffer for the crimes
> of the guilty) but turn the inclination your master had for you into the

---

76 [Haywood], *Present for a Servant Maid*, 1743 edn, pp. 44–6; S. Richardson, *Pamela; or, Virtue Rewarded* (1740; Harmondsworth, 1985), p. 52: emphasis in the original.

extremest hatred. He may endeavour to clear himself by throwing the odium on you.[77]

In denying intimacy between mistress and maid and putting the husband/ wife relationship above that of master/servant, Haywood was highlighting a cruel aspect of patriarchal relations, rammed home in her stock but evocative cautionary observation: 'Every street affords you instances of poor, unhappy creatures who once were innocent till seduced by the deceitful promises of their undoer; and then ungratefully thrown off, they become incapable of earning their bread in an honest way'.[78]

Haywood advocated female–servant passivity to some degree, but also advised her readers to use words and wiles to deter predatory masters, and — while she appears to have denied servants the potential of sexual desire for these men most of the time — autonomy was still possible. Wade's infuriated rejection of her master may not have been condoned, but the last resort of departure was certainly a real escape route and form of empowerment in a service labour market in which demand exceeded supply. However, Haywood failed to pursue other avenues for autonomous action: Vose attempted a variety of strategies to save her reputation and to do what she could for her own livelihood and that of her child. Parochial assistance and the inefficiencies of London's employer networks for the passing on of references gave her the openings for at least some degree of agency in the outcome of her predicament. The reverse-gendered 'fraternity' possible between servants and their mistresses discussed above may well have rendered irrelevant Haywood's plea for secrecy, and several of the female producents (plaintiffs) suing for marital separation at the London Consistory court on the grounds of violence relied on testimony from servants of the failed or successful attempts upon their own chastity to reinforce their mistresses' claims.

A case from 1684 demonstrates that Wade and Vose's master was not alone in serial rape or attempted rape. Mr Vesey 'did attempt the chastity' of at least two of his servants: Elizabeth Taverner complained to her mistress, while Elizabeth Wilcox spoke to her aunt, and both, when the attempts did not stop, left their jobs. Jane Peareth described her master, Mr Hall, as 'a person of low, lewd and wicked life'. When attempting to rape her, he told Jane 'he had lain with all his maids and that he would lie with her, and in all appearance he did then design and with all his power

---

77 R. Filmer, *Patriarcha, or the Natural Power of Kings* 2nd edn (London, 1685), p. 39; [Haywood], *Present for a Servant Maid*, 1743 edn, pp. 5, 46–7.
78 [Haywood], *Present for a Servant Maid*, 1743 edn, p. 44.

then endeavour so to do'. In a perversion of Filmer's 'natural rights' of patriarchs, this particular master considered he had the privilege of his servants' sexual favours, or at least made full use of the power his status gave him. The presence of his wife certainly did not deter, and may even have encouraged him: she told her husband 'that if he must have a whore he should go abroad for one and not meddle with her maids, for as they came honest into her house she desired they might go away so'. Like Wade, Taverner and Wilcox, Peareth 'for preserving herself . . . was obliged to quit her service'.[79]

However, mistresses were not always prepared to put their servants' concerns over and above the sexual demands of their husbands: Isabel Bagnall's master came home drunk one evening and her mistress, fearing his blows, asked Isabel to go to bed with him. But when she refused, the two women shared a bed together in the parlour instead for mutual protection. The ever-present threat of recourse to neighbourhood publicity surfaced in 1732, when Ann Musgrave deposed that she 'heard the cookmaid cry out murder and thereupon she opened the casement of her room and cried out thieves, and then her master came down from the garret where the cookmaid lay in his shirt and cap only'. When the cookmaid came down to Ann and her mistress, she 'told them her master had endeavoured to force into her room and to fling the door off the hinges'.[80]

Fear of assault was greatly heightened by the knowledge that the master had syphilis or other venereal diseases, usually known by anyone in close proximity with their employers or washing sheets and clothes. One servant had her sleeve torn off by her master in an attempt at rape; he promptly gave her half a crown to have it mended, but despite this apparent gesture of contrition she resorted to getting female friends to share her bed with her at night to discourage him because she knew he had the pox 'by his sheets'. In a ghastly case from 1687, Susannah Yeareley was raped by her master when she was in the midst of an epileptic fit. She did not realise what had happened until a few weeks later when she overheard him boasting about his conquest to another woman, saying he had done it because Yeareley was too kind to her mistress, his wife; it was only then that she discovered she had the pox, and her master paid the surgeon £10 to have it cured.[81]

79 LMA, DL/C/241 f. 5, Elizabeth Taverner, 17/3/1684; f. 31, Elizabeth Wilcox, 8/4/1684; DL/C/264 f. 149, Jane Peareth, 2/2/1727: see also f. 163, Dorothy Evans, 28/4/1727; and f. 177, Elizabeth Banfield, 19/7/1727; Filmer, *Patriarcha*, p. 24.
80 LMA, DL/C/267 f. 50, Isabel Bagnall, 15/12/1729; DL/C/635 f. 49, Ann Musgrave, 27/6/1732. See also DL/C/269 f. 66, Elizabeth Mead, 15/11/1731; DL/C/244 f. 256, Lucy Oates, 10/12/1694; DL/C/262 f. 327, Mary Dodd, 5/5/1725.
81 LMA, DL/C/244 f. 78, Christianna Lovegrove, 5/5/1693; DL/C/242 f. 80, Susannah Yeareley, 2/6/1687.

Unfortunately, we will never know whether either of these masters was moved to pay out of remorse, as bribery for what they hoped would be silence, or as the result of blackmail by the servant's threat to inform mistress, neighbourhood or magistrate.

Samuel Pepys is probably the most famous master-groper of servants in the seventeenth century, having as keen an interest in the appearance of his female servants as he did in most of the women he knew or met. But his conquests of servants occurred largely in the fevered realms of his imagination, since, of the thirty-one or so female servants employed in his household in the *Diary* period, he fondled and kissed five of them (according to his own diary entries), and only went any further in his dreams.[82] He seems to have adopted a certain code of behaviour towards them: regardless of a servant's length of service in his family, the code authorised his casual groping, especially when a maidservant engaged in a relatively intimate task like combing his hair. Pepys's fondling of Jane Birch seems to have begun relatively late, and at least did not intensify until he had known her for the best part of a decade, while he caressed Nell Payne after she had been in his employ for only a month or so. But he felt guilty when his hands strayed beyond a servant's 'mamelles' to her 'thing': coming home one evening, 'I did put my hands under the coats of Mercer and did touch her thigh, but then she did put by my hand and no hurt done'.[83]

It would appear (although reliance on Pepys's account alone makes this point uncertain) that while they were employed by him, Pepys initiated sexual acts but allowed the servants to dictate how intimate they went. He only conducted relations that might be termed an affair with one of his servants, Deb Willet, but it was only when she was on the point of departure that he wrote, 'the truth is, I have a great mind for to have the maidenhead of this girl, which I should not doubt to have' had she stayed longer in his household.[84] Willet was dismissed at his wife's insistence after she walked in on them kissing and caressing in Pepys's chamber, and this, 'which [in Pepys's words] occasioned the greatest sorrow to me that ever I knew in this world', was the most disruptive of any of his relations with servants to domestic peace. Elizabeth Pepys was horrified at her

---

82 Earle, *English Middle Class*, p. 224 and n. 35; Pepys, *Diary* X, pp. 177–80; the individual servants kissed and caressed were: Susan, the 'little girl', VI, p. 185; Mary Mercer, his wife's companion, VII, pp. 104, 172 and 364, VIII, pp. 37 and 150, IX, p. 55; Nell Payne, cookmaid, VIII, pp. 274, 276, 280, 293 and 315; Jane Birch, chambermaid and cookmaid, IX, p. 307; Deb Willet, VIII, p. 585, IX, pp. 143–5, 274, 277, 282, 328, 337–8, 366; he fantasises at, for example, III, p. 152, IX, pp. 180 and 502.

83 Pepys, *Diary* VI, p. 185, IX, pp. 337–8; VIII, p. 274, and IX, p. 307; VIII, pp. 276, 280, 315; IX, p. 55.

84 Pepys, *Diary* IX, p. 361.

servant-companion's behaviour and it severed relations between them irrevocably; but even this seems to have affected his marriage more than employer–servant relations in the 'family' generally (though the *Diary* is less forthcoming on this issue). Yet for aggressiveness and the manipulation of his position of power, his sexual relations with his servants cannot compare with Pepys's attitude towards women married to men in need of his help to procure a post or other material gain, where he applied another sexual code altogether.[85]

Illegitimacy and infanticide

Pepys's more restrained strategy towards his female servants might have saved him: it was the birth to a servant of a bastard child fathered by her master, especially if it came to the attention of the parish, that was almost guaranteed to create a permanent breach in the fabric of the family. Manual writers like Hayward tried to prevent such a cataclysm but nonetheless, of course, it still happened. In 1698, for example, the matrimonial dispute of *Harrington* c. *Harrington* came before the London Consistory court, in which the wife of the steward to the Earl of Warrington demanded a separation from her husband on the grounds of adultery, because he had got their maid Jane Burton pregnant. It seems that Burton's mistress discovered the pregnancy when she returned from the country, whereupon Burton promptly left the house and her service to go to a midwife's, giving birth to a male child.[86] It is unclear whether Burton remonstrated with her master as recommended by the manuals; whether the sexual liaison was the result of coercion or seduction by her master, or arose from mutual attraction and/or consent; whether she resigned her post or was sacked; nor do we have a record of what happened to Burton thereafter. It is clear, however, that the servant who had been made pregnant usually had to leave her job and the shelter in which she may well have formed bonds of friendship. Again, the role played by the wife and mistress was crucial to the servant's experience: Burton's mistress had been absent (presumably facilitating the liaison in the first place) and her return signalled the break-up of their family.

Historians have linked this aspect of service employment with the prosecution of infanticide. Sharpe has written that 'the typical infanticidal

---

85 Pepys, *Diary* IX, pp. 337, 339–40; for non-servants, see, for example, VI, p. 40.
86 LMA, DL/C/245 f. 422, Amy Robinson; f. 425, Hanna Gery, 13/1/1698 (housekeeper). Mr Harrington was nominally a servant himself, though his managerial or even professional status, and the fact consistently averred by witnesses that his income was in the order of £200 a year, puts his rank into perspective.

mother was an unmarried servant girl, and her motives were usually the desire to avoid the shame and consequent loss of position which unmarried motherhood would bring'. Affirming the consensus on this issue, Hill asserts that pregnancy was 'grounds for immediate dismissal', adding: 'Little wonder that of those women convicted of infanticide whose occupation was known, the majority were domestic servants, and there must have been many cases which never came to light'. This is confirmed by a recent study of seventeenth-century infanticide largely based on northern English rural evidence, and also reflected in research on seventeenth- and eighteenth-century France. Beattie's data reveal that 'perhaps as many as two-thirds' of unmarried women charged with infanticide at the Surrey assizes were servants; at the Old Bailey in the eighteenth century, 70 per cent of those indicted for the same offence for whom occupation is known, were servants.[87]

The early Jacobean Act punished the concealment of the birth to an unmarried mother of a child subsequently found dead, and servants were clearly the largest group of unmarried women for whom such concealment was generally obligatory. But prosecutions were extremely rare, and perhaps these cases are more important for the insights they provide of disrupted household relations: 'Ambivalent and equivocal figures', writes Gowing, 'mistresses were as likely to threaten as to help pregnant servants', and may have been responsible for concealing the birth process and disposing of some servants' still-born or even live bastards.[88]

Just as the manuals foresaw the seductive nature of promises by men of higher status within the household, there could be real ambiguities inherent in master–servant liaisons particularly if the master was not married. Roberts has suggested that 'one consequence [of the growing insecurity of service] was an increase in the number of "quasi-uxorial relationships" between migrant women and single male employers' in late sixteenth- and early seventeenth-century urban England. Concubinage could be an act of choice rather than coercion. 'But', Roberts continues, 'these relationships were also vulnerable to exposure, particularly by an unwanted pregnancy . . . for some women at least intimacy with an "employer" may have represented a high-risk strategy for the acquisition of economic security'. The will disputes

---

87 J.A. Sharpe, *Crime in Early Modern England, 1550–1750* (London, 1984), p. 110; Hill, *Women, Work and Sexual Politics*, pp. 137, 138; L. Gowing, 'Secret births and infanticide in seventeenth-century England', *Past and Present* 156 (1997); J.-L. Flandrin, Familles: Parenté, Maison, Sexualité dans l'Ancienne Société (Paris, 1976), p. 178; Fairchilds, *Domestic Enemies*, pp. 178–9; J. Beattie, *Crime and the Courts in England, 1660–1800* (Oxford, 1986), pp. 113–24, esp. 114; R.W. Malcolmson, 'Infanticide in the eighteenth century', in Cockburn, ed., *Crime in England, 1550–1800* (Princeton, 1977), p. 202.

88 21 *Jas.* I, *c.* 27 (1624); Gowing, 'Secret births', p. 104; Beattie, *Crime and the Courts*, pp. 114, 124–32.

discussed in Chapter Five reveal that the master-husband's premature death might also leave them high and dry, but in general domestic service in London during the late seventeenth and early eighteenth centuries was less insecure than its earlier counterpart. In the light of this, Fairchilds overstates her case when she writes that 'force [in master–servant sexual relationships] was rarely needed; in most cases the economic power of the master sufficed'.[89]

It may well be that the realms of emotional choice for female servants were circumscribed both by patriarchal norms and the vulnerability of some subordinate young women in other men's households, and continued to mean near-certain dismissal. But for many of these relationships the emotional calculations were far more complex than Fairchilds's blunt analysis allows; in many others, force was absolutely essential to overcome servant resistance. Nor were all masters immune from community sanction or damage to household reputation in cases of alleged sexual harassment. One servant witness told the court clerk that her former master was bringing a case (presumably of defamation) against another maid who had claimed publicly that he had propositioned her, and put his hands up her skirts 'to know whether she was a man or a woman'. The master had brought the case to clear his name which 'is much disgraced among his neighbours', and his wife was 'much disturbed about it'.[90]

It is important to remind ourselves that reports of master–servant sexuality often emerged incidentally in matrimonial disputes where a request for separation was founded on allegations of violence by the husband against the wife, as further evidence of masters' violent actions and bad characters. Some female servants were clearly resourceful enough to ensure that they were heard in a public forum when the golden opportunity to speak and be listened to arose, in a manner parallel to the way that defamation disputes allowed women to take conflicts which arose in shops or streets and continue them in the judicial realm, one which carried greater weight and which proved more resonant.[91]

Records of illegitimate births and extramarital motherhood — French *déclarations de grossesse*, English bastardy examinations and applications to the

---

89 M. Roberts, 'Women and work in sixteenth-century English towns', in P. Corfield and D. Keene, eds, *Work in Towns 850–1850* (Leicester, 1990), pp. 92–3; Fairchilds, 'Female sexual attitudes', p. 175: for the 'decline of concubinage' in France in the early modern period, see Flandrin, *Familles*, pp. 176–80.
90 LMA, DL/C/241 f. 92, Elizabeth Collingwood, 3/10/1684; for a similar case from the early seventeenth century, see L. Gowing, 'Language, power and the law: women's slander litigation in early modern London', in J. Kermode and G. Walker, eds, *Women, Crime and the Courts in Early Modern England* (London, 1994), p. 37.
91 Meldrum, 'Women's court', 13; Gowing, 'Language, power and the law', p. 41.

London Foundling Hospital — are documents of a different nature. They seem to offer historians the opportunity for broader analysis and the quantification of servant sexuality in particular: given that most young women in the relevant age cohorts were in some form of service in western Europe for much of the eighteenth century, it is no surprise to find that most of those in surviving evidence who gave birth to bastards were servants. It is unfortunate that the Foundling Hospital for orphaned or abandoned children, in the first few decades after its opening in 1741, ensured the anonymity of the children's mothers by not recording their details. But Gillis concluded that 'servants of all types accounted for 65.6 per cent of the women successfully applying to the Foundling Hospital' across the nineteenth century, while Seleski wrote that of those applying between 1800 and 1809 'about 90 per cent [had been] employed at some time or another as domestic servants'.[92] Fairchilds found that in Aix-en-Provence, over half of the unwed mothers making *déclarations* throughout the eighteenth century were servants, while Rogers's study of Westminster parish bastardy examinations between 1712 and 1786 revealed that between 80 and 95 per cent of those examined by the JPs were spinsters, and most of those 'were in their early to mid-twenties and had entered the London job market as servants' of the lower ranks. Both historians found that most of the fathers of their children (as declared) were of similar social status to the servants and were far less likely to be masters, who formed only 4–6 per cent of all fathers in these urban areas.[93]

This would be a fascinating finding were it not for the fact that liaisons between these women and higher-status men were more likely to involve the avoidance of parochial intervention and its attendant publicity. As a consequence, in Rogers's words, 'one should not place too much explanatory weight upon the changing sociology of illegitimacy' since such affairs were more likely to go unreported: this was especially the case in the three West End parishes he examined, St Margaret and St John, St Martin-in-the-Fields, and St Clement Danes. Indeed, since few using the parochial bastardy examination named masters as fathers of their bastard children, Rogers believes that the pressure applied by community and parish on wealthier fathers to hand over lump sums for the care of the child meant

---

92 Wilson, 'Illegitimacy and its implications'; J. Gillis, 'Servants, sexual relations and the rise of illegitimacy in London, 1801–1900', repr. in J. Newton, M. Ryan and J. Walkowitz, eds, *Sex and Class in Women's History* (London, 1983), p. 116; P. Seleski, 'The women of the labouring poor: love, work and poverty in London, 1750–1820', unpublished Stanford University Ph.D. thesis (1989), p. 15 and Chapter 4.

93 Fairchilds, 'Female sexual attitudes', Appendix I, Table 3 Rogers, 'Carnal knowledge', pp. 358, 360.

that in their case, 'a bastardy deposition was often an admission of failure to secure a suitable maintenance by informal means'. And although the *déclarations* of illegitimate births are widely available as a source in France, their proportion of total bastard births, let alone the total of pre- or extra-marital affairs is difficult to judge. Intuitively it would appear that servants were the largest group of women giving birth to illegitimate children in metropolitan England and urban France, and that masters are under-recorded as fathers; but the degree to which these sources are representative of servants' sexual lives remains unclear.[94]

Yet they should not be ignored, and Rogers's finding that socially symmetrical relationships were more likely to result in a bastardy deposition in London's West End as the eighteenth century proceeded is significant. Relationships between those of similar status were 'not usually a casual encounter', and may have grown 'out of work situations, out of domestic settings or neighbourhood associations'. Often, 'illicit unions, in fact, took place within the same household', and some 6 per cent of the Westminster bastardy depositions were due to births from relations between servants and apprentices. Haywood's manual taught the female domestic servant to be wary of the apprentice's designs and her own capacity for self-deception, but many of them working in the smaller households of the metropolis ignored the advice: Margaret Lichfield, for instance, married a hempdresser who had also been an apprentice or journeyman in her master's family. Robert Kemp was butler in a household in which his mistress's waiting-maid married the apprentice; and Judith Hilliar's sister, servant to an ivory-turner in the City parish of St Bride's, also married her master's apprentice. And of course fellow servants certainly married after they had left the house-hold's confines.[95]

Moreover, marriage between fellow servants did not always result in departure from employers' households. In a number of cases, servants were permitted to stay on by masters and mistresses who displayed flexibility and understanding, and a high degree of affection, for these contractual members of the family. In a fascinating example, Elizabeth Cole deposed that upon the marriage of a maidservant and apprentice, both from the household in which Cole used to work, the maid came to her for a temporary bed because she was pregnant. Cole agreed and the maid went off to her master,

---

94 Rogers, 'Carnal knowledge', 360; Fairchilds, 'Female sexual attitudes', p. 166.
95 Rogers, 'Carnal knowledge', 358; LMA, DL/C/245 f. 228, Margaret Lichfield, 3/5/1697; DL/C/249 f. 23, Robert Kemp, 5/2/1706; DL/C/249 f. 40, Judith Hilliar, 4/1/1706. See also DL/C/250 f. 409, Elizabeth Newbold, 15/6/1709; *Wilson c. Wilson*, esp. DL/C/631 f. 28, Margaret Clay, 20/1/1700; DL/C/250 ff. 461–3, William and Sarah Ashley, 7/7 and 14/7/1709.

a gunsmith, to obtain a character reference; to her surprise, he told her that she and her apprentice husband could both stay in his house until they found jobs elsewhere. If the apprentice had not yet finished his indentured term, this would have been an even more generous offer and one in breach of Company rules. Mary Kirke, also servant to a gunsmith, married her master's journeyman and both still appeared to be at the house ten or eleven years later (although it is not entirely clear if they continued to live in). A widowed woman named Mary Dorrington testified for a servant who had married her master's apprentice 'from [her mistress's] house'. Her mistress paid the marriage fees for the couple, and they appear to have set up on their own, because master and mistress supplied the servant and her new husband 'with some necessaries'.[96]

Between 15 and 18 per cent of the Westminster bastardy examinations gave servants as the father; in the French *déclarations* the proportion of births resulting from affairs between servants fell to 6 per cent by the end of the eighteenth century from 15 per cent earlier on. While recognising that 'we have to work from inference' when using these kinds of documents, Rogers suggests that the way 'female servants were vigorously solicited' by male servants with 'a reputation as sexual predators' to keep up meant that many maids were under a great deal of sexual pressure. Of course, some of these relationships fail to give impressions of coercion: Jane Morgan, for example, married a male servant who also lived in the household of Lady Mary Roberts. They both promptly moved into lodgings, although he stayed on as servant living out while she took up needlework at home. Judith Lush, servant to Lady Altham, met the coachman who became her husband, John, while she and Lady Altham were lodging at the inn where John stabled his master's horses, and they lived together at her mistress's house for at least three months after the wedding. Penelope Barrett and her husband married and managed to maintain parallel domestic servant careers, sometimes within the same household, for over a decade or more.[97]

However, Haywood's 'pert and saucy' male domestic servants are visible in the church court depositions: Anne Saunders, servant to a joiner, testified in a defamation case at the London Consistory court, but, no doubt to

---

96 LMA, DL/C/273 f. 248, Elizabeth Cole, 2/2/1744; DL/C/637 f. 534, Mary Kirke, 21/2/1745; DL/C/631 f. 233, Mary Dorrington.

97 Rogers, 'Carnal knowledge', 359, 362–5; Fairchilds, 'Female sexual attitudes', pp. 179–80 (quote from p. 171), and her *Domestic Enemies*, 88–9; see also Maza, *Servants and Masters*, pp. 70–1 and 91–2; LMA, DL/C/632 f. 337, Jane Morgan, 14/7/1712; DL/C/253 f. 26, Judith Lush, 3/11/1712, and f. 38, John Lush, 19/11/1712; DL/C/250 f. 478, Penelope Barrett, 6/9/1709: see P. Earle, *A City Full of People: Men and Women of London, 1650–1750* (London, 1994), pp. 193–4 for a transcription of her testimony.

discredit her as a witness, a midwife was later brought in to swear that Saunders had come to her when pregnant by a coachman, and had asked her whether she would deliver her bastard child. She agreed, but advised Saunders to go to the churchwardens to ensure the father paid for the costs of the birth and lying in. McGlashan's testimony (discussed above in the context of spatial privacy) against Mrs Anderson, a married female servant whom he claimed had given him 'the pox', sounds more like the thwarted lover rather than a liberty-stealing blade.[98] But the stories in the examinations and *déclarations* are too frequently of false promises, arm-twisting and rape for footmen's predatory *machismo* to be dismissed lightly.

Marriage between household members does not necessarily imply prior sexual relations, but some forms of sexual intimacy were more than likely given the repeated tales by bastard-bearers in the examinations and *déclarations* that fathers procured sex upon promises of marriage, and if London was precocious in terms of changes in sexual behaviour. However, Hitchcock's accounts from the Chelsea bastardy records of servants abandoned by lovers when they became pregnant points to the frequent disintegration of relationships under pressure. What Rogers has identified as 'the economic imperatives towards conjugality and the pragmatic heterosexuality of the London poor' could lead servants into trouble: Anne Tisdale, servant to a peruke maker, was courted by one of his journeymen 'in the way of marriage and she believing him to be a bachelor did accept of such courtship, and he afterwards prevailed on her to tell her father and mother that she was married to him'. She seems to have stayed in the service of the peruke maker, but her father did not believe her, and when proof was not forthcoming the bigamous journeyman left her to return to his real wife. At least Anne Tisdale avoided pregnancy. Mary Vaughan's sister was servant to a Mr Wright, and was made pregnant by her master's apprentice; Vaughan denied her sister was married, and anyway, her master had searched the marriage registration books of the local parish church to confirm that the birth was illegitimate and, presumably, to justify their removal from his household.[99]

The female servant making a bastardy examination before a magistrate in London was more likely to have been made pregnant by someone without

---

98   LMA, DL/C/249 f. 145, Anne Saunders, 24/5/1706 (the midwife's testimony is at
      f. 199); DL/C/254 f. 71, John McGlashan, 12/3/1714. For servant sexual relations
      with lodgers, see Meldrum, thesis, pp. 210–11.
99   T. Hitchcock, '"Unlawfully begotten on her body": illegitimacy and the parish poor in
      St Luke's Chelsea', in Hitchcock, King and Sharpe, eds, *Chronicling Poverty*; Rogers, 'Carnal
      knowledge', 363; LMA, DL/C/261 f. 293, Anne Tisdale, 25/1/1723; f. 299, George
      Tisdale, 25/1/1723; DL/C/241 f. 153, Mary Vaughan, 30/10/1684. See also DL/C/635
      f. 286, Jane Burworst, 27/3/1734; DL/C/245 f. 254, Mary Aldin, 5/2/1697.

rather than within her household, and the examinations, *déclarations* and church court depositions show female servants involved in casual and longer-term relationships with men outside their place of employment: this is to be expected given the opportunities for interaction with possible partners in market-places, taverns, streets, shops and at the doorstep. Mary Slicer, for instance, was a servant in a household in which her fellow servant married a man named Symonds. The union was recognised by her employers, and she only left their household when she was ready to give birth to her child. Anne Whitehead, wife of a tobacconist, met the man her servant claimed to be married to when he came to visit at their shop. Later, Whitehead allowed him to lodge in the household for a fortnight, 'when they lived together as man and wife'. The husband, a sailor, then went off to sea again. When the man who had made a servant named Martha pregnant declared his paternity before a midwife to reassure the parish overseer of the poor, Martha promptly 'did penance in the parish church of St. Giles'. This appears to have guaranteed the goodwill of her employers, and in a fascinating declension, her status within the household changed from that of servant to lodger.[100] The degree to which these cases are exceptional cannot be known, but they are a useful counterweight to the frequently traumatic accounts found in bastardy examinations and *déclarations de grossesse*.

Homosexual relations

What we call today homosexual relations between household members, both male and female, appear on the depositional evidence to have been extremely rare. There is an ongoing debate about the availability of clear sexual categories like 'homosexual' and 'lesbian' to the minds of contemporaries. Evidence of homosexuality within French households, presented by Fairchilds, is largely anecdotal; but eighteenth-century London has been identified as the site of a gay subculture centred around 'molly houses' and other outdoor places of assignation like Moorfields. McCormick's valuable reprinting of trial reports in particular demonstrate male servants as both objects of desire in the eyes of older and wealthier men, and also as initiators and active participants in same-sex relations. There must remain more than a possibility that menservants, particularly those of this subculture's gentleman-participants, also took part, and it would appear from the trial

---

100 Rogers, 'Carnal knowledge', 359; Fairchilds, 'Female sexual attitudes'; LMA, DL/C/252 f. 185, Mary Slicer, 19/4/1711; DL/C/249 f. 386 and *passim*, *Pickard c. Pickard*; DL/C/256 f. 75, Elizabeth Dally; f. 78, Anne Beck.

accounts that servants working in victualling households were occasionally propositioned by passing trade.[101]

While there is evidence for cross-dressed marriages of women in the late seventeenth century, the strong social taboos against sodomy and tribady, and the threat of the gallows for prosecuted cases of sodomy, meant that the likelihood of such activities being reported was small. Memories of the execution of Lord Castlehaven in 1631 for sodomising his male servants, among other perceived travesties of patriarchy, will have stayed in the minds of elite employers at least. But one titillating 'confession' by an anonymous author in the early eighteenth century used a chambermaid's erotic fondling of her mistress's daughter to illustrate his cautionary tale against lesbian relations; and Jane Barker's tale of *The Unaccountable Wife* (1723) offered a warning of the topsy-turvy degeneracy caused by one mistress's infatuation with her maidservant. Commenting on the practice (discussed above) of female servants and their female employers or children sharing beds for comfort, consolation and mutual protection, Hitchcock has written that 'it is . . . difficult to believe that a proportion of the female population didn't progress from the almost mandatory hug and kiss at night to more profound forms of sexual satisfaction'.[102]

Menservants and mistresses

'The one sexual relationship that was totally outside the bounds of the moral order in eighteenth-century England', Stone has written with characteristic exaggeration in the third volume of his study of divorce, 'was adultery between an upper-class woman and a lower-class male, especially

101 R. Trumbach, 'Sodomitical subcultures, sodomitical roles, and the gender revolution in the eighteenth century: the recent historiography', and G.S. Rousseau, 'The pursuit of homosexuality in the eighteenth century: "utterly confused category" and/or rich repository?', both in R.P. Maccubbin, ed., *'Tis Nature's Fault: Unauthorised Sexuality During the Enlightenment* (Cambridge, 1987); Fairchilds, *Domestic Enemies*, pp. 185–8; R. Norton, *Mother Clap's Molly House: The Gay Subculture in England, 1700–1830* (London, 1992); I. McCormick, *Secret Sexualities: A Sourcebook of 17th and 18th Century Writing* (London, 1997), esp. Chapter 2. A very useful summary is provided in Hitchcock, *English Sexualities*, Chapters 5 and 6.
102 P. Crawford and S. Mendelson, 'Sexual identities in early modern England: the marriage of two women in 1680', *Gender and History* **7** (3) (1995); C. Herrup, 'The patriarch at home: the trial of the second Earl of Castlehaven for rape and sodomy', *History Workshop Journal* **41** (1996); J. Barker, *A Patch-Work Screen for the Ladies; or, Love and Virtue Recommended* (London, 1723), cited in McCormick, *Secret Sexualities*, pp. 202–4; Hitchcock, *English Sexualities*, pp. 79, 86.

a mere domestic servant'. Yet for all the revulsion for this, the 'gravest of social inversions', several well-documented cases of these liaisons from the eighteenth century exist which suggest that some mistresses considered such relations too compelling to resist, or worth the risk of opprobrium. Aristocratic correspondence recorded the notorious marriage of Lady Harriet Wentworth to her footman, and the cases of *Middleton* c. *Middleton* (1796) and *Dormer* c. *Dormer* (1715) came before the church courts. The Middleton case emerged when a landowner took his wife to law for conducting an affair with the groom; the Dormer case when a wealthy member of the London gentry sought separation from his wife on the grounds that she had committed adultery with the footman (and she may also have begun a second affair with another male servant). [103]

The Dormer case embodies many of the elements of household tension discussed above, but because of the nature of this form of affront to patriarchy, other aspects of servant–employer relations exhibited in the extensive testimony allow unique insights. In an overturning of the norm in separation suits at the church courts, when abused wives could look forward to support from important servant witnesses, almost all of the more than twenty servants who came forward to give evidence condemned Diana Dormer with tales of sexual encounters and pregnancy, but most frequently, of the disruption caused to a relatively large family of male and female servants. Aside from these more or less direct accusations of incontinence, the Dormer family servants backed up their master's case with accusations of their mistress's favouritism towards the footman Thomas Jones, by her 'constantly [speaking] to him in a very smooth and soft style', and by allowing him to monopolise her time and space. After one encounter between Jones and another servant, Mrs Dormer shouted, 'Well I don't care, if he uses you all like dogs you shall take it . . . if he were a villain she should not live with a villain', and she dismissed the complaining servant soon afterwards. As one footman observed, what Jones said 'was law'. [104]

Not content with usurping other servants' roles, Jones sought to steal all those of his master: when Mrs Dormer's waiting woman informed her

---

103 Stone, *Broken Lives*, pp. 162–247, esp. p. 243; P. Seleski, 'The footman's revenge: masculinity and the "feminisation" of domestic service in late eighteenth and early nineteenth-century London', unpublished paper to the Berkshires Conference on Women's History (June 1993), pp. 24–7; D. Marshall, 'The domestic servants of the eighteenth century', *Economica* **9** (25) (1929), 34; LMA, DL/C/255 f. 80 and *passim*.

104 LMA, DL/C/255 f. 116, Mary Horne, 14/3/1715; f. 137, Elizabeth Cotton, 17/3/1715; f. 129, Thomas Lewin, 16/3/1715; f. 151, Thomas Edwards, 24/3/1715; f. 141, Alice Hogger, 18/3/1715; f. 166, Mary Davis, 25/3/1715; f. 129, Thomas Lewin, 16/3/1715: for a fuller account see Meldrum, thesis, pp. 214–17.

master that Jones 'had beat and very much abused' his wife, John Dormer sacked Jones and warned that any servant letting him into the house faced instant dismissal. Jones then attempted to conduct a *charivari* outside the house, inviting neighbours to pass judgement on his affair and exclusion, and the crowd ensured his escape. Diana Dormer had often told Alice Hogger, her chambermaid, 'that if Mr Dormer turned away Jones she would turn away all her servants', and a number of servants were removed, both from the Dormers' employ and that of their later employers when pursued vindictively by their former mistress. Others 'voluntarily quitted and left their service' because they incurred Diana Dormer's displeasure in their attitudes to her affair with Jones, and she made working for her very uncomfortable. Mrs Dormer's behaviour managed to alienate even the closest of her female servants, and at least one maid empathised whole-heartedly with her master, as 'she verily believes him to have been much abused' by his wife.[105]

At least until Diana's infatuation with a second footman, Jones seems to have been in receipt of a private income. Drinking with a footman from another household who asked him 'after what manner he lived since he had been out of place for so long', Jones replied that 'he had no occasion to take any more places, for his Lady maintained him . . . for he had debauched her' and made John Dormer 'a cuckold'. Later on in the conversation, he 'took his privy members from out his breeches and let them hang down bare and exposed for some considerable time', saying (in a pungent phrase which summarised many of his rural contemporaries' impressions of the life of the idle metropolitan footman) that 'his prick was his plough'. But such bravado could not disguise the fact that just as his mistress-lover had disrupted servant–employer loyalties, Jones had put himself outside any solidarity between the family's male servants, leading another of the footmen to claim that 'he would break Jones's neck before he should come into the house'.[106] It is clear how an affair between mistress and manservant was not just a sexual but, like the Castlehaven case, a social inversion. The male lover interposed himself between mistress and master by taking his master's place in the matrimonial bed in a dastardly act of disloyalty, and in so doing, usurped his power over both mistress and servants. Here, Jones had the audacity not just to obtain mastery over the family by overturning

---

105 LMA, DL/C/255 f. 181, Francis Warrington, 17/5/1715; f. 162, Joseph Morris, 25/3/1715; f. 133, Robert White, 17/3/1715; f. 107, Alice Rigby, 12/3/1715; f. 157, Charles Whiston, 24/3/1715; ff. 129, 141, 151, 166.
106 LMA, DL/C/255 f. 178, Richard Haynes, 17/5/1715; f. 168, James Webster, 12/4/1715; f. 145, Richard Morris, 19/3/1715; ff. 162, 181.

Table 4.1   Reasons London servants gave for departure, 1660–1750

Reason	N	Reason	N
Employers' marital breakdown	38	Bankrupt/Household economies	7
Illness	13	Violence/Sexual assault	7
Differences with employers	13	Indiscipline/Bad company	6
Employers' death	12	Better place	6
Marriage	11	Slander/Defamation	5
Reputation	8	Date/Season	4
Unsuitable/Unqualified	8	Miscellaneous/Unknown	14
Remuneration	7		
		Total N	159

Source: church court depositions.

work-roles, but also to exercise all the conjugal rights of the husband, even including physical chastisement under the eyes of the whole household.[107]

Departure from the household

The day-to-day rubbing along of employer–employee relations is difficult to delineate even in the records of the church court depositions, but further insight into the parameters of the acceptable can be gained from an examination of the reasons servants gave for leaving their places. Illness, violent confrontation and sexual assault, as the chapter so far suggests, were all reasons for leaving a place. Indeed, illness together with 'differences with employers' formed the second largest category of reasons for leaving. Both dismissal and departure could be used as a form of punishment or as a strategy for coping with chastisement and violence, by employers and servants respectively, and while it was an essential element in the employer's armoury of discipline, the market for service made it more potent in the hands of servants. Table 4.1 shows that the most frequently-given reason for departure was violence or other dispute between master and mistress

---

107   Compare to cases in which mistresses fell in love with apprentices: LMA, DL/C/249 f. 423, Mary Revell, 17/10/1707; and the case of *Clifton* c. *Clifton*, esp. DL/C/265 f. 47, Ellen Slater, 27/6/1728; f. 55, Mary Gould, 29/6/1728; f. 57, Martha Metton *née* Astbridge, 3/7/1728.

and the marital breakdown which usually resulted in the disintegration of the household.[108]

The death of an employer had a similar effect in dissolving the domestic arrangements: for instance, Thomas Edwards 'lost his service by the death of Peregrine Bertie, Esq.', his then master. So did an employer's decision, forced (by bankruptcy or the exposure of fraud) or unforced (by the desire to economise) to diminish the size of the household: Francis Warrington 'quitted [the Duchess of Devonshire's] service by reason of the Duchess retrenching the number of her family'. The one servant prepared to tell the London Consistory court he had been sacked for theft, Robert White, denied the offence, yet it has been included under the only employer-defined category in the table, 'indiscipline/bad company', which also included dismissals for drunkenness, illicit sex, keeping 'bad company', or 'disobliging' other members of the household.[109] In fact, because of the negative implications for those servants concerned, several of these reasons for departure were reported by their fellow servants.

Robert White, the alleged thief, gave reasons for a succession of places which provide an interesting insight to the sackings or decisions that encouraged menservants in wealthy households to move on: Lord Longueville discharged him because he was 'going into the country where he kept but one footman'; Lieutenant-General McCartney turned him out because 'of another person being recommended to him who could brew and do other matters which he was ignorant of'; he 'voluntarily quitted and left his service' in the Dormer family because 'it became very difficult in him to oblige' his mistress; Lord Rosnieram, the Danish Envoy, turned him out as a footman 'upon an accusation of his having said that the Lord's Lady would ruin her husband by play'; and the Duke of Schomberg turned him out 'upon an accusation of stealing some fruit out of his garden of which he was innocent'.[110] But none of these jobs lasted less than five months, and the longest (with the Duke of Schomberg) lasted five years, so their relative precariousness must not be exaggerated.

However, this list does demonstrate the role of whim and contingency in the lives of London servants: fewer than a third of the decisions in Table 4.1 can be said to be those of servants determining their own fate (from the 'marriage', 'reputation', 'unsuitable or unqualified' as deemed by servants, 'remuneration', 'better place', 'defamation or slander' and 'date or season'

---

108 A full set of references for this section can be found in Meldrum, thesis, pp. 180–3.
109 LMA, DL/C/255 f. 151, Thomas Edwards, 24/3/1715; DL/C/255 f. 181, Francis Warrington, 17/5/1715; DL/C/255 f. 133, Robert White, 17/3/1715.
110 DL/C/255 f. 133.

categories), and even then some of those servants may have felt their hands were forced. Of course, such categorisation also highlights the part of fate in determining the fortunes of London households for all their members. The combined effects of the market for service and the state of relations between employer and employee helped foster a moral economy of service (a concept explored in Chapter Six), but this customary context was shorn of seasonal hiring times: only four servants left at distinct times of the year, Christmas, Whitsuntide, Michaelmas and Easter. The impression those accounts gave was that, although White's testimony indicated the continued importance of the London Season as a recruitment cycle in the early eighteenth century,[111] such dates provided markers to jog servants' memories rather than weighty seasonal turning points for employer or employee. Betterment, in the search for greater remuneration or a better or more suitable place, formed a small minority of the reasons given for departure here, and it is this which renders the data somewhat problematic. While they have their uses, the data are drawn from less than 10 per cent of the population of servants from the London church court depositions, and seem to reflect the nature of the matrimonial or defamatory disputes more than the fortunes of servants themselves. Nonetheless, in those households in which servants were sucked into their employers' crises, the disruption of involuntary departure was mollified by the strength of demand for servants: the striking factor about Robert White's account is the speed with which he found alternative employment.

Conclusion

If the section on departure paints an ambiguous picture of the severance of some servants' relations with their employers, the extended discussion of servant sexuality before it provides a valuable lens through which to look back to the broader issue of household relations, not least because recent accounts seem to treat the coercive nature of some servants' sexual relations as symptomatic of the lives that particularly female servants led in the long eighteenth century. Some historians seem unable to dissociate patriarchal relations from an all-embracing and vicious oppression. But in ideal terms contemporaries associated patriarchal ideology with duties of care as well as obligations of command and obedience. This chapter has discussed a wealth

---

111   L.D. Schwarz, *London in the Age of Industrialisation: Entrepreneurs, Labour Force and Living Conditions, 1700–1850* (Cambridge, 1992), p. 104.

of types of relations between servants and other household members, especially their employers, by refusing to rely on elite or institutional sources
alone. It is apparent now by setting *déclarations*, bastardy examinations,
prescriptive literature and diary entries alongside church court depositions
— in which servants themselves (mediated through clerks) told the stories
of their own lives — that 'vulnerability' cannot encapsulate the diversity of
servant interaction with those around them. Domestic servants were not
simply victims. To reduce them to life-cycle pawns is both jaundiced and
one-dimensional.

Two potential models of servant relations were presented — Maza's
'threshold' and the 'growth of privacy' — but neither was found to be
satisfactory. The idea that servants led a liminal existence between the
privileged world of their employers and the plebeian world everyone else
inhabited may be attractive at the intellectual level, but is not supported by
the evidence. Most domestic servants, for most of the time, were engaged
in too much interaction with others who lived in their households and
many beyond it, some of that interaction intimate, for them to be in any
way aloof or withdrawn. For some of the time, that interaction was deeply
satisfying as they struck up friendships and more with fellow servants,
employers and neighbours: even in documents whose genesis lay in crisis
and conflict, the warmth of many of these human encounters is evident. But
before this conclusion appears to be opposing 'vulnerability' with cosiness,
it is also plain that many other servants, or occasionally the same servants
at different times, experienced discomfort, aggression, violence or even
rape. The testimonies of Elizabeth Wade and Martha Vose cast too sharp
a shadow to be ignored; but their experiences of service and the interventions of parish authorities could hardly place them on the cusp, in
limbo, between worlds. Domestic servants were certainly ubiquitous in late
seventeenth- and early eighteenth-century London, but they were far from
invisible.

The evidence discussed in this chapter fails to lend much support to a
teleological 'growth of privacy', nor to domestic servants' participation in
the creation of 'separate spheres', but confirms instead the utility of a contemporary household/family elision. Privacy might be seen in two ways in
this context: as the gradual divorcing of employers and their immediate
blood kin from the servants they employed, and as the increasing isolation
and seclusion of servants within the household. It is apparent from earlier
discussion in this chapter that the development of technology designed to
create distance between employer and domestic employee refused to fit into
prescribed linear patterns, and anyway had little impact on the lives within
most households. If there appears to be a stark division between the argument based on spatial analysis with the sections that followed, it is because

very few church court depositions gave adequate spatial information, and that it is a near-impossible task to collate 1,500 servant biographies over 90 years with probate inventories or house-plans (if they existed).

However, it is also clear that what might be called the Gormenghast model — isolated, excluded servants flitting wraith-like from shadow to shadow — does not fit the London of our period, is most likely inappropriate for the hundreds of thousands of domestic servants employed in urban western Europe at this time, and its relevance to even the largest rural households in this period has yet to be shown convincingly. Servants, like most others, were embedded in local networks of information and gossip, playing an active role in mediating their own and their households' reputations as well as being objects of such networks. Conversely, within the hierarchical and spatial subdivision of large houses, as in the compact proximity of small households, some forms of private seclusion were possible some of the time to servants or employers. The extensive evidence of the sexual activities of servants with or under the noses of fellow household members, including employers, might suggest a possible model of cultural trickle-*up* rather than trickle-down: were servants in the van of increasingly-identifiable categories of metropolitan homosexual relations? Was London's precocious adoption of penetrative heterosexuality practised by plebeians first, and only then taken up by the middling sort and elites who employed them? The managerial mistress — whose late eighteenth-century novelty is dispelled here — was even, occasionally, an active participant. The point is, the quality of the interaction between household members was more important in determining the degree of 'privacy' available than bricks, mortar, wainscot or 'separate spheres'.[112]

Both the threshold and privacy models preclude servant-employers from acting *in loco parentis* but the evidence on illness, pregnancy and general care of their charges demonstrates that ideals of patriarchal duty still had a purchase on the minds of some. It is certainly true that sick or pregnant servants were more likely to be removed from the household, and predatory masters and ambivalent mistresses could shatter a servant's illusions that they might act like a surrogate father or mother. If, for instance, Pepys is even remotely representative of middling masters, then they and some of their servants considered a low level of sexual harassment/play as part of the relationship. But in Pepys's mind, and certainly in the minds of those

---

112 For an excellent recent interrogation of this ideological construct, see R.B. Shoemaker, *Gender in English Society, 1650–1850: The Emergence of Separate Spheres?* (Harlow, 1998), esp. Chapters 4 and 5; also important is H. Barker and E. Chalus, eds, *Gender in Eighteenth-Century England: Roles, Representations and Responsibilities* (Harlow, 1997).

servants who resisted his more intrusive attentions, there were limits to the sexual scope of mastery, beyond which lay assault and rape. There has been some evidence of the conscious cultivation of female solidarity, especially around issues of sexuality and pregnancy,[113] even if the church court depositions throw up mistresses who try to persuade servants to sleep with their drunken husbands, or servants who were prepared to bear witness to their mistresses' poor housewifery or adultery. Unlike apprentices, for whom such semi-parental duties were clearer, even contractual and legally-enforceable, domestic servants had fewer safeguards, but also could change employers far more easily. And it must be appreciated that the availability of extra-household routes of redress or support, whether formal (magistrates, church courts or parish officials) or informal (neighbourhood opprobrium, ostracism and the *charivari*), highlights the permeability of household boundaries in London. Harm could be done to servants but they were far from isolated.

In the face of such diversity it is difficult to substitute a redundant old model of vulnerability with a new one. It is possible that a servant's age influenced the richness or precariousness of his or her relations with employers and other household members, though the depositions are far from definite on this point: older female servants were not necessarily more able to resist the determined master. The size of household and the gradient of the servant hierarchy, or degree of specialisation, affected a servant's proximity to an employer, and will also have governed to some extent the chances for friendship or enmity among fellow servants. But the clearest distinguishing factor was gender: the evidence on reputation suggests that menservants constructed identities for themselves; yet those for female servants were so often based around their sexual 'honesty' that they required greater levels of vigilance.

While bearing in mind that only a small minority of London's servant-employing households kept menservants, Jones's affair with his mistress, for instance, exposed sharp differences with sexual relations between master and maid. Mrs Dormer had far more to lose in the gossip-ridden world of London society than had Jones the footman, and he completely subverted his own master, while boasting of his sexual prowess with a fellow footman under the terms of an alternative code of conduct that validated his actions (at least among menservants outside the household). Free of the risk of

---

113   See the essays by L. Pollock, A. Wilson and esp. P. Crawford in V. Fildes, ed., *Women as Mothers in Pre-Industrial England* (London, 1990); for modification, see Gowing, 'Secret births', and for scepticism, U. Rublack, 'Pregnancy, childbirth and the female body in early modern Germany', *Past and Present* **150** (1996).

pregnancy, it is no wonder he did not appear to be saddled with the sort of concerns that bedevilled Martha Vose. We must be careful not to put too much emphasis on a male servant 'brotherhood', given that much of the evidence of this is anecdotal and from the pens of commentators and employers. As Jones's experience shows, male solidarity could be just as fragile as female through the competing pressures of favouritism and jealousy. Domestic servants, united in their subordination under the patriarchal demands of servitude, lived lives in which household relations were fractured by gendered experience. The following chapter will examine through a gendered lens the extent to which domestic service can be portrayed as work.

CHAPTER FIVE

Domestic service as work

With labour I must earne / my bread; what harme?
Idleness had bin worse; my labour will sustain me
Milton, *Paradise Lost* x, 1054.

Introduction to the meaning of work

Hard labour

Twentieth-century historians of service have been much more absorbed by the implications of service for social relations than by the work servants performed; similarly, seventeenth-century writers were generally more concerned to clarify a servant's place in the ideal hierarchy of labour, rather than the nature of his or her tasks. In his anti-Cromwellian paean to kingship, *Patriarcha*, Filmer asserted that the 'community of man and wife differs from the community of master and servant, because they have several ends. The intention of nature by conjunction of male and female, is generation; but the scope of master and servant, is preservation'. The natural place for servants was in the patriarchal household but in a socially rather than a biologically reproductive role, with a significant degree of division of labour: 'even as several servants differ in the particular ends or offices; as one to brew, and another to bake; yet they agree in the general preservation of the family'.[1] Filmer was using a metaphor that he took to have both

---

1 R. Filmer, *Patriarcha, or the Natural Power of Kings*, 2nd edn (London, 1685), pp. 38–9.

profound scriptural authority and the virtuous simplicity of common-place wisdom, to illuminate and lend weight to his view of the self-evident merits of kingship. According to Schochet 'the social and political presumptions to which patriarchalism belonged were even then [in the 1650s] losing their relevance';[2] but at one remove, Filmer had in fact written the labour of servants into the political canon as an essential component of the patri-archal family, and this would remain influential long after the revolutionary embers of mid-century had cooled.

In his classic analysis of labour in seventeenth-century England, Coleman noted that the 'necessity to "employ the poor" is a theme which is reiterated time and time again in this period, enlivened by frequent blasts against "idleness".' Baxter, the eminent seventeenth-century divine, firmly advo-cated the godly discipline of labour, and counselled servant-employers to choose a servant 'that is not of a flesh-pleasing, or lazy, sluggish disposition . . . Yea though they should have grace, a phlegmatic, sluggish, heavy body will never be fit for diligent service, no more than a tired horse for travel'.[3] Divine injunctions to work drove most thought on the subject, based on both Old and New Testament teachings on the sacred necessity but curse of labour. Fundamental were the words, elaborated upon by Milton in this chapter's epigraph, to Adam as he and Eve were cast out of Eden forever to work for their livelihoods: 'cursed is the ground for thy sake; in sorrow shall thou eat of it all the days of thy life; thorns also and thistles shall it bring forth to thee; and thou shalt eat of the herb of the field; in the sweat of thy face shalt thou eat bread' (*Genesis* iii, 17–19). Preachers also looked to the life of Jesus, one linking divine servitude with work by declaring that 'Christ is expressly called God's servant . . . It was his father's business he was employed in, and to him he behoved to work', citing St John's gospel: 'I must work the works of him that sent me' (*St John* ix, 4). The use of these formulae were far from new but as Keith Thomas highlighted years ago, they received greater emphasis from the sixteenth century.[4]

Likewise, Slack has observed that 'the ideal of labour as a remedy for idleness was, of course, as old as the hills', but he and Roberts recognise something qualitatively different here: 'the emphasis was particularly char-acteristic of vocational doctrine, and increasingly so during the course of

---

2   G.J. Schochet, *Patriarchalism in Political Thought: The Authoritarian Family and Political Speculation and Attitudes Especially in Seventeenth-Century England* (Oxford, 1975), p. 57.

3   D.C. Coleman, 'Labour in the English economy of the seventeenth century', reprinted in E.M. Carus-Wilson, *Essays in Economic History*, 3 vols (London, 1954–62), II, p. 292; R. Baxter, *Works*, 4 vols (London, 1707), I, p. 386.

4   T. Bouston, *The Mystery of Christ in the Form of a Servant* (Edinburgh, 1742), pp. 16, 18; K. Thomas, 'Work and leisure in pre-industrial society', *Past and Present* **29** (1964).

the seventeenth century'.[5] Appleby notes that the 'men who wrote about [the labouring classes] evaluated them in terms appropriate to their own participation in a developing economy', and 'economic pamphleteers [of the later seventeenth-century] repeatedly hailed the value of disciplined, economic effort in appraising the various elements in their society'.[6] Yet though conservative proponents of patriarchy and more 'radical' advocates for labour discipline and effort may have differed over the purpose of servants' labour, they were agreed on their place in the commonwealth: preservation or vocation, servants' divinely allotted station was subordinate, working for their superiors.

Commentators often referred to manual service work as 'drudgery', in the sense of 'mean or servile labour, wearisome toil, dull or distasteful work' (*OED*). This is what Defoe alluded to when he mentions the 'menial servants who do her ladyship's drudgery', and certainly is Mandeville's meaning in his *Essay on Charity, and Charity-schools*: to 'do something or other that turns to profit as soon as they are able, be it never so little', the exertions of the scriptural hewers of wood and drawers of water 'where hard labour is required, and dirty work to be done'. Yet as Earle has shown, Pepys did not disparage such drudgery, particularly not when it served his household: 'Willingness to work hard was obviously an important asset and a servant who was "a drudging, working wench" would receive due praise, as did [Pepys's servant] Susan, who was described as "a most admirable slut", not at all an opprobrious term'.[7]

Occupational labels

Domestic servants themselves recognised their subordination, and were under no illusions about the laborious nature of their work. When Mary Fibbs told the clerk of the Bishop of London's Consistory court she had been 'going backwards and forwards in [her mistress's] house', something had

---

5 P. Slack, *Poverty and Policy in Tudor and Stuart England* (London, 1988), p. 29; M. Roberts, '"Words they are women, and deeds they are men": images of work and gender in early modern England', in L. Charles and L. Duffin, eds, *Women and Work in Pre-industrial England* (Beckenham, 1985), p. 134.

6 J.O. Appleby, *Economic Thought and Ideology in Seventeenth-Century England* (Princeton, 1978), pp. 132–3.

7 D. Defoe, *Everybody's Business is Nobody's Business; or, Private Abuses, Public Grievances* (London, 1725), p. 11; B. de Mandeville, 'An essay on charity, and charity-schools', added to the second edition of his *The Fable of the Bees* (1723; Harmondsworth, 1970), pp. 278, 293, 306; P. Earle, *The Making of the English Middle Class: Business, Society and Family Life in London, 1660–1730* (London, 1989), p. 224.

clearly been keeping her busy; Ann Hopson related in 1738 that she had maintained herself 'by her labour' for the two years prior to her deposition, a period that overlapped with a four-year 'place' in service.[8] Yet many domestic servants, if asked explicitly by church court proctors how they were maintained, answered by default. One said she 'was bred up by her aunt from her youth and was bred to no trade and follows no trade but she hath sometimes gone to service to wait on a gentlewoman'; another described herself as 'of no trade or calling and maintains herself by going to service' to a barber and periwig-maker; yet another said 'she goes to service for her livelihood being of no trade or profession'; and a fourth 'follows no trade or employment but gets her living by going to service as she hath done for most part of these seven years'.[9]

Conventionally speaking, many of London's female domestic servants described themselves by default as having neither trade, profession, calling, nor even employment, but simply that they 'got their living by going to service'. Initially, this type of self-ascription appears to encapsulate the ambiguity of domestic service in hierarchies of both work and status. It lay outside the jurisdiction of the early modern institutions that organised manufacture and trade, the Livery Companies, and constituted a quite different form of service from craft apprenticeship: in Campbell's classic description of London trades, he acknowledged the occasional female apprentice, to capmakers for example, but only mentions female domestic servants when writing homilies such as his tuppenny wisdom in the entry on the Chandler's shop.[10] These testimonies also illustrate how domestic service might lie beyond contemporary occupational categories: for instance, Gregory King's 'scheme of the income and expense of the several families of England' for 1688 mentions 'outservants', but *domestic* servants do not feature under those that 'decrease' the wealth of the nation because they are subsumed under the household heads of those 'increasing' it.[11]

Yet these phrases were used frequently by church court witnesses, by witnesses apparently ingenuous in intent and seemingly certain of comprehension

---

8 LMA, DL/C/252 f. 191, Mary Fibbs, 19/11/1710; DL/C/272 f. 21, Anne Hopson, 2/2/1738.

9 PRO, PROB 24/48 f. 150v, Anne Watson, 24/5/1709; LMA, DL/C/254 f. 207, Mary Stackhouse, 13/5/1714; DL/C/255 f. 308, Mary Coleman, 7/7/1715; f. 238, Mary Cross, 18/5/1715.

10 R. Campbell, *The London Tradesman* (London, 1747), pp. 210, 280.

11 G. King, *Natural and Political Observations upon the State and Condition of England* (1695), reprinted in J. Thirsk and J.P. Cooper, eds, *Seventeenth-Century Economic Documents* (Oxford, 1972), pp. 780–1; London servants do appear earlier in the work when King disaggregates by marital status, pp. 772–3.

within the quasi-judicial context in which they were spoken. These female domestic servants reflected the 'consignment of so much of women's work to a residual sphere, occupationally unlabelled and outside the well-documented male "occupational structure"'; or, as Mary Prior puts it, 'What men did was definite, well-defined, limited. . . . What the women did was everything else'.[12] But the fact that these servants 'went to service', a state of being or living in an intensely hierarchical society as much as an employment, also suggests that the duty implied in Filmer's 'preservation' still had purchase, however unfashionable his politics had become around the turn of the eighteenth century. Like apprenticeship, service involved the socialisation of young people (especially the young labouring poor) into the socially-stratified patriarchal society of early modern England. But to stop here would limit the phrase's interpretative scope and deny its complexity. As it did for the man 'going to sea' or the older woman who 'goes out nursekeeping', the social breadth of the master–servant dichotomy gave the girl 'going to service' entry into a nexus of functions, customs and conventions by which she could 'get her living'.[13]

Male domestics, on the other hand, tended to be far more precise in the terms they used to describe how they maintained themselves in the metropolis: they gave occupational labels like footman, butler, groom, coachman, clerk of the kitchen, or cook. Such self-ascription expressed a kind of certainty over occupational role and identity, and an assurance of working status that did not need to define itself by reference to a superior but instead could stand alone in its own right. There were exceptions, like 'gentleman's gentleman'; one manservant even let pride in his title overlook his master's death when he told the court clerk he was a 'gentleman's servant' to a 'widow gentlewoman' in Drury Lane.[14] But even here, enhanced status was gained (albeit vicariously) by direct reference to the gentle employer.

Earlier historians of domestic service certainly took the familiar roster of status and task-oriented labels at face value. Hecht devoted most of his chapter on 'The Servant Hierarchy' to the finer gradations of male service, while his discussion of wages detailed 25 separate male posts but only

12 Roberts, '"Words they are women"', p. 140; M. Prior, 'Women and the urban economy: Oxford, 1500–1800', in M. Prior, ed., *Women in English Society 1500–1800* (London, 1985), p. 95.
13 D. Simonton, 'Apprenticeship: training and gender in eighteenth-century England', in M. Berg, ed., *Markets and Manufacture in Early Industrial Europe* (London, 1991), p. 253; P. Earle, *A City Full of People: Men and Women of London, 1650–1750* (London, 1994), pp. 138, 208.
14 LMA, DL/C/638 f. 41, Nathaniel Morgan, 8/11/1749.

eleven female. To some degree this was a reflection of the gendered difference in specialisation in the eighteenth century, and the far greater range of tasks open to men in the largest households.[15] The *Plan of a Person of Quality's family*, for instance, illustrates the ideal contemporary range of potential tasks and the domestic servants required to fulfil them, detailing a full complement of 69 servants, thirteen women and 56 men, including six chaplains, four cooks, and two 'Gentlewomen of the lady's bed chamber'.[16] But it was elite sources similar to the *Plan* which led Hecht to portray servants' stations of rank with a deceptive mathematical exactitude, and service work simply as errand-running by languid lackeys.

In addition to a wariness about the provenance of our sources, we must be careful not to overdraw the gender distinction apparent in occupational labels. Those of male servants could become blurred if they were employed by victuallers in public houses, taverns or inns, for instance, despite the apparent occupational precision of terms like 'tapster' and 'chamberlain'. In 1715, Arthur Babit called himself a 'hostler' when a former female servant of his master's revealingly described him simply as a 'servant': he was at pains to don a gendered occupational label, but she reminded him of his simple subordinate status.[17] Historians have cautioned against the uncritical use of early modern occupational titles and the misleading appearance of certainty they convey. In particular, Woodward's research into the building trades in the north of England have shown that men who worked as masons and carpenters actually engaged in a multiplicity of earning strategies. The diversity of their employment was hidden by the craft titles they adopted and by which they were described in probate inventories or other surviving documents, reaffirming the gender-free connotations of Hufton's pungent but often misquoted phrase, 'an economy of expedients, multiple makeshifts which together permitted some kind of existence'. Sonenscher's research into the 'bazaar economy' of male trades in eighteenth-century France emphasises how trades established and maintained work identity in the face of economic fluctuations, worker mobility and the limited range of

---

15 J.J. Hecht, *The Domestic Servant Class in Eighteenth-Century England* (London, 1956), Chapters 2 and 6. In fairness, the sources used in this thesis were not available to him.
16 Anon., *Plan of a Person of Quality's family* (1690?).
17 A tapster was 'a woman who tapped or drew ale or liquor for sale in an inn', or 'a man who draws the beer etc. for the customers in a public house'; a chamberlain was an 'attendant at an inn, in charge of the bedchambers' (*OED*): see the discussion of service and retail below; LMA, DL/C/255 f. 455, Arthur Babit, 5/12/1715; f. 457, Frances Carter, 5/12/1715: 'hostler' (and in its abbreviated form 'ostler') in its usage from the sixteenth century was 'a man who attends to horses at an inn; a stableman, a groom' (*OED*).

skills and raw materials used in manufacturing: the legal defence of custom was sometimes the only way craft differences could be affirmed.[18]

Work in theory

Sonenscher's has been a prominent voice in the reconsideration of the historical meaning of work in the last few decades, an intellectual development that has been mirrored across the humanities and social sciences thanks to the reinvigoration of Marxism within academia during the 1970s, and the responses that this inspired in revision. A variety of historians have attempted to move beyond neo-classical economic categories or those of over-stratified Marxism to a more keenly-contextualised and nuanced understanding of 'getting a living' in the past. Joyce edited a volume in 1987 which was entirely preoccupied with 'the historical meanings of work', acknowledging 'the significance of work as a social construct' and 'the need to look beyond the realm of the economic and of production if work is to be understood'. This book gives striking prominence to studies on historical discourses about men and women's work in the last three centuries, and perhaps unwittingly (given that most of the contributions cover the nineteenth and twentieth centuries) draws us back to older definitions of 'œconomy' which encompassed factors, over and above material production or the generation of monetary resources, such as the management of the household.[19] The sociological response to these intellectual shifts has been profoundly influenced by the development of labour process theory, but the participation of feminists in response to the relative omission by Marx and his interpreters of women's work and domestic labour, and the growth of women's history as a sub-discipline, has most relevance to the subject here.[20] Many years ago Alice Clark stressed the value of work conducted within the domestic sphere and the centrality of the pre-modern household as an economic institution, a place now recognised as one where

---

18 D. Woodward, 'Wage rates and living standards in pre-industrial England', *Past and Present* **91** (1981), 39–42; his *Men at Work: Labourers and Building Craftsmen in the Towns of Northern England, 1450–1750* (Cambridge, 1995), pp. 236–44; O. Hufton, 'Women without men: widows and spinsters in Britain and France in the eighteenth century', *Journal of Family History* **9** (4) (1984), 363; M. Sonenscher, *Work and Wages: Natural Law, Politics and the Eighteenth-Century French Trades* (Cambridge, 1989), p. 178 and *passim*; his *The Hatters of Eighteenth-Century France* (Berkeley, 1987), esp. Chapter 3.

19 P. Joyce (ed.) *The Historical Meanings of Work* (Cambridge, 1987), p. 1; *OED*, 'economy'.

20 P. Thompson, *The Nature of Work: An Introduction to Debates on the Labour Process* 2nd edn (Basingstoke, 1989), Chapter 7; R.E. Pahl, *On Work: Historical, Comparative and Theoretical Approaches* (Oxford, 1988).

people developed (in Pahl's words) a 'household work strategy'. 'The house-hold' historically differs in size and composition, of course, but as an ideal or theoretical space it has proved useful in comprehending the gendered nature of work in the past. A new emphasis is now put on the assertion that Marx and Engels made, in Paul Thompson's summary, that 'the conditions for producing commodities are bound together with the reproduction of people as social beings, particularly in the family', especially since it is now recognised that 'the household persisted as a site for wage earning well into the twentieth century'.[21]

Social anthropologists have demonstrated similar preoccupations by view-ing work in terms of physical transformations, social transactions, economic activities and personal identities: 'In each of these respects', writes Wallman, 'work is "about" control — physical and psychological, social and symbolic', and, she might have added, 'about' power in Foucault's sense that it gener-ates discourses of authority and subordination.[22] This perspective assists us in understanding a major concern of the Marxist-feminist 'domestic labour' debate, the power relations that created sexual divisions of labour. We might recognise that this debate 'argued itself into a cul-de-sac' by the inability of the theories upon which it was founded to deal with, firstly, the complexities of households in the present or the past, eliding 'household' and 'family' without clarity about the nature of their overlap; and secondly, by getting bogged down by the nature of the intersection between capital-ism and patriarchy while trying to decide which was the 'determining' factor.[23] It also presupposed a monolithic transition from household work to factory work at some point in the late eighteenth or early nineteenth centur-ies, a widely-held view which the latest research tends to undermine. But it did establish 'one point quite clearly: that domestic labour is production, it produces goods and services which contribute to the standard of living in . . . society',[24] i.e. it is avowedly work rather than non-work, which has tangible value whether it lends itself to calculation or not.

---

21 A. Clark, *Working Life of Women in the Seventeenth Century* (London, 1919; 1992 edn); Pahl, *On Work*, p. 10; Thompson, *Nature of Work*, p. 188; S.O. Rose, ' "Gender at work": sex, class and industrial capitalism', *History Workshop Journal* **21** (1986), 114.

22 S. Wallman, ed., *Social Anthropology of Work* (London, 1979), p. 1; 'Truth and power', in C. Gordon, ed., *Michel Foucault. Power/Knowledge. Selected Interviews and Other Writings, 1972–1977* (Brighton, 1986).

23 M.M. Mackintosh, 'Domestic labour and the household', and C. Middleton, 'The familiar fate of the *famulae*: gender divisions in the history of wage labour', both reprinted in Pahl, *On Work*, pp. 392 and 41–5 respectively. See Chapter Two for more on the family/household elision, and the Bibliographical essay later for 'work'.

24 Mackintosh, 'Domestic labour', p. 405; H. Barker and E. Chalus, eds, *Gender in Eighteenth-Century England: Roles, Representations and Responsibilities* (Harlow, 1997), esp. the discussion in pp. 10–15.

Current debates have revolved around the nature of long-term historical change. The idea that there might have been some kind of 'golden age', when working women had fulfilling economic roles usually within the household, which disintegrated with the transition to 'separate spheres' of gender-distinct work in which women were marginalised (be that due to advances in seventeenth-century capitalism or eighteenth-century industrialisation), has undergone sustained challenge.[25] On the one hand, some researchers assert that certain forms of work persisted as 'feminine' realms of labour over long periods of time. While much changed in broader social and macro-economic terms, continuities in patriarchal gender relations and therefore in sharp sexual divisions of labour were more striking than structural shifts in society or economy, and this has been borne out particularly in the English metropolis.[26] On the other hand, some historians stress the significance of wider change, particularly the industrial revolution, but stress that women and men responded differently and, especially given the variety of circumstances women found themselves in, the effects on attempts at 'making shift'[27] often fail to fit a linear model of change. The stress today is less on grand theorising and more on regional and local studies of gendered work from which a clearer overall picture will emerge,[28] and this chapter hopes to perform that role for London domestic service in the late seventeenth and early eighteenth centuries.

The present chapter began with an appreciation of the way female domestic servants effaced, and male domestic servants affirmed, their working status and identities, allowing us to explore how historical discourse about 'work' has been deconstructed in the last few decades. Writing and research by historians, anthropologists and sociologists take the debate beyond orthodox neo-classical and Marxist categories that frequently exhibited production-dominated perspectives concerned with male labour. Now we have moved towards an analysis that sees work as a set of activities involving

---

25 Succinctly summarised in R.B. Shoemaker, *Gender in English Society, 1650–1850: the Emergence of Separate Spheres?* (Harlow, 1998), Chapter 5.

26 J.M. Bennett, 'Medieval women, modern women: across the great divide', in D. Aers, ed., *Culture and History 1350–1600: Essays on English Communities, Identities and Writing* (Brighton, 1992); P. Earle, 'The female labour market in London in the late seventeenth and early eighteenth centuries', *Economic History Review* 2nd series, **42** (3) (1989); L.D. Schwarz, *London in the Age of Industrialisation: Entrepreneurs, Labour Force and Living Conditions, 1700–1850* (Cambridge, 1992), Chapter 1.

27 P. Sharpe, *Adapting to Capitalism: Working Women in the English Economy, 1700–1850* (London, 1996), p. 1.

28 Sharpe, *Adapting to Capitalism*, p. 4 and *passim*; P. Hudson and M. Berg, 'Rehabilitating the industrial revolution', *Economic History Review* 2nd series, **45** (1) (1992), 44; A. Vickery, 'Golden age to separate spheres? A review of the categories and chronology of English women's history', *Historical Journal* **36** (2) (1993).

social reproduction and the generation of identity, as much as economic transactions and the physical transformation of material resources. The household, the site of domestic service, has become the focus again of a reinvigorated enquiry into gendered work and the sexual division of labour. These arguments inevitably return us to the 'politics of place' by requiring the historian to see service work within the early modern household as embedded in contexts of gendered social relations, in which the meanings as well as the value of work were contestable and negotiable.

The sexual division of service labour is striking, and the remainder of this chapter explores the usefulness and also the limitations of a model of service work based on gender divisions. This book has repeatedly stressed the key distinction between smaller households, mostly employing female servants, and the larger households which employed menservants as well, often in greater numbers than female; but this distinction informs rather than determines the structure of what follows. We examine the concept of 'housewifery' as the ideal locus of (particularly female) domestic work, and attached to this is a smaller section on service and retailing; secondly, the chapter details the 'idle luxury' of the livery and upper servants in larger households in the metropolis. These subjects are tackled in two integrated ways. Firstly, a much-needed typology of the work that domestic servants actually undertook in metropolitan households during the late seventeenth and early eighteenth centuries is provided: it is essential that discussion proceeds with an evidential base rather than a continuing reliance on the impressionistic words of employers alone. Secondly, testimony by servants is analysed in terms of contemporary comment and the relevant theory and historiography to recover domestic service from its unsatisfactory place in the interstices of pre-modern work.

Housewifery and the drudgery of service

Housewives and servants

The concept of 'housewifery', as an embodiment of much of what the early modern period understood to be appropriate work for women, has a long pedigree. The *OED*, with examples dating as far back as the thirteenth century, defines 'housewife' as 'a woman (usually, a married woman) who manages or directs the affairs of her household; the mistress of a family; the wife of a householder', a definition combining managerial tasks with marital and middling status. It adds: 'often (with qualifying words), a woman who manages her household with skill and thrift, a domestic economist'. Penelope Corfield recently observed that while 'there is no shortage of evidence to show that women have . . . been familiar to toil' in a range of orthodox sectors of the economy throughout the past, they were also 'the chief suppliers of the routine support services within the household'. In other words, 'housework' for many women was supplementary to other (often waged) work, but for many more these services constituted their principal tasks as 'housewife' and helped to define their role. 'The relentlessness of these chores was proverbial', she notes, citing Thomas Tusser's observation in 1570 that 'Huswives affaires have never none ende'. He added 'an uncompromising motto for the hard-pressed housewife', writes Corfield: '"I serve for a day, for a week, for a year / For a lifetime, for ever, while man dwelleth here".'[29] The commonplace nature of these sentiments is emphasised by their echo in a seventeenth-century ballad whose first verse chirped that '. . . a maid may set still, go or run, but a woman's work is never done', and in Mary Collier's heartfelt cry, 'Alas! our labours never know an end'.[30]

'Housewifery' as an ideal formulation of women's household labour was most clearly elaborated during the Elizabethan and early Jacobean period, in the large body of prescriptive literature usually known now as household manuals. Tusser's was only one: Gervase Markham's *The English Housewife*, professing to be a book *containing the inward and outward Vertues which ought to be in a Compleat Woman*, was first published in 1615 but was reprinted throughout the seventeenth century. Like Tusser's text, it was the mirror to another volume for men: originally volume two of *Country Contentments*, the first volume was entitled *The Husbandman's Recreations*. It set out to describe 'the office of our English housewife, who is the mother and mistress of the family, and hath her most general employments within the house'.[31] But perhaps the sub-title ought to have read 'complete virtues', since the woman he described deserved to be canonised: 'it is meet that our English housewife be a woman of great modesty and temperance, as well inwardly as outwardly' — she should greet her husband's 'mis-government of his will' with a 'mild sufferance', and in one of the very few references throughout to

29 P.J. Corfield, 'Defining urban work', in P.J. Corfield and D. Keene, eds, *Work in Towns 850–1850* (Leicester, 1990), p. 208, citing T. Tusser, *A Hundred Good Points of Husbandry, lately Married to a Hundred Good points of Huswifery* (London, 1571).

30 Ballad cited by C. Davidson, *A Woman's Work is Never Done: A History of Housework in the British Isles, 1650–1950* (London, 1982); M. Collier, *The Woman's Labour* (1739; London, 1989), p. 23.

31 G. Markham, *The English Housewife, containing the inward and outward Vertues which ought to be in a Compleat Woman*, 9th edn (London, 1683), pp. 1–2.

domestic staff, 'calling into her mind, that evil and uncomely language is deformed, though uttered even to servants'.[32]

The manual describes how to make cures and ointments, to grow herbs and legumes, use kitchen implements, preserve and prepare food, make distillations and perfumes, to order, preserve and serve all sorts of wines, and imparts knowledge of wool, hemp, flax and dyeing so the housewife could clothe her family; it also describes the making of malt, butter, cheese, bread and beer. If these instructions are only marginally more realistic in intent than his injunctions regarding housewifely behaviour, Markham for one perceived housewifery to encompass an extremely wide range of skilled tasks, within the ambit of the virtues of domestic economy and thrift. Berg has pointedly remarked that 'the very definitions of skilled and unskilled labour have at their root social and gender distinctions of far greater significance than any technical attribute', and Markham in his manual reinforced conventional perceptions of the household as a legitimate realm of female accomplishment. According to Best, the modern editor of the first edition, 'Markham's book describes the activities of a large rural household', although its commercial success and the unrivalled access to books in the metropolis meant the readership of this generic piece of literature was almost certainly urban too.[33] Nevertheless, in this early ideal form the housewife was an 'œconomist' in charge of household resources within the bounds of rural self-sufficiency.

In the chapter on food preparation, Markham wrote: 'Now we have drawn our housewife into these several knowledges of cookery, in as much as in her is contained all the inward offices of household, we will proceed to declare the manner of serving and setting forth of meat for a great feast'. He continued, 'It is then to be understood, that it is the office of clerk of the kitchen, (whose place our housewife must many times supply) to order the meat at the dresser, and deliver it unto the sewer, who is to deliver it to the gentlemen, and yeomen-writers to bear it to the table'. But he was only teasing when he referred to this battalion of servants: 'Now because we allow no officers but our house-wife, to whom we only speak to this book . . .' and he proceeded to direct his elaborate instructions to her alone.[34] Best remarks that dairying is one of the few tasks at which Markham assumes the help of a servant, and seems to suggest that he was appealing to as wide a readership as possible, even to housewives with very few or no servants:

32   Markham, *English Housewife* (1683 edn), p. 3.
33   Roberts, '"Words they are women"', p. 142; Berg, *Age of Manufactures*, p. 155; G. Markham, *The English Housewife*, ed., M.R. Best (1615; Kingston and Montreal, 1986), p. ix.
34   Markham, *English Housewife* (1683 edn), p. 98.

implicit in this, given his former remarks about large rural households, is that Markham's readers tailored the ideal to their own needs.[35]

Markham's manual is very interesting in the way it sublimated servants and their work under the assumed authority and competence of the housewife. It was certainly not a managerial tract in the sense of an instruction manual informing mistresses how to govern their 'family' of servants. But the apparent elision of the tasks of housewife and servant in the household is disentangled somewhat by the direction of this advice to the 'mother and mistress of the family'.[36] Roberts has observed that these tasks 'were primarily viewed as the social obligations of the wife rather than as the "occupation" of a married woman',[37] pointing to housewifery's liminal place in the early modern discourse of work; but this finding also illuminates its conjunction of status and work-role. Domestic skills taught in books like Markham's were at least implicitly shared between mistress and maid, and the tack taken by the author is a function of both an assumed managerial role of mistress and the width of the market at which it was aimed. Best acknowledges that supervisory role, yet insists that 'the truth of the housewife's life of unremitting labour should never be far from the mind of the reader'.[38]

The ninth edition of *The English Housewife* (published in 1683) differed from the first only in its publication as a separate volume, but by the late seventeenth and early eighteenth centuries, several distinct but related genres developed. Books on housewifery still appeared, like Eliza Smith's *The Compleat Housewife; or, Accomplished Gentlewoman's Companion*, which was 'a collection of upwards of five hundred of the most approved receipts . . . to which is added a collection of near two hundred family receipts of medicines'. She makes use of an interesting marketing ploy that would not have been seen in Tusser's or Markham's day: 'what I here present the world with', wrote Smith, 'is the product of my own experience, and that for the space of thirty years and upwards, during which time I have been constantly employed in fashionable and noble families'.[39]

Cookbooks, often written by former servants, had become established as a discrete genre yet their texts failed to mention servants explicitly, making

35 Markham, *English Housewife*, ed., Best, pp. xxvii, xlvi.
36 Markham, *English Housewife* (1683 edn), pp. 1–2.
37 Roberts, '"Words they are women"', p. 144.
38 Markham, *English Housewife* (repr. 1986), pp. xxviii, li. Provincial JPs' understanding of tasks performed by 'best' servants or housekeepers, exhibited in their wage assessments, mirrored those assumptions made by Markham: M. Roberts, 'Wages and wage-earners in England: the evidence of the wage assessments, 1563–1725', unpub. D.Phil. thesis (Univ. of Oxford, 1981), pp. 168–70.
39 E. Smith, *The Compleat Housewife; or, Accomplished Gentlewoman's Companion* 2nd edn (London, 1728), n.p.

no apparent assumptions about their readership bar literacy. For instance, *Mrs Mary Eales's Receipts* was penned by the former confectioner to Queen Anne; mentioned above was Smith's, written by a cook who professed to have worked in the largest households; Mrs Lydia Fisher's *The Prudent Housewife* followed Markham by including a monthly bill of fare, marketing advice, and recipes for cures 'for most distempers incident to human bodies[, c]ollected by eminent physicians'. Although it is a late example, the anonymous author of *The Housekeeper's Pocket Book* included the following statement about his or her aims: 'I do not intend to teach professed cooks; but my design is to instruct the ignorant and unlearned (which will likewise be of great use in all private families) and in so plain and full a manner, that the most illiterate and ignorant person, who can but read, will know how to do every thing in cookery well': the author assumed that 'private families' employed a cook and later on, a nurse when members were ill.[40] None of these books made even one direct reference to domestic servants, yet it would seem fair to assume that servants would have formed a significant proportion of their readership given their growing rates of literacy.[41]

As we have seen, from the late seventeenth century a new sub-genre developed of advice aimed explicitly at mostly female domestic servants themselves. But even a classic like Eliza Haywood's *Present for a Servant-Maid* oriented itself towards cookery over time. The edition of 1743 devoted two-thirds of its 76 pages to a treatise on serving with honour, diligence and chastity, the 'due observance' of whose rules 'cannot fail of making every mistress of a family perfectly contented, and every servant-maid both happy and beloved'. By its 1771 edition, the treatise had been reduced to a mere 17 pages, and it had become largely 'a good and useful system of the art of cookery' for mistresses and particularly maid-servants. Incidentally, its cover price in 1743 of 1*s.* — or '25 for a Guinea to those who give them away' — had risen to a 2*s.* flat rate, suggesting a near doubling in the cost of philanthropy, or, when the treatise was reduced to a third of its former length, a six-fold rise in the value of pearls of wisdom.[42] The special rate for bulk purchasers of the 1743 edition — be they charitable donors or heads of

---

40 M. Eales, *Mrs Mary Eales's Receipts* (London, 1718); L. Fisher, *The Prudent Housewife; or, Complete English Cook for Town and Country* (London, 1750); anon., *The Housekeeper's Pocket Book* (London, *c.*1780), p. 3. I am grateful to Sara Pennell for help in tracking down cookbooks.

41 Before 1700, 27.5 per cent of female domestic servants could sign their name on their depositions (63.9 per cent of the male), but from 1700 on that proportion rose to 49.8 per cent (87.0 per cent of male): church court depositions.

42 [E. Haywood,] *Present for a Servant Maid; or, the Sure Means of Gaining Love and Esteem* (London, 1743), Preface; [E. Haywood,] *Present for a Servant Maid* (London, 1771), p. iii.

large families — adds to the impression that it was not just the servants who
were intended as readers of this tract.

The kitchen

This literary device does not blind us to the fact that cooking was a key part
of the servant's work in the household. The kitchen, which in terraced
houses actually built in the early eighteenth century was often found in the
basement, in many ways formed the focal point for servants in all but
the largest households, for several obvious reasons: it was almost certainly
the warmest room in the house, with fires that burned longer and were fed
more frequently than those in other rooms, and increasingly with ovens for
baking that gave out heat in a controlled fashion. These devices might take
some getting used to: Elizabeth Pepys, using her new oven in 1660, managed to 'a little overbake' her pies and tarts, 'but', as her husband smugly
observed, she 'knows how to do better another time'.[43]

The kitchen was where much of the work in the less-specialised household would have to be done — food and drink preparation, water-heating,
washing (unless there were separate facilities for that purpose) — and as
such, it was probably the room most likely to be lit after dusk. Most everyday cooking, spit-roasting meat, boiling vegetables or simmering stews on a
trivet or tripod, was still done on a grate over an open fire, generating mess
in the form of coal-dust, fat dripping and spillages; yet the cleanliness of
English kitchens was repeatedly reaffirmed by foreign commentators like
Saussure. Well-kept houses were washed twice a week, he observed, 'and
that from top to bottom; and even every morning most kitchens, staircases
and entrances are scrubbed. All furniture, and especially the kitchen uten-
sils, are kept with the greatest cleanliness.'[44] It was one of the single most
frequently-mentioned locations for servant witnesses at the church courts,
demonstrating its centrality not only to the activities that went on within it,
but also its position in lowlier housing on the threshold between house and
communal yard. In the thousands of multi-occupancy houses in the capital,
it could also be a busy place whose use at all times of the day and night
might generate arguments among neighbours.[45]

43 D. Cruickshank and N. Burton, *Life in the Georgian City* (London, 1990), pp. 52–3, 60–1,
    63–6, 248; S. Pepys, *The Diary of Samuel Pepys*, 11 vols, eds, R. Latham and W. Matthews
    (London, 1971), I, p. 291.
44 Earle, *English Middle Class*, pp. 222–3; Cruickshank and Burton, *Georgian City*, pp. 79–81; C.
    de Saussure, *A Foreign View of England in the Reigns of George I and II* (London, 1902), p. 157.
45 E.g. LMA, DL/C/236 f. 158; DL/C/237 f. 68; DL/C/237 f. 73; DL/C/240 f. 291; f. 296
    (the servant slept at the kitchen door); f. 382; f. 399ᵛ; Cruickshank and Burton, *Georgian
    City*, pp. 60–1.

Elizabeth Davis, the domestic servant whose description of the tasks undertaken within her mistress's household supplied us with a model of the moderate-sized family in the Introduction, testified to the importance of one of the tasks carried out in the kitchen. 'Dressing' the family's meat was one of the named tasks for which she was hired, but her 'unskilfulness in dressing' meant that the meat supper was not done on time, angering her master. Yet Davidson has observed that cookery was the only area of servant work where servants were clearly creative and influential in writing or contributing to cookbooks;[46] it was one of the activities in which many mistresses participated, particularly in the smallest households, a point which we saw above was exploited by Gervase Markham. Elizabeth Pepys's cooking is noted on a number of occasions in her husband's diary, especially at Christmas, and servants were assisting her. When domestic servant Elizabeth Shepherd's master gave a feast for the local watch a year after the publication of the ninth edition of Markham's *English Housewife*, it was Shepherd and her mistress who provided the supper together.[47]

A household with the income to employ a second servant was likely to hire a cookmaid to supplement the labour of their maid-of-all-work, or may even have hired an occasional cook: Pepys hired a 'man-cook' just 'to dress dinner' on Lady Day, 25 March 1662, the day he re-hired the maid Jane (incidentally, Pepys hired a total of eleven cookmaids over the diary period and, briefly, one under-cookmaid). The largest houses would have employed at least one full-time cook, and ideally several, and the *Plan of a Person of Quality's family* recommended the following: 'Cooks are in number according to the grades of the lord's house-keeping and are usually as follows. Viz. one cook for the French way / one cook for the English way / one cook for the pastry / one cook for the larding and the roast'.[48]

This degree of specialisation, of course, was out of the question for all bar the West End resident nobility, and cooks living in households like that of Pepys were expected to be versatile enough to cook and 'dress meat' for family and guests: his cookmaid Hannah 'doth dress my meat very well and neatly', and cooked a nine-dish meal. While most households would have had fairly regular meal times, a cook was often expected to prepare food as

---

46 LMA, DL/C/250 f. 197, Elizabeth Davis, 18/11/1708; Davidson, *History of Housework*, Chapter 8.

47 Pepys, *Diary*, I, pp. 29, 291; II, pp. 170, 293, 295 (with her maid Jane); IV, pp. 62, 361, 363, 433; VII, p. 420 ('my people busy making mince pies'). Throughout the diary period the family had a maid, and for most of it had a cookmaid too, first hired in September, 1661: II, p. 176; LMA, DL/C/240 f. 399, Elizabeth Shepherd, 17/3/1684.

48 Pepys, *Diary*, III, p. 53; VIII, p. 225; Hecht, *Domestic Servant Class*, pp. 65, 43–4; anon., *Plan of a Person of Quality's family*, n.p.

and when it was required, particularly in unusual circumstances. Diana Dormer, wife of an esquire and mistress of a family of around ten male and female servants in 1715, gave birth at 4 or 5 a.m.; 'after Diana had lain in some time, she had a roasted chicken and a pint of wine for her dinner which [Thomas Edwards, footman] carried up to her, and attended her'.[49]

In households of that size, cooks would have had a particular place in the hierarchy of employer–employee intimacy: footmen did the mediating between Mistress Dormer and her cook, but we have other evidence that such servants were, by the nature of their work and their physical place in the kitchen, more distant from their employers. Jane Fordin was 'cook and housekeeper in the [parties'] family at their town house and country seat', but she claimed that she only learned of the deterioration in her master's relations with her mistress 'by what she heard from her fellow servants who were more immediately about the person of her mistress'. A task related to food preparation that probably required servant–mistress consultation when performed by servants was marketing. In one household, a cook was apparently 'turned out of the family for not being a housewife nor understanding her business as a cook', making a distinction between the thrift of domestic economy and the dextrous skills of cooking (though her employers sacked her for lack of either).[50] Servants can be seen in the depositions on their way to buy fruit and 'herbs' for the household or returning from the market with their purchases. This was not an exclusively female task: even John Perrott, servant to Lady Stradling who 'collecteth her rents in the country' also 'goeth some time to market to buy provisions for her house'.[51]

Disputes in the Prerogative Court of Canterbury over wills offer further evidence of the importance of the preparation and presentation of food in the construction of housewifery during our period. These cases sometimes involved what may be termed 'quasi-uxorial' relationships in which female servants lived with their masters as if they were married,[52] and the transmission of property would usually be contested by blood kin of the deceased man who did not recognise their alleged matrimonial bond. A case from

---

49 Pepys, *Diary*, IV, pp. 90, 95; for French female cooks, see C. Fairchilds, *Domestic Enemies: Servants and their Masters in Old Regime France* (Baltimore, 1984), pp. 15–16, 51; S. Maza, *Servants and Masters in Eighteenth-Century France: the Uses of Loyalty* (Princeton, 1983), p. 316; for mealtimes see Cruickshank and Burton, *Georgian City*, pp. 27–45; LMA, DL/C/255 f. 151, Thomas Edwards, 24/3/1715.

50 LMA, DL/C/637 f. 586, Jane Fordin, 11/3/1748; DL/C/633 f. 94, Humphrey Cook, 16/2/1716.

51 LMA, DL/C/250 f. 23, Hannah Ayers, 5/12/1707; DL/C/236 f. 304, Margaret Lloyd, 17/11/1671; PRO, PROB 24/42 f. 133, John Perrott, 8/7/1703.

52 A term borrowed from M. Roberts, 'Women and work in sixteenth-century English towns', in Corfield and Keene, eds, *Work in Towns*, p. 92.

1721 took evidence from Susannah Beardsley, who twice dined at the deceased bookseller Henry Rhodes's house, 'at which times Jane Lillington [whose role as either housewife or housekeeper was at question] sat at the upper end of the table and carved as mistress of the family, and the servants both at London and at Peckham attended upon her and addressed themselves to her as their mistress'.[53] This witness supported Lillington's claim to be entitled to a wife's share of the estate by demonstrating that, in a family with several servants and two houses, she did not just have a managerial role, which could have left her simply at the head of the servant hierarchy within the household. What proved crucial in this account was the manner in which she was addressed by the servants, and the particular symbolic role she adopted when carving the joint.

The same court took evidence from several witnesses in 1715 over Edward Atwood's disputed will; Eleanor Coote's deposition listed her answers to questions regarding Elizabeth Vickers, who took the name of Atwood after Edward's death. Coote 'often observed her to dress his victuals and wash the dishes, wait on him at table, and weed the garden, and to behave herself in all respects as a common servant in doing all the mean and servile work of Atwood's household'. Coote and friends

> stayed with Atwood one evening till 'twas night, and Elizabeth lighted them out of the door, and [they have] given money to [her] when they so dined . . . Elizabeth complain[ed] that washing Atwood's linen was hard upon her since he would allow her no more help than a char woman . . . [she] constantly and on all occasions say Sir when she spoke to him . . . Elizabeth did not dine at his table but waited on him, and . . . used frequently to dine and sup with the char woman [and] with Coote's maid.[54]

Elizabeth Vickers was clearly being portrayed here as a domestic servant rather than as Atwood's wife, and again status, work and skill are the key determinants. The housewifery exhibited by Vickers was 'mean and servile', she ate with servants (both resident and non-resident), accepted tips, and addressed her master in terms understood by Coote to denote servility. Yet she exercised skills in the preparation of food and did the sort of

---

53 PRO, PROB 24/59 f. 223, *Popping c. Rhodes*, ?/11/1721. A similar case arose from a matrimonial dispute at the London Consistory court — a servant reported that the housekeeper 'lived and lodged at his master's houses . . . and converse and keep company with him and sat at table and managed his affairs as wives usually do', adding that 'there was a report in the neighbourhood that they . . . live together in a lewd and scandalous manner': LMA, DL/C/263 f. 63, Thomas Cox, 26/2/1726.

54 PRO, PROB 24/54 f. 093, *Atwood/Bedell c. Downes*, 14/7/1715.

laundry work that would otherwise have been purchased entirely, instead of just partially, on the market.

The records of will disputes inevitably exhibit a bias towards larger household size and greater employer wealth, and the heightened circumstances of conflict over the allocation of probate resources in all likelihood led to exaggeration in the clarity of household relations. Nevertheless, this evidence suggests that a clear distinction had to be made on occasions in London between wife and servant, but that housewifery could blur apparently clear boundaries. The cases turned on the symbolic as well as legal or spiritual relationship between the master of the house and the woman who had initially benefited from the will, and the degree to which her role matched that of the managerial housewife. The latter was defined by her place at the head of the table or as the giver of orders, and the domestic servant, with due deference, undertook 'housewifery' under her guidance; yet food presentation, the place where and the company with whom it was eaten assumed major cultural significance in the delineation of housewifery.[55] Work in the household was about control and the fostering of identities, and gendered housewifery was more complex than a list of tasks: Filmer's clear ideal distinction between the 'generation' of wives and the 'preservation' of servants may have been a good guide to ideals of appropriate sexual relations within the household, but was too cut and dried when it came to work.

Washing and cleaning

Two other central components of contemporary housewifery were clotheswashing and general cleaning. In an urban environment where dirt, coaldust and effluent were ever-present, much of servants' time was taken up by washing clothes. A number of servants engaged in it spoke — like Elizabeth Vickers — of having the assistance of hired help: Mary Sewell worked with a 'washer and scourer' in 1684.[56] Others had help from their mistresses or even neighbours, like Susannah Burnaby, whose mistress helped her with hanging the washing out in the house's gallery in 1679, or Ann Miller, working in the kitchen in 1689 while her mistress 'scoured in the back washing house'. Martha Arrowsmith was helped in her washing by next

---

55   Elizabeth Pepys's companions ate with her but Samuel's younger sister Pall, their chambermaid, did not: Pepys, *Diary* II, p. 4; see Earle's discussion, *English Middle Class*, pp. 226–7.
56   LMA, DL/C/241 f. 181, Mary Sewell, 24/11/1684; see also DL/C/252 f. 260, Jane Weston, 8/2/1711.

door's maid and apprentice in 1697, who seem to have taken it as an opportunity to be together outside the surveillance and prying eyes of their own household; while Margaret Denton went to her mistress's daughter's house to assist the maid with the washing and stayed three or four days in 1704. In Pepys's household, his wife Elizabeth 'used to make coal fires and wash [Pepys's] foul clothes with her own hand' when they lived without servants early in their marriage, and even when they had servants she assisted in the arduous process; occasionally she merely supervised, waking the servants up early at 4 or even 2 o'clock in the morning. Needless to say, Samuel followed the conventional view that washing was women's work and never took part himself.[57]

Sharing this job must have made it less onerous, but it could still be especially memorable: Elizabeth Young was recovering from illness when she returned to service in St Giles in the Fields, but 'particularly remembers this day because it was washing day', and her mistress helped her with the washing 'for all the whole day'. Historian Bridget Hill has reminded us of the laboriousness of washing in country and town when water had to be fetched then heated over the fire or stove, and servants seem to have made full use of specialised or communal facilities for washing and water-fetching. In London by the end of our period, 'the wives and servant-girls of mechanicks and day-labourers, who live in courts and alleys, where one cock supplies the whole neighbourhood with water' could be seen at 4 a.m. on Sunday mornings 'taking the advantage before other people are up, to fill their tubs and pans, with a sufficiency to last them the ensuing seven days'. A domestic servant named Sarah Hill in 1687 washed her family's laundry in the wash-house common to the houses built around the same yard; in 1695 Mary Brock did the washing near her aunt's door at a sink in St James's market while a hackney-coachman's wife hung hers out.[58]

It was mentioned above that clothes-washing was often done in the kitchen, and in their study of the Georgian town-house, Cruickshank and Burton note the use of sinks made of stone and timber then lined with lead, or even carved whole from stone in the eighteenth century. Large houses with basement kitchens might have a lead cistern in the open area in front

---

57 LMA, DL/C/238 f. 11, Susannah Burnaby, 8/7/1679; DL/C/243 f. 19, Ann Miller, 6/5/1689; DL/C/245 f. 255, Martha Arrowsmith, 5/2/1697; DL/C/248 f. 140, Margaret Denton, 1/2/1704; Pepys, *Diary*, VIII, p. 82; I, pp. 19, 296, 301; IV, p. 65; V, pp. 11, 55, 62.
58 LMA, DL/C/259 f. 220, Elizabeth Young, 12/2/1720; B. Hill, *Women, Work and Sexual Politics in Eighteenth-Century England* (Oxford, 1989), pp. 107–13, esp. p. 108, citing *Low Life, or One Half of the World Knows Not How the Other Half Live* (London, 1764); DL/C/242 f. 145, Sarah Hill, 11/11/1687; DL/C/244 f. 281, Mary Brock, 12/3/1695.

of the kitchen collecting rain water with a tap over a butt, or one inside the kitchen itself, fed by the water-pipe through which one of the private water companies delivered water for a fee from reservoir or river. The wealthiest houses would have had their own wash-houses, probably at the back of the basement, and there is certainly evidence from the end of the eighteenth century of back-garden washing lines in the London town-house.[59] Defoe related a story about a haughty prospective domestic servant who insisted to her future employers that 'if you wash at home, you should have a laundry maid', and setting aside for the moment Defoe's impatience with servant 'impudence', employers in extensive households would have had specialist laundry staff. The *Plan of a Person of Quality's family* recommended three in total, 'according to the largeness of the family': 'The first is to wash the Lord and Lady's wearing linen, all the laces, heads, ruffles and all the small linen in general; the second to wash the wearing linen of such domestics as are allowed their washing; the third to wash all the great linen such as the table linen, napkins, towels, sheets and such like'. But by the late seventeenth century in London, the washerwoman taking in washing in her own house was a firm fixture, and other more specialist facilities were available: in 1667, Elizabeth Pepys took her household wash out to be bleached at the 'whitsters' on the south bank, a process that took over two days.[60]

In the intimate proximity of a household, washing clothes and linen could have an extra importance, and in matrimonial disputes heard at the London church courts servants were explicitly asked about evidence on the sheets of their masters' or mistresses' extra-marital sexual behaviour.[61] Mary Davis, laundry maid in the jealousy-riven family of the Dormers, 'was turned out by her mistress because she refused to take mouldy starch unfit for her business from one of her trades people'; however, this was only the pretext for dismissal, because she refused to put up with Mrs Dormer's footman-lover, who came down to the laundry room 'and there pretended to pry into matters which did in no wise belong to him'. When Mary told him to go, 'he took hold of the door of the laundry and flung it backwards and forwards several times therewith making a great noise; Mary thereupon taking her advantage shut the door and locked him out'. She clearly saw the laundry room as her territory (as much her province as the purchasing of the household starch), and refused to tolerate an intervention by an interfering footman; she clearly had far greater work autonomy compared

<hr/>

59 Cruikshank and Burton, *Georgian City*, pp. 64–5, 84–9, 203, 248.
60 Defoe, *Everybody's Business is Nobody's Business*, p. 18; Earle, *City Full of People*, pp. 116, 126–7; anon., *Plan of a Person of Quality's family*, n.p.; Pepys, *Diary*, VIII, pp. 383–6.
61 E.g., LMA, DL/C/271 f. 54, Mary Thomas, 3/12/1737; DL/C/272 f. 188, Martha Owers, 9/7/1740.

to the servants who had to use public rather than special in-house facilities.[62] For all intents and purposes, in this example work had taken spatial control from the hands of the employer and put it into a particular employee.

In addition to laundry, servants' other principal sanitary tasks revolved around cleaning, dusting and sweeping in the rest of the house and its environs.[63] Thomas Tryon noted that 'Most people take care that their furnitures are daily brushed and rubbed, and their very floors washed, as though they were to eat their food on them', and many employers had high expectations of their servants in this regard. Pepys, for instance, observed his cookmaid Hannah's staying up all night to clean the kitchen and yard; a week later, however, he scolded her for not keeping the house clean. In the Consistory court depositions, servants described themselves as 'sweeping the kennel before her master's door', upstairs on the first floor above the shop 'washing a room' and sweeping the stairs, or 'sweeping a chamber up one pair of stairs' and opening 'one of the casements of such room to let out the dust'. Mary Serjeant washed down her master's yard by letting the water from the water-cock flow through the gate; Sarah Chamlett fetched pails of water from the cock in the nearby yard so the gardener could wet the gravel he was laying, 'it being a very dry season'.[64] Like washing, this might involve the concentration of resources, permanent and temporary, on a particular day. Ann Davis was hired as a maid 'to do all work', but got help from a char on Saturdays 'to clean the house down'. Employers with rooms let to lodgers often placed special emphasis on cleaning the bedrooms and it was the maid Ann Seymour's 'particular business to make the beds'. Likewise, it 'was the business of [Anna Peter] to be often in the [two bedchambers] to make the beds and do the other work which has to be done there'.[65]

That would include the removal of chamber pots to the cesspools, which were usually found at the back of yards or gardens at the rear of houses. According to Cruickshank and Burton, 'the drainage of Georgian houses was unpredictable: some had main drains, some did not', and 'older and poorer parts of town were less well provided' than the newer building developments of the late seventeenth and early eighteenth centuries; the

---

62 LMA, DL/C/255 f. 166, Mary Davis, 25/3/1715.
63 Cf. Hill, *Women, Work and Sexual Politics*, p. 127. See also Hecht, *Domestic Servant Class*, p. 67; Earle, *English Middle Class*, p. 222.
64 T. Tryon, *A Treatise of Cleanness* (London, 1682), p. 6; Pepys, *Diary*, IV, pp. 253, 264; LMA, DL/C/244 f. 13, Elizabeth Edwards, 22/3/1693; DL/C/245 f. 32, Mary Bibby, 6/3/1696; DL/C/257 f. 319, Elizabeth Cotterell, 10/11/1718; DL/C/240 f. 269, Mary Serjeant, 4/12/1682; DL/C/241 f. 183, Sarah Chamlett, 27/11/1684.
65 LMA, DL/C/638 f. 292, Ann Davis, 15/10/1749; DL/C/251 f. 189, Anne Seymour, 3/12/1709; f. 166, Anna Peter, 22/11/1709.

dwellings of richer middling and gentry Londoners may even have had water closets, but even here most members of these households will have used something more portable. Fortunately for the domestic servants, many would have worked for employers who paid others to dig up the accumulated deposits: 'nightsoil' was so named for the simple reason that it was collected after dark by the nightman, and when Pepys's 'house of office was emptying' overnight the nightmen did not leave till just before 6 a.m., the stench making the idea of eating at home the next day thoroughly unpalatable.[66]

The bedchamber

Working in bedchambers, like washing laundry, involved servants in the most intimate parts of the household and demonstrates just how different notions of personal space were in early modern life (see the discussion on privacy in Chapter Four). Servants were always going into their mistresses' or lodgers' bedrooms in the morning while they were still in bed to light the fires, or in the evening to warm the beds before employers or lodgers got into them: a lodger aroused Margaret Ellsdon's suspicions when 'she always sit up an hour or half an hour after her bed was warmed and therefore would not permit Margaret to stay with her or assist her in going to bed'.[67] Ann Eldridge's master's lodgers 'ordered her to fetch up the sheets saying that they should go to bed immediately'. Her mistress told Ann the sheets had not been aired but the lodger said she would have them anyway, and helped her make the bed saying 'two people can do it quicker than one'. Meanwhile, her lover ordered Ann to fetch 'a lighted rush candle and he set it in the chimney and put to the window, shut and drew the window curtains closed and when Ann went out of the chamber he held the door and shut it after her and locked it so that no person could go into the chamber without their leave or consent'.[68]

Servants could be, indeed had to be involved in their employers' indiscretions if masters and mistresses were to retain any control over the dissemination of gossip and information about their affairs, and their work in and about rooms containing beds made this imperative. Just as servants' work involved them in the more intimate aspects of their employers' lives, working in households that specialised in providing illicit services for others

---

66 Cruikshank and Burton, *Georgian City*, pp. 91–6; Pepys, *Diary* IV, pp. 252–3.
67 LMA, DL/C/251 f. 390, Margaret Ellsdon, 21/1/1710; DL/C/247 f. 9, Catherine Holland, 13/2/1701.
68 LMA, DL/C/272 f. 50, Ann Eldridge, 19/7/1738.

made such intimacy a matter of course. Lydia Painter knew 'that the house [where she worked] was a house of ill reputation', where unmarried strangers 'did often come to the house and lie there together'. Lydia 'by the order of [her mistress] . . . made and sheeted a bed in the parlour' for one couple, unlaced the woman's stays and fetched her a clean shift. Afterwards, Lydia's mistress called her into the parlour and she 'laced the stays and helped to dress' the woman. On the rare occasions when servants admitted to working for women who were for all intents and purposes prostitutes, they were party to intimacies of the closest kind in bedrooms. Susannah Bucktent admitted to liaising between her mistress and two men, and her mistress tried to get her 'to have driven the same truck'.[69]

Childcare and nursekeeping

Caring for employers or their children during illness or infancy was part of many a servant's brief when such needs arose. Elizabeth Smart 'lived and lodged at [her master's] chambers in the Middle Temple Lane' but described herself as his 'nurse and chamber-keeper' rather than simply 'servant' since she cared for him in the last two years of his life. In 1726, Elizabeth Daniel said of her master's child that she 'is so troubled with convulsion fits that she is almost deprived of her senses and is almost a servant's work to look after her', and while she did not describe herself as a nurse, much of her daily labour involved caring for this child.[70] Evidence on the female labour market in London around the turn of the eighteenth century suggests that 'nursekeeping' in the sense of tending to the sick was well established as a discrete occupation in the capital by then, particularly for married or widowed women, but Margaret Pelling has rightly highlighted 'the difficulty of defining nursing' in the early modern period. Nursekeepers might spend considerable time in their employers' households attending to longer-term illness, but their employment was on a different basis from that of domestic servants, who were much more likely to be involved in care as one of the 'expedients' open to households for shorter-term sickness or incapacity.[71]

---

69 LMA, DL/C/257 f. 225, Lydia Painter, 12/6/1718; DL/C/240 f. 130, Susannah Bucktent, 2/6/1681.
70 PRO, PROB 24/55 f. 27, Elizabeth Smart, 5/1/1716; DL/C/263 f. 65, Elizabeth Daniel, 26/2/1726.
71 Earle, *City Full of People*, pp. 116, 130–9; M. Pelling, 'Nurses and nursekeepers: problems of identification in the early modern period', in her *The Common Lot: Sickness, Medical Occupations and the Urban Poor in Early Modern England* (Harlow, 1998), pp. 179, 200.

Employers whose work brought them into contact with children meant that their servants were likely to come into contact with them too. Lydia Everington was a midwife's servant, although did not appear to be directly involved in her mistress's work since she said she waited at home for her return; but she did fetch a client's baby, took it to a nurse and saw it several times thereafter. Wet-nurses, those who 'got their living' by breast-feeding others' children, were also found within the household when wealthier mistresses gave birth, and the advice literature certainly dealt with this topic. The ninth edition of *The Complete Servant-Maid* (published in 1729) gave explicit instructions to servant-employers, observing that 'it will be proper to give some rules for choosing a good wet-nurse' (an aspect of specialisation, since this replaced a section on nursery-maids in earlier editions). The manual then proceeded to advise mistresses on the ideal size of breast and most appropriate temperament, 'for children generally take after their nurses'.[72] Valerie Fildes may have described the eighteenth century as 'perhaps the most significant period' of wet-nursing's history before the decline set in, but she freely acknowledges that advice on the requisite physical qualities of the best women for breast-feeding had ancient precedence: a Renaissance tract by the German medical writer, Bartholomaeus Metlinger, after making suggestions like those above, adds that the wet-nurse 'should have a strong thick neck' and 'good praiseworthy habits'.[73]

Occasionally, care for employers' children was concealed in servants' own accounts of their work. Lucy Young talked simply of 'her service' in Lady Morice's household but a fellow servant described how Lucy 'came to live as a nursery-maid in their master's family'. But in the largest households, the increased division of labour often meant that the family included named nursing or child-rearing servants whose place was much less ambiguous. Grace Armourer was 'dry nurse to the children . . . and continued in the nursery till the children under her care were sent to school'; but she was still 'living in the town house' after the children were gone and her mistress had separated from her master, presumably fulfilling another role. Both her case and that of Lucy Young, cited above, suggest that in households where children had to be cared for, servant careers could be strongly influenced by the life cycle of the children as much as that of the servants

---

72 LMA, DL/C/255 f. 47, Lydia Everington, 21/2/1715; anon., *The Complete Servant-Maid; or The Young Maiden's and Family's Daily Companion* (9th edn, 1729), pp. 2, 7.

73 V. Fildes, *Wet Nursing: A History from Antiquity to the Present* (Oxford, 1988), pp. 111 and 70, citing B. Metlinger, *Ein Regimen der Junger Kinder* (Augsburg, 1473): for continuities in this literature, see pp. 69, 111–13. See also R. Perry, 'Colonizing the breast: sexuality and maternity in eighteenth-century England', *Journal of the History of Sexuality* 2 (1991), 204–34, for the resurgence of maternal breast-feeding.

themselves. Gaining the affections of noble children could have distinctly benevolent effects on the long-term careers of the servants who cared for them: Ursula Hobson had been governess to the Marchioness of Carmarthen in her childhood, and after her young charge's marriage she became house-keeper in the new matrimonial home, and claimed to be 80 when she gave her deposition.[74]

The position of governess was clearly established by the late seventeenth century in the most eminent of households. An early eighteenth-century advice manual was more precise in subject matter than in its target audi-ence: in its 'Dedication to the governesses of Great Britain', *The Accomplish'd Housewife; or the Gentlewoman's Companion* prefaced 70 'Instructions for the better regulation of your future conduct' with statements addressed to 'a wife and prudent mistress'. It sardonically observed that 'We meet with plenty of books that teach [the fair sex] the art of cookery, pastry, pickling, and several others which they may have occasion to practise when they come to years of maturity, and have the care of providing for a family'. But, it complains, 'none of them lay down rules and instructions for a governess to train up her little pupils, or point out the studies and employments that are proper for their tender minds'. The book's title may have been close to that of Smith's *The Compleat Housewife; or, Accomplished Gentlewoman's Compan-ion*, one of its literary targets, but the locus of the *Accomplish'd Housewife*'s dominion was the nursery rather than the kitchen.[75]

Domestic service in retailing households

Shopkeeping

This brings us to two categories of servant who have featured indirectly in this survey of servant work but deserve separate treatment, since their very status as domestic servants may be thought problematic: servants in coffee houses, taverns, inns and public houses; and servants working in shops. The first set of tasks to be examined in this section relates to shopkeeping, an area of the work in many servant-employing households which reminds the

---

74 LMA, DL/C/271 f. 63, Lucy Young, 15/12/1737, as described by Francis Yeo, f. 67, 19/12/1737; DL/C/637 f. 582, Grace Armourer, 9/3/1748; DL/C/632 f. 208, Ursula Hobson, 3/5/1712.

75 Anon., *The Accomplish'd Housewife; or the Gentlewoman's Companion* (London, 1745), n.p.; Smith, *Compleat Housewife*. For the French *Gouvernante*, see Fairchilds, *Domestic Enemies*, pp. 200–3.

historian that any consideration of urban domestic service merely as the precursor of 'Upstairs, Downstairs' is thoroughly anachronistic. But Ann Dewey's description of herself 'sitting in the door between her master's shop and the rest of the house' highlights the historian's dilemma and the ambiguity of her own position: was she specifically a shopworking servant, or simply a domestic servant?[76] While this is impossible to quantify with any certainty, many of the households in which servants could be found had retailing or manufacturing 'shops', usually on the ground floor or in the basement.

Female servants were frequently found in the households of retailers of textiles and their tasks were rarely limited to housewifery as it has been illustrated thus far. For instance, Mary Gill was servant to a haberdasher, but spent time in her mistress's booth at Stourbridge Fair in addition to her shop in St Andrew's Holborn. Martha Hulme was servant to a linen draper whose mistress had two shops, 'the one almost over against the other' in narrow Middle Row, in the parish of St Giles in the Fields. When a dealer came to one of the shops to sell her mistress a shirt, Martha was present in the shop but not directly involved in the negotiations. As a final example, Hannah Humphreys and her mistress were sitting drying sheets at the fireside 'in the room behind the counting house' in her master's house. Her master came home drunk and asked why Hannah was there, and 'why was she not in the counting house?' But 'it being very bad weather and no fire place in the counting house her mistress said, "Why, the maid cannot sit in the counting house altogether [in] this cold weather without coming to warm herself".' It is not clear in the deposition who had washed the wet sheets, but it is certain that Hannah lived in with her master and mistress, and also that one of her tasks was to take her mistress's baby to and from its nurse. The relative importance of these tasks is obscure, but it seems that her shopwork was an intrinsic part of her job as servant in this household.[77]

It is instructive to note Higgs's words in the context of the late nineteenth-century professionalisation of shopkeeping and the growth in the numbers of female shopworkers: 'The shop assistant was not a new phenomenon but a specialist, fulfilling some of the functions of household servants, as retailing came to be dissociated from household work'. Such work cannot, therefore, be divorced from domestic service but was to some extent a sub-category of housewifery, which increasingly came to have a separate existence as retailing and the household were gradually divided into discrete

---

76 LMA, DL/C/238 f. 54, Ann Dewey, 12/6/1678.
77 LMA, DL/C/249 f. 179, Mary Gill, 23/11/1706; DL/C/272 f. 238, Martha Hulme, 4/6/1740; DL/C/269 f. 75, Hannah Humphreys, 10/3/1732.

realms. Although only discussing retailing, he correctly analyses the 'decline of the domestic servant in the late nineteenth century' as 'merely a change of nomenclature' rather than 'a change in the nature of the work done'.[78] In London in the late seventeenth and early eighteenth centuries, a degree of specialisation had begun to occur in the nature of service work; but it would be perverse, more than a century before the change Higgs identifies, to split domestic service from retail. Domestic servants were recognisably distinct in role and status from apprentices, with their indentures and long-term contracts, and journey-workers, paid weekly or even daily wages. Yet domestic servants in London households were frequently engaged in primary productive or ancillary tasks related to their employers' livelihoods, and these tasks were performed within the context of their service.

Victualling

The drawer, characterised by Ward as a soberly-dressed drunk who kept his drunker clients' glasses full, sat at the bottom of the male servant hierarchy in public houses since his job was literally to draw pints at the bar from the barrel. His job was also described by the simple term 'serving man', but this seems to have been synonymous with the usual term 'servant', which applied to women as well, and men and women appear to have shared the tasks performed within these establishments, including pulling pints and serving drinks at the bar. James Penner called himself a 'serving man', then detailed how 'he was hired by his master who then kept the Thistle and Crown in Denmark Court . . . to be his drawer or servant', while Elizabeth Tylett related how she drew a pint for a customer,[79] and servants such as these would be found in the smallest establishments as well as the largest. Conversely, the 'hostler' or 'ostler' would only be found in hostelries large enough to have stables attached and may be seen as the inn's equivalent of the groom (for the liveried version in gentry or aristocratic households, see below). While these outdoor servants were exclusively male, their work was largely though not exclusively outdoors.

The 'chamberlain' acted in a foreman-like, sub-managerial status, if the victualling household was large enough to have an internal hierarchy, but

---

78   E. Higgs, *Domestic Servants and Households in Rochdale, 1851–1871* (New York, 1986), pp. 239, 240.

79   N. Ward, *The London Spy*, ed. P. Hyland (East Lansing, 1993), pp. 63–4; LMA, DL/C/270 f. 1, James Penner, 1/7/1735; DL/C/240 f. 304, Elizabeth Tylett, 12/5/1683.

while he may have had more of a role dealing with the establishment's guests, much of his work did not differ markedly from that of servants in general. According to the satirist Richard Head, there were chances for promotion within these households, and if fortune smiled on them, even a meteoric rise: 'they commence boot-ketchers; from thence they proceed gradually to under hostlers', then 'his mistress . . . (out of pity for the stripling, whom for the kindling love she bears him, thinks him better born than he is), removes him from the stables to be a chamberlain', and, 'entrusting him with the sheets, has a month's mind to lie in a bed of his making'. Twenty-two-year-old John MacDaniell, who from 1698 to 1701 had been 'a drawer in taverns' and before that 'a soldier in Colonel Coyes's regiment' for four years, had let it all go to his head. He styled himself 'gentleman' on the somewhat optimistic grounds that, 'if he could get his debts in he would be worth sixty pounds'.[80]

There are two good reasons for including servants who worked in victualling establishments among a general category of 'servants'. The first is that most servants who worked in this employment also worked in other types of London household: while there appear to have been some servants who made a career out of working with victuallers, most servants joined them as they would any other employer. Take the career of Margaret Gamlyn, from Faversham in Kent: she began her service career at the age of eighteen, after spending a year at her aunt's in Bloomsbury, by becoming a servant at the Dolphin Tavern in St Giles in the Fields. She only spent three months there the first time around, and for the following nine months to a year she held two other service jobs, one with a widow in Covent Garden, and another for six months with a gentleman's family in Surrey. But immediately after that she 'went to live again at the Dolphin Tavern in order to learn to keep a bar and to assist the gentlewoman of the tavern, who was then much out of order and continued so all the time Margaret remained with her', which was fifteen months.[81] The second reason for embracing these individuals under the umbrella of domestic service is the more pressing one that much of the work in these specialist food- or drink-retailing households was very similar to that done in those other households: they performed housewifery. The servants worked for their masters and mistresses but also for the lodgers that abounded at these establishments: servants in victualling households made and lit fires, made and aired

---

80 R. Head, *Proteus Redivivus: The Art of Wheedling or Insinuation, in General and Particular Conversations and Trades* (London, 1684), pp. 139–40; PRO, PROB 24/40 f. 305, John MacDaniell, 7/3/1701.
81 LMA, DL/C/266 f. 7, Margaret Gamlyn, 11/6/1729.

beds, lit people to bed with candles, and brought food and drink up to people's bedchambers.[82]

Even a chamberlain, charged with the responsibility of locking the inn gates just before 11 p.m., can be seen in the Consistory court records letting in a couple who wanted to spend the night there. John Barnes had a bed made for them by one of the servants under him, and the next morning, when he noticed the woman dressing, he fetched a mirror for her in just the way a footman might. Servants at victualling houses could occasionally be seen working as a husband-and-wife team. Thomas Pearson was chamberlain at the Bull Inn in the City of London parish of St Ethelburga, and while he took some guests upstairs to their rooms, his wife (who, with a male drawer, appear to have been the only others employed at the inn) laid sheets on their bed, and then they both brought the couple tea in bed. Of course, some of these households gained their main source of income from 'inmates', but the housing of lodgers was relatively widespread and vital to some families' livelihoods, and the volume of work created by lodgers in victualling houses of various sorts may not have been much more than in non-victualling households. A singular difference lay in the way servants in victualling houses could be called on to feed and water individuals beyond the bounds of their masters' own four walls. Ann Tilly worked in a coffee house, and 'several times carried victuals and drink' to a couple who had taken lodgings in the same road as her master's establishment; on at least one occasion this involved serving chocolate to them while they lay in bed one morning, the sort of task Ann would expect to perform if she were their own servant. Meanwhile, servants to victuallers, bakers or other food manufacturers had further food-related duties, and Elizabeth Dixon testified she had been 'crying of pies' as late as 9 p.m. in Grays Inn Lane.[83]

The role victualling houses played, however, as local centres of exchange (of information and services as well as trade) gave them several specialist functions in metropolitan society in the late seventeenth and early eighteenth centuries that were not mirrored in the other households in which servants worked. Firstly, the obvious concentration on the production of food and drink kept drawers and other servants busy for much of the time. Secondly, inns and taverns in London, particularly in the ecclesiastical

---

82   LMA, DL/C/247 f. 322, Ann Wilder, 4/2/1702; DL/C/248 f. 229, Elizabeth Croon, 2/12/1704; DL/C/252 f. 77, Mary Pollard, 13/7/1710; DL/C/264 f. 171, Rebecca Green, 21/6/1727.

83   LMA, DL/C/248 f. 365, John Barnes, 10/5/1705; DL/C/632 f. 154, Thomas Pearson, 7/2/1712; DL/C/262 f. 244, Ann Tilly, 15/12/1724; DL/C/236 f. 327, Elizabeth Dixon, 22/1/1672; for lodgers, see Earle, *English Middle Class*, pp. 209–18; Cruickshank and Burton, *Georgian City*, pp. 60–3.

liberties of the Fleet and the Mint, had become centres for the business of 'clandestine' marriages.[84] Servants in the victualling houses where the clerics-for-rent plied their trade were frequently called in to the Consistory court as the best witnesses on the scene.

Elizabeth Jones, for instance, took a couple up into a private room carrying drinks and a prayer book for them, and then, with her master's permission, went into the next room to watch through a crack in the wall while the couple were married with an orange-peel ring. Hannah Aldridge was witness to a wedding in the tavern where she worked, and was given half a crown by the couple. She claimed she 'hath been present at and seen several clandestine marriages solemnised in the house of one Mr Bennett at the Goat near Fleet Street, during the time of her being a servant to Mr Beckly'. But occasionally a servant became much more involved in what must have been a fairly lucrative sideline. A former sailor, who at the time of making his deposition kept the Three Tunns public house within the liberty of the Fleet, admitted that eighteen months previously 'he came to live at the Bull and Garter near Fleet Prison as a servant and as a plyer at Elizabeth Lilly's door to pick up marriages or to persuade people going by inclinable or intending to be married within the liberty of the Fleet to be married at her house'.[85]

Prostitution and common fame

The other thriving business within victualling houses in London was prostitution. This is a notoriously problematic subject to document as work, and is not assisted by the obvious unwillingness of the servants who appeared at the church courts as witnesses, to condemn themselves (or sometimes even their mistresses) by confessing to selling sex. But both contemporaries and historians have explicitly linked service and prostitution, particularly in London. Daniel Defoe warned that the mobility of servants and their inability to set money aside while they had employment meant that 'if they are out of place, they must prostitute their bodies, or starve; so that from chopping and changing, they generally proceed to whoring and thieving'; and Henry Fielding promoted his Universal Register Office by stressing 'its usefulness to young people who were coming from the country to be servants or

84 L. Stone, *Road to Divorce: England 1530–1987* (Oxford, 1990), pp. 106–8; J. Boulton, 'London widowhood revisited: the decline of female remarriage in the seventeenth and early eighteenth centuries', *Continuity and Change* 5 (3) (1990), 329–31.
85 LMA, DL/C/252 f. 471, Elizabeth Jones, 17/5/1711; DL/C/258 f. 1, Hannah Aldridge, 2/1/1719; f. 371, Zachary Taylor, 3/12/1719.

apprentices in London and who were too easily led into crime, prostitution or poverty by being badly placed'.[86]

Research in London's criminal records demonstrates that there was a seasonal frequency of commitments for prostitution, peaking 'in the late spring and summer when the demand for servants was lowest', i.e. when the largest employers had left London for the country. This impression is compounded by the observation that not only did prostitutes in eighteenth-century London possess 'autonomy and relative independence', but they also appear 'to have participated in a life-cycle choice. The most reliable figures available suggest that most prostitutes were between the ages of fifteen and twenty-five', the age profile of a large proportion of the capital's female domestic servants. A few servants in place, and some of them out of place, must have used prostitution as one means of 'making shift' in the capital during personal periods of debt, bouts of unemployment, or during cyclical economic fluctuations. But the evidence of London prostitutes' working origins points to the needle and other sweated trades, or the vast range of casual work, as the impoverished stimulus drawing young women into prostitution: if only because of the relative buoyancy of the market for service, the commentators' fears seem to have been misplaced, at least before the late eighteenth century.[87]

However, the cases cited above show how blurred the lines could be, either between entertaining lovers and prostitution, or between lodgings and brothel. The couples for whom fires were lit and drinks served in tavern beds were described in the church courts as adulterous or as consummating marriage, making identification of prostitution difficult; but even when the sex was known to have taken place elsewhere, victualling houses made good rendezvous points. Elizabeth Bedolph, whose mistress met different men in lodgings 'and frequently made Elizabeth be with her or attend on her', dragged her around numerous public houses in pursuit of assignations. Complicity could be more oblique, like the way James Harris (who worked at the Bear tavern in the Strand for nearly seven years) took messages written by his gentlemen customers from his master's victualling house to an alleged prostitute nearby. When Ann Power, sacked for drunkenness, admitted meeting men at the tavern next door to her master's, and her fellow servant Amy Middleton was condemned as a whore by three

---

86 Defoe, *Everybody's Business is Nobody's Business*, pp. 8–9; H. Fielding, *The Covent-Garden Journal and A Plan of the Universal Register*, ed., B.A. Goldgar (Oxford, 1988), p. xx.

87 R. Shoemaker, *Prosecution and Punishment: Petty Crime and the Law in London and Rural Middlesex, c.1660–1725* (Cambridge, 1991), pp. 184–6; T. Hitchcock, *English Sexualities, 1700–1800* (Basingstoke, 1997), p. 95; O. Hufton, *The Prospect Before Her: A History of Women in Western Europe vol. I, 1500–1800* (London, 1995), p. 325.

former employers, they were insinuating that this watering-hole had served as the site of their assignations.[88]

Defamation disputes demonstrate that women in London taverns were vulnerable to accusations of whoredom by slanderers impugning their sexual reputations, but whether this was due to the plausibility for contemporaries of the link between a woman's presence in a victualling house and prostitution is by no means clear.[89] What is clear, however, is the link perceived by the authorities between victualling houses and vice, and the potential connections of servants (male and female) with this vice: they were certainly committed to houses of correction for drinking and other 'disorderly conduct', although Robert Shoemaker thinks that, to a certain extent, these institutions 'were viewed by parents and masters as a type of reform school where young offenders could be punished without incurring the social stigma of having been formally prosecuted'.[90] The resurgent societies for the reformation of manners directed their attentions particularly at female servants around the turn of the eighteenth century, initiating many of the prosecutions against them in that period. Even if it was not the servants themselves, it was certainly the company they were perceived to be keeping that exercised those concerned about 'order'.[91]

From this diffuse evidence, there is one main conclusion that can be made regarding servants in victualling households or shops. These workers can be regarded as servants who, due to the nature of their households, spent a part of their working day engaged in tasks associated with their employers' primary economic activities. The following factors contribute to their remaining 'domestic servants' according to the definition supplied in the Introduction: they named themselves 'servant' or 'domestic servant'; they had subservient relationships with masters and/or mistresses; they lived in as full-time members of their households; and they appeared to do 'housewifery' in addition to their tasks of pulling pints or counting cash. As far as

---

88 LMA, DL/C/245 f. 91, Elizabeth Bedolph, 12/6/1696; DL/C/259 f. 172, James Harris, 11/11/1720; DL/C/239 f. 131, Ann Power, 16/7/1680; f. 139, Amy Middleton, 24/2/1680.

89 T. Meldrum, 'A women's court in London: defamation at the Bishop of London's Consistory court, 1700–1745', *London Journal* **19** (1) (1994), 9, 14; for an earlier period, see L. Gowing, *Domestic Dangers: Women, Words and Sex in Early Modern London* (Oxford, 1996), pp. 67, 70, 82.

90 For servant committals to houses of correction, see Shoemaker, *Prosecution and Punishment*, p. 174.

91 Shoemaker, *Prosecution and Punishment*, Chapter 9; his 'Reforming the City: the reformation of manners campaign in London, 1690–1738', in L. Davison, T. Hitchcock, T. Keirn and R.B. Shoemaker, eds, *Stilling the Grumbling Hive: The Response to Social and Economic Problems in England, 1689–1750* (Stroud, 1992). See the discussion of servants and social order in Chapter One, this volume.

prostitution is concerned, it seems to have been a marginal part of the lives of most servants. There are two groups who cannot be considered a servant for the purposes of this chapter: firstly, those who were engaged only in shopwork, and secondly, where there is a suspicion that the master ran a manufacturing concern in which the 'servant' (and most doubts surround male servants in these cases) appears to be an apprentice or journeyman.

Apprenticeship and service work

The issue of apprenticeship, of course, is not without its complexity when considering service work. Girls in a variety of towns in the early modern period were bound to apprenticeships in housewifery as many of their male contemporaries were to the variety of corporate trades, but certainly 'by the seventeenth century most girls bound to housewifery were paupers'. For instance, two-fifths of all female apprentices in early sixteenth-century Bristol were bound as 'housewife', while a century later (when about a fifth were apprenticed by the urban or parish authorities) 89 per cent of them were bound to some form of 'service'. Over the course of the seventeenth century, 'domestic service now replaced what was earlier described as "housewifery" . . . by the seventeenth century household service became not simply an additional duty which, like their male counterparts, women might on occasion be obliged to perform, but a formal and major obligation of their apprenticeships'. But female apprentices formed only a tiny proportion of all early modern Bristol apprentices, only 2.2 per cent in the seventeenth century.[92]

As for London, Brodsky Elliott has written that 'the apprenticeship registers for 15 London companies disclose over 8,000 entries but fail to reveal a single woman apprentice between 1580 and 1640', consonant with Ben-Amos's suggestion that the larger the town, the fewer women bound in apprenticeship. But the picture in the metropolis for the late seventeenth and early eighteenth centuries is far less clear. Ben-Amos has found that some London livery companies took on a small number of female apprentices in the later seventeenth century when demographic stagnation (and possibly the impact of the 1665 plague) dented the supply of young men, and there is evidence for the granting of some female apprenticeships in

---

92 J. Lane, *Apprenticeship in England, 1600–1914* (London, 1996), pp. 127–8; I.K. Ben-Amos, 'Women apprentices in the trades and crafts of early modern Bristol', *Continuity and Change* **6** (2) (1991), 229; her *Adolescence and Youth in Early Modern England* (New Haven, 1994), p. 140.

housewifery in that period.[93] By far the greatest activity stemmed from the London parishes, about whose disregard for their child charges George is damning. While she is complementary about the Foundling Hospital's inspection procedures regarding girls apprenticed to 'housekeepers', the fate of 'the workhouse child' at 'the bottom of the scale' was likely to be apprenticeship in the '"art of housewifery"', [where] there was no pretence of teaching anything'. Compare this with Snell's data, which show that over 30 per cent of southern English rural parish apprenticeships went to women or girls, including 48.7 per cent of women in the seventeenth century, and 37.6 per cent in the eighteenth century, into housewifery alone; and Hill points out that in southern England parents were still choosing to send their daughters to apprenticeships in housewifery in the eighteenth century.[94]

Historians have noted the young age at which parish apprentices started and the greater length of their terms relative to craft or trade apprenticeships generally. The standard printed parish indenture for an apprenticeship in housewifery bound Myrtilla Kirton to Henry Golder of Brentford in 1747 at the age of nine. This document is very quiet about the work or training entailed: her master 'Henry Golder the said apprentice in housewifery will teach and instruct or cause to be taught and instructed', though exactly what should be 'taught and instructed' is not elaborated upon here (and in Brentford 'housewifery' may have included husbandry). For Kirton, 'during all which term', i.e. until she reaches the age of 21, 'the apprentice her said master faithfully shall serve in all lawful businesses, according to her power, wit and ability; and honestly orderly, and obediently in all things demean and behave herself towards her said master and all his during the said term'. The emphasis here was more on discipline rather than on the work content, and although Kirton's indenture is very similar to trade indentures of the period, it also demanded that Kirton 'be not any way a charge to the parish'.[95]

This appears to make explicit the parish's main concern, to remove a potential future burden from their books, and Hill raises the question of the

---

93   V. Brodsky Elliott, 'Single women in the London marriage market: age, status and mobility, 1598–1619', in R.B. Outhwaite, ed., *Marriage and Society: Studies in the Social History of Marriage* (London, 1981), p. 91; Ben-Amos, *Adolescence and Youth*, pp. 135–6.
94   M.D. George, *London Life in the Eighteenth Century* (London, 1925, 1966 edn), pp. 227, 229, 245; K.D.M. Snell, *Annals of the Labouring Poor: Social Change and Agrarian England 1660–1900* (Cambridge, 1985), pp. 279–82, Table 6.1, p. 283 n. 30; Hill, *Women, Work and Sexual Politics*, p. 99.
95   M. Pelling, 'Child health as a social value in early modern England', reprinted in her *Common Lot*, p. 119; LMA, DRO 3/F6/1/45, Housewifery Apprenticeship Indenture, Myrtilla Kirton, Brentford, 1747; Simonton, 'Apprenticeship', p. 229; Lane, *Apprenticeship in England*, pp. 14, 249–51.

real nature of housewifery apprenticeships: was 'housewifery' in this context just an excuse for the parish to discharge its duty, or for parishioners to obtain cheap labour with a small premium as George suggests? According to Simonton, girls were often apprenticed to mistresses or to a married couple, and when apprenticed to a master, as here, it tended to be for formal purposes only, which implies that most discipline would have been in the hands of the mistress. It is possible that some masters or mistresses were compelled to take apprentices by the threat of a fine, but whether as compensation or inducement, the premium they received for an apprentice in housewifery was certainly cheap: Ben-Amos states that it was around £2 in early seventeenth-century Bristol, 'substantially lower than premiums normally paid for males', while in eighteenth-century London, George notes that £6 was a 'large fee' for a parish apprentice when Earle finds that such a sum was near the lowest limit for trade or craft non-pauper apprenticeships.[96]

Even so, many historians accept that for the seventeenth and early eighteenth century, an apprenticeship in housewifery might teach girls a 'number of skills', especially shopkeeping, sewing and other textile skills, as well as more mundane tasks of household upkeep and domestic economy. But the suspicion lingers that for many poor masters and mistresses, the offer of long-term unwaged labour was too good to turn down, and their emphasis would not have been on training their apprentices so much as exploiting them. Ben-Amos blames the seventeenth-century 'loss in the prestige of female apprenticeship' on its tendency towards domestic service: the contractual rigidity and potential impoverishment of an apprenticeship in housewifery clearly resembled what contemporaries dismissed as drudgery when contrasted with domestic service's ever-expanding market in London, its rising wages and its relative contractual informality.[97] Housewifery, implicit in the household manuals and explicit in will disputes and here in the experience of parish apprenticeship, was not a neutral repository of domestic skills but a concept sharply riven by gender and status. In a period in London during which many young people possessed relative autonomy in their choice of 'place', institutions like charities and the parochial authorities

---

96 Hill, *Women, Work and Sexual Politics*, p. 98; George, *London Life*, p. 228; D. Simonton, 'The education and training of eighteenth-century English girls, with special reference to the working classes', unpublished Ph.D thesis, University of Essex (1988), p. 258; Lane, *Apprenticeship in England*, pp. 84–7; Ben-Amos, *Adolescence and Youth*, p. 141; George, *London Life*, pp. 221–2, 228; Earle, *City Full of People*, pp. 64, 118.

97 Roberts, '"Words they are women"', p. 142; P. Sharpe, 'Poor children as apprentices in Colyton, 1598–1830', *Continuity and Change* 6 (2) (1991), 256; Simonton, thesis, pp. 211, 257–63; Schwarz, *Age of Industrialisation*, pp. 19–21; Ben-Amos, *Adolescence and Youth*, p. 143.

could set others on servile work under terms and conditions the non-indentured would not have tolerated for long.

Idle luxury

Conspicuous consumption

'People are the wealth of the nation', wrote Sir Thomas Dalby in 1690, but 'serving men' along with the gentry, clergy, lawyers and beggars were 'wholly unemployed' and therefore excluded (from 'people' as much as from creators of the nation's wealth). The serving men whose self-ascription was cited at the beginning of this chapter may have been clear about their occupational labels, but they were not immune from criticism which called their bluff. Some of the loudest commentators thought that domestic service (and particularly male service) was hardly work at all but licensed idleness, usually going hand-in-hand with arrogance and insubordination. Mandeville complained about servants as he railed against the over-education of the labouring poor: 'Ask for a footman that for some time has been in gentlemen's families and you'll get a dozen that are all butlers. You may have chambermaids by the score, but you can't get a cook under extravagant wages . . . Nobody will do the dirty slavish work, that can help it', he whined, leaving one at the mercy of 'raw ignorant country wenches and boobily fellows that can do, and are good for, nothing'.[98]

Akin to Defoe's double-standard inherent in his advocacy of a high-wage economy for all bar domestic servants, there is a certain irony in the satiric advocate of private vices in pursuit of public benefits refusing the same occupational group the joint status of luxurious consumers *and* objects of luxurious consumption. Even those who echoed Filmer in the early eighteenth century, in the didactic literature directed at servants, could not bring themselves to make an unequivocal alliance of service and work. The author of *The Servants Calling* declared: 'Every family bears a likeness to a kingdom, for as a family is a contracted government, a kingdom is an extended family'. But the nature of the work servants did was not even of secondary importance. This writer declared that he proposed 'to treat of some moral and Christian duties, in the relation they bear to the office of servant', whose 'fundamental duties' were listed as 'humility of mind' and 'fidelity to their [masters'] trust'. 'Diligence' came a poor fifth among 'some

---

98 Cited in Appleby, *Economic Thought and Ideology*; Mandeville, 'Essay on charity', p. 307.

other duties that complete the character of a good servant'. Humorists certainly played on the lack of diligence in lackeys: when Ned Ward's 'London spy' and his man-about-town friend are thrown overnight into the Poultry Compter, they observe that some of the prisoners 'were lain upon benches, as if they had been bred up courtiers' footmen'.[99]

The most influential writer in this vein has been Adam Smith, who in 1776 reformulated an ancient theme. He elegantly linked service with luxury in a new guise, as Corfield has observed, by 'applauding "productive" labour (the generation of tangible goods) over "unproductive" services'. 'A man grows rich by employing a multitude of manufacturers', wrote Smith. 'He grows poor, by maintaining a multitude of menial servants'. Smith emphasised that

> the labour of menial servants does not continue the existence of the fund that maintains and employs them. Their maintenance is altogether at the expense of their masters, and the work which they perform is not of a nature to repay that expense. That work consists in services which perish generally in the very instance of their performance.[100]

Writing a century after Appleby's pamphleteers, the emphasis on godly asceticism that fuelled so much of the seventeenth-century writing had diminished, while that on efficient economic productivity had become paramount. At Smith's hand, service had ceased to be labour with divine blessing, and had become instead a burden to the economy.

The consignment of servants to a realm of luxurious, idle, non-work through the reification of economic activities that generate quantifiable products — particularly when propagated by a writer of the posthumous stature of Adam Smith — has been extremely influential in the post-Enlightenment characterisation of work. Marx's discussion of the labour process as it was subsumed under capitalism led to his assertion that human interaction with, and use of, the means of production generated social relations, i.e. class society.[101] As a consequence, a century or more of historical and sociological dispute over the origins and trajectory of western society has been conducted within economic realms which inherently marginalise occupational groups like domestic servants. Jan de Vries confessed only

99 P. Earle, *The World of Defoe* (London, 1976), p. 175; [Mr. Zinzano], *The Servants Calling; with some Advice to the Apprentice* (London, 1725), pp. 7, 11, 17, 46–7; Ward, *London Spy* IV, p. 71.
100 Corfield, 'Defining urban work', p. 209 and n. 21; A. Smith, *The Wealth of Nations*, eds, R.H. Campbell and A.S. Skinner (Oxford, 1976) 2 vols, I, p. 330 and II, p. 675.
101 Elaborated in K. Marx, *Capital* vol. I (Harmondsworth, 1976), p. 1035 and *passim*.

recently that 'the economist's great fault [in the eyes of social and cultural historians] . . . is the privileging of production': this tendency has resulted in the exclusion of unpaid household work from conventional economic indices and therefore its devaluation, and spurred on many of the participants in the Marxist-feminist 'domestic labour' debate, as we saw earlier in this chapter.[102]

However, this is not the only sense in which service has been marginalised in debates on work. Classical sociology, too, must take some responsibility for cementing the link between service and idleness. Thorstein Veblen posited a cultural stage theory which achieved something of an intellectual impact in the early twentieth century, in which a model of domestic service's historical development played a crucial role. By the stage of 'predatory culture', 'conspicuous abstention from labour becomes the conventional mark of superior pecuniary achievement'. Then, 'in the economy of the leisure class the busy housewife of the early patriarchal days, with her retinue of hard working handmaidens, presently gives way to the lady and the lackey'. These servants formed the 'vicarious leisure class', and in his most pungent phrase, Veblen wrote: 'The need of vicarious leisure, or conspicuous consumption of service, is a dominant incentive to the keeping of servants'.[103] For Veblen, the growth of surplus wealth in the hands of the social elites during what we may take to be the 'long' eighteenth century — and he is not explicit about chronology — is characterised by domestic service's transition from labour to idleness.

Norbert Elias was uncomfortable with unilinear processes or teleological stages, but like Veblen he was repelled by what a nineteenth-century tradition was wont to call 'civilization'. He developed a theory of 'the civilizing process', and in his discussion of the development of *habitus* servants were not explicitly mentioned. But in this process whereby the social norms generated by society seem habitual within the individual, the family is given a 'primary and dominant' role in 'installing drive control', or what Elias later describes as the 'social constraint towards self-constraint'.[104] In other words, it is the realm which servants inhabit in which manners are generated. It is a historian deeply influenced by Elias's theory who develops one

102 J. de Vries, 'Between purchasing power and the world of goods: understanding the household economy in early modern Europe', in J. Brewer and R. Porter, eds, *Consumption and the World of Goods* (London, 1993), p. 85; Pahl, *On Work*, pp. 349–54.
103 T. Veblen, *The Leisure Class* (New York, 1899), pp. 38, 54, 56–7, 59, 62.
104 N. Elias, *The Civilising Process* vol. I, *The History of Manners* (1939; Oxford, 1978 edn), p. 137; vol. II, *State Formation and Civilization* (1939; Oxford, 1982 edn), p. 229. For useful introductory comments, see S. Mennell and J. Goudsblom, eds, *Norbert Elias On Civilization, Power, and Knowledge: Selected Writings* (Chicago, 1998), pp. 14–22.

of the possible implications of 'the civilizing process' for domestic servants. Georges Vigarello's study of concepts of cleanliness in France from the fifteenth century detects over time the emergence of a new intimacy, generating a *private* behaviour that tended to exclude the attendance of servants. He cites the example in the mid-eighteenth century of the Marquise de Châtelet bathing naked while her male valet poured in the water, making sure it was not too warm to burn her: 'What [the valet] might see was irrelevant', writes Vigarello; 'he did not belong to the same universe as the young woman. She did not see him'. He contrasts this with the French development of the separate bathroom at the end of the nineteenth century, where he comments that 'an ever more private place was created, where one attended oneself without witnesses . . . The employment of new devices made it possible to dispense with the traditional servants'.[105] The attendance of the Marquise's valet looks very much like Veblen's 'conspicuous consumption of service', but the alleged chronological change results in not merely idleness but unemployment.

Waiting and attending

The evidence presented in previous sections of this chapter has demonstrated a wide range of laborious activities performed by servants which, within current broad-based formulations, would certainly be termed 'work'. Yet even for those at work in households whose primary economic activities drew servants into retailing, it is extremely difficult to calculate the value of that labour or its opportunity cost. For the domestic servants whose work forms the subject of this section — that of footmen, waiting women, butlers and the like — such an exercise would be impossible and probably pointless. But like housewifery, considering the definition of 'work' in its fullest form means understanding how 'work' also embraces social reproduction and the construction of identity, 'the application of human energy to generate social as well as economic value'.[106] Those of the livery were only the most visible tools in the construction of their employers' high-status identity. This section proceeds in that vein to consider service work such as waiting and attending, running errands, acting as close companions, and looking after or using horses and carriages.

Waiting and 'attending' were the tasks of service most derided by commentators as symptomatic of idle luxury, classic instances of what Adam

105 G. Vigarello, *Concepts of Cleanliness: Changing Attitudes in France Since the Middle Ages* (Cambridge, 1988), pp. 93, 216.
106 Corfield, 'Defining urban work', p. 208.

Smith (as noted above) dubbed 'unproductive labour . . . work [that] consists in services which perish generally in the very instance of their performance'.[107] This indignation may have had some justification when well-dressed 'ladies' women', 'waiting women' or simply 'women' acted as their mistresses' hands and limbs to, as the *Plan of a Person of Quality's family* put it, 'attend their lady in the dressing room'. Margaret Tweedy demonstrated in her depositional evidence in 1736 that the job entailed more than simply running and fetching indoors: she served the wife of a baronet as 'her Lady's woman', waiting on her as she travelled to and from York races and when she had 'company of the best fashion', and generally acting as her confidante. When a wealthy mistress fell in love, a waiting woman's workload could be doubled but her customary access to her mistress could also be thwarted. In 1740 Martha Owers and the other servants 'were ordered not to come into the room at any time when Lord Conway was with [their mistress] till the bell rung', and when they tried them they found the doors 'fastened on the inside, which was not usual'.[108] In this state employers could be most demanding, requesting from the bedside poached eggs at night, chocolate in the morning, and the emptying of chamber pots at any time.[109]

Contrary to Maza's 'threshold' model in which servants existed in social limbo between their employers and the rest of the world (discussed in the previous chapter), the job of the servant in the largest households in important respects could often be seen as one of intercession between the household and the neighbourhood or metropolis at large, and running errands, fetching and carrying took up much of a servant's time. Servants were summoned in the night by bells; sent to fetch masters or mistresses home from taverns and neighbours' houses (with or without candles and lanterns), or drink from taverns for employers and lodgers, or doctors for sick family-members; and carried letters and delivered packages often in clandestine circumstances.[110] Manservant Ralph Stockton made the perfect messenger but a hopeless witness to his master's infidelities: 'not being able to read or

---

107 Smith, *Wealth of Nations*, II, p. 675.
108 Anon., *Plan of a Person of Quality's family*, n.p.; LMA, DL/C/271 f. 158, Margaret Tweedy, 5/2/1736; DL/C/272 f. 188, Martha Owers, 9/7/1740.
109 LMA, DL/C/251 f. 82, Sarah Brackley, 5/12/1709; DL/C/242 f. 138, Francis Dobson, 1/6/1688; DL/C/250 f. 511, Jane Wadley, 8/7/1709; DL/C/249 f. 214, Hannah Washbourne, 9/10/1706.
110 E.g. LMA, DL/C/243 f. 23, Sarah Pritchard, 13/5/1689; DL/C/238 f. 13, Judith Cuthbert, 16/7/1679; DL/C/241 f. 112, Elizabeth Gill, 4/11/1684; DL/C/245 f. 160, Sarah Blith, 18/6/1696; DL/C/248 f. 205, Mary Barr, 24/11/1704; DL/C/258 f. 108, Elizabeth Davis, 24/2/1719; DL/C/271 f. 180, Griffin Cresswell, 5/3/1736; DL/C/270, f. 187, Benjamin Halley, 10/3/1736; Maza, *Servants and Masters*, Chapter 3.

write [he] does not know the contents' of the notes he carried. It was not the monopoly of the richest to employ servants in the sending and receiving of notes and messages, of course. Alice Foster delivered a letter from her mistress to her master, a naval captain in Virginia, by the circuitous route of the wife of the captain of another man-of-war which was about to sail for the Americas.[111] But they tended to be the sort of elite masters and mistresses both sufficiently romantic (or fearful of exposure) and sufficiently wealthy to afford to employ footmen instead of the regular post.

Indeed, some footmen had to go to some lengths to comply with their employers' orders to ensure a degree of secrecy. While his master was away, William Dibble 'did carry great numbers of letters from his mistress to Lord Conway [her lover] and brought answers back and has received others from the hands of porters and delivered them to his mistress'. Once he took a letter for Lord Conway to Tonbridge 'and sent it to him by the drawer of the inn where he put up his horses and he by the order of his mistress shift his livery and dress himself out of livery in a coat that he had borrowed of a fellow servant'. Lord Conway met him at the inn and gave him a letter which he delivered the same day (although it is unclear whether he stayed overnight at the inn or not). When Lord Conway came the following day William was 'ordered to be the only servant to attend her both at Grosvenor Square and at Woodcot when she expected Lord Conway to come to her . . . William was sent out on messages by her, and orders were given to the other servants to say she was not at home'.[112]

By sending servants on certain sorts of errands, employers placed a great deal of trust in them, as did Elizabeth Smallpiece's mistress when on her death bed she gave Elizabeth a note to collect £100 from a debtor. Elizabeth felt entrusted enough — and presumably sure enough of her mistress's capacity to hang on for a little while longer — to use her discretion in accepting £50 in cash immediately and the other £50 in a bond a few days later. Not surprisingly, running errands frequently roped servants into assisting with their masters' or mistresses' livelihoods: for example, a hackney coach-keeper's servant can be observed fetching corn for the horses, the servant of a wine and brandy merchant carrying four-gallon jars round to a customer's house, or an apothecary's servants delivering medicines.[113] The tasks these servants were performing might constitute 'idleness' rather then

---

111   LMA, DL/C/270 f. 277, Ralph Stockton, 14/7/1736; DL/C/249 f. 49, Alice Foster, 12/12/1705.
112   LMA, DL/C/272 f. 192, William Dibble, 23/7/1740.
113   LMA, DL/C/240 f. 280, Elizabeth Smallpiece, 11/1/1683; DL/C/248 f. 160, Mary Webb, 19/5/1704; DL/C/242 f. 326, Ann Bales, 28/6/1688; DL/C/258 f. 108, Elizabeth Davis, 24/2/1719.

housewifery, but in other respects their work would have constituted 'retail' labour like others employed by trade or victualling masters.

In slightly smaller households, the job definition could absorb functions that in a larger one would have been separate. Ann Clements had been nursery maid before the breakdown of Lady Calvert's marriage, when she 'could observe very little otherwise of her Lady's conversation during the said time other than what she collected now and then by chance from the giggling and coughing of the servants concerning the Lady' and her lover. But upon her promotion to lady's woman when her mistress took lodgings after the separation, another servant commented that she 'served in the station of a Lady's woman and housekeeper, and her business was to dress and undress her mistress and to dress the victuals when there was no cook, and to look after the dressing thereof when there was one, that she had the care of the Lady's linen and clothes'. She was also fully involved in the preparations for and the concealment of her mistress's bastard birth.[114]

This is avowedly an elite case and therefore not necessarily representative, since it was only the wealthy who could afford menservants; but the clandestine birth to mistresses of bastard children was not an exclusively female affair. Her mistress asked James Shortell, her butler, 'to take care of the funeral' of the dead baby, and James 'procured the same to be buried in the parish church of St. Martin-in-the-Fields'. It is important to note that Shortell was not present at the birth itself, and only dealt with the aftermath, taking the corpse from the nurse's house to the church, so Gowing's recent assertion that childbirth 'in early modern England took place in a female world of ritual and secrecy' is not contradicted. She is also right to note the precarious nature of illegitimate births: Rublack sensibly urges us to recognise the place of husbands in particular in the legitimate birth process, but illicit relationships made childbirth and its consequences much more fraught and sharpened gender distinctions. Deposing in 1699, Samuel Allam related how he had to leave the house for a week while his master's mistress lay in, and his only role in the birth of the illegitimate child was to pay 46s. in birth and burial duties on his master's behalf.[115]

Close personal attendance upon a lady could bestow vicarious status to the servant concerned: Abigail Dew 'was principally [hired] to attend upon [her mistress's] daughter', but attained a more elevated position in the household when she sat with her mistress during her illness. However, such

---

114 LMA, DL/C/250 f. 431, Ann Clements, 3/6/1709; Shortell James, f. 435, 4/6/1709.
115 LMA, DL/C/250 f. 435; DL/C/246 f. 217, Samuel Allam, 7/3/1699; L. Gowing, 'Secret births and infanticide in seventeenth-century England', *Past and Present* **156** (1997), 87; U. Rublack, 'Pregnancy, childbirth and the female body in early modern Germany', *Past and Present* **150** (1996).

posts could also have distinct disadvantages: servants occupying them were more vulnerable to changes in the household, employers' whims or jealous gossip within the household, and occasionally, had to perform extremely unpleasant tasks. Judith Wright's master was undergoing what she described as a 'salivation' treatment for syphilis when, during an argument with his wife he threw his basin of spittle over her: the results 'stunk so intolerably that Judith could hardly come near to help her mistress off with her clothes'.[116]

Footmen and boys

Male personal servants were also expected to wait on their masters or mistresses in the house and beyond. Carl Chame, fourteen-year-old footboy, had to attend on his master when he went for a morning drink, and had to wait downstairs while his master joined two women upstairs at a tavern. But as observed above, it was the footmen who did most of the errand-running and general carrying and fetching (over and above manual lifting and shifting) in the larger houses, in addition to personal attendance. According to the *Plan of a Person of Quality's family*, they 'are to attend their Lord and Lady both at home and abroad and are under the directions of such chief domestics attending the Lord and Lady and go on all such messages relating to them both'. This meant they played a major role in displaying their masters' wealth and status, particularly when dressed in livery, and therefore a key part of their labour lay in playing a part in the construction of their employers' social identity. Of course, that was sometimes a mixed blessing, particularly when footmen rioted over the loss of vails, for instance, and as the discussion on household reputation in Chapter Four demonstrated, employers' public personas could be compromised by their servants' behaviour at large.[117]

'It is an interesting point to notice', wrote Marshall, 'what a very prominent part the footmen play in the eighteenth century', and she stressed that it was their (rather than female servants') public behaviour as much as that within the household that excited elite comment. Their prominence and notoriety saw Mandeville write that 'there is not one in fifty [footmen] but what overrates himself', and Swift used in his *Directions to Servants* what

---

116 LMA, DL/C/241 f. 46, Abigail Dew, 26/5/1684; DL/C/246 f. 167, Judith Wright, 3/12/1698.

117 Anon., *Plan of a Person of Quality's family*, n.p.; LMA, DL/C/242 f. 303, Carl Chame, 19/6/1688; DL/C/246 f. 202, John Mould, 6/2/1699; Hecht, *Domestic Servant Class*, pp. 51–7. For French *laquais* and *gens de livré*, see Fairchilds, *Domestic Enemies*, pp. 31–5; Maza, *Servants and Masters*, pp. 119–23.

Thaddeus calls the 'footman-persona' as his prototypical servant and mouth-piece for satirical advice.[118] Footmen could be observed accompanying a mistress on horseback when she travelled by coach, on foot in the garden, long gallery and dining room, or attending her at the opera, playhouse, court or masquerade. While his mistress held dancing meetings, George Pearcifull was 'waiting on the company with coffee and passing from the drawing room to the dining room on the first floor'. In Joseph Clark's case, 'attendance' meant going on country strolls while leading a mastiff called Tiger 'to defend his mistress from gypsies and other vagabonds she might chance to meet with on her walks'. Bartholomew Hyatt, originally hired as a manservant 'to dress, shave, go out with and attend on [his master] as he had occasion of him', was sent to his master's lover with a message 'to give his service to her': his service had become temporarily part of the commerce of affection.[119]

Mistress Diana Dormer's whim and favouritism played havoc with her household's order. For her footman Richard Haynes, waiting upon his mistress was a matter of pride, or at the very least a duty pertaining to his station that ought not to be usurped. It 'was his business to wait and attend on her at the drinking of tea, coffee or chocolate, yet she would frequently discharge him and call for Lawrence [her then favourite] even sometimes out of the stables (where his business principally lay) and that he was in a very dirty condition to wait on her at such times'; and Richard 'often observed that at dinner times, when it was his place to wait on her or to give or exchange her plates, she would put him by and call on Lawrence to do it'. It must be emphasised that the footman was not as close to the 'person' of the employer as the lady's woman, and wearing the servile badge of livery helped to emphasise that status.[120]

The case of *Jenyns* c. *Jenyns*, heard at the London Consistory court in 1728–9, allows us to observe these gender differences at close quarters. The parties had separated (in fact if not yet in law) and Madam Jenyns had rented various lodgings, generally with a household that comprised a footman and two female servants, a cookmaid and a waiting woman. Her cookmaid Ann Maguire related how, as she returned from the local chandler's shop,

---

118 D. Marshall, 'The domestic servants of the eighteenth century', *Economica* **9** (25) (1929), 17; Mandeville, 'Essay on charity', p. 308; Swift, *Directions to Servants*, pp. 18, 33–45 and *passim*; J. Thaddeus, 'Swift's *Directions to Servants* and the reader as eavesdropper', *Studies in Eighteenth-Century Culture* **16** (1986), 111.

119 LMA, DL/C/271 f. 181, John Wastenays, 8/3/1736; DL/C/265 f. 96, Thomas Long, 13/12/1728; DL/C/271 f. 189, George Pearcifull, 21/4/1736; DL/C/637 f. 570, Joseph Clark, 26/2/1748; DL/C/251 f. 223, Bartholomew Hyatt, 19/1/1710.

120 LMA, DL/C/255 f. 178, Richard Haynes, 17/5/1715.

she bumped into Francis Hughes, the footman, 'who told her that her mistress was come home very ill and was angry that she was abroad whereupon she made haste home and went up directly into mistress's bedchamber in order to have attended her if she had been ill'. On another occasion, when both the maids were out, Francis resorted to asking the maid of the gentleman in whose lodgings the family lived, Elizabeth Viner, to attend on his mistress when she complained — again — of being ill. All the while, Francis was down at an alehouse where he kept the footman of his mistress's jilted lover (who had been set to watch her door for visitors) drinking and distracted. Francis had a strategy for coping with his mistress's indiscretions, but he and the maids had clearly-demarcated territories of competence, where the female servants did the work closest to their mistress's 'person' and the footman deferred to serving women, even when they were not directly employed by his mistress.[121]

Butlers and gentlemen's gentlemen

A closer equivalent for the male employer's personal servant was the butler, especially in smaller households. Ideally, his role was much more precisely related to the management of food and drink, albeit at a more personal level than cook or footman: 'his station', says the *Plan of a Person of Quality's family*, 'is to take care of the wine to bottle it off and fine it down; to take of the beer and bread and to see it is not wasted; [he] lays the cloth for his Lord and Lady and attends the table and side board at the time of dinner and supper, and has the care of all the silver plate belonging to the table &c'.[122] James Shortell demonstrated that the distinction between footman and butler was quite clear in his mind: he had been footman to Lady Calvert 'and wore her livery for one year of his said service but no longer, and then became her butler and caterer which he continued to be until he left her service'. However, in circumstances with less specialised divisions of labour, Richard Oughton was butler (in a household with around four servants) who usually accompanied his master as a personal manservant to London and France: to illustrate the intimacy of his service, while his master dressed he fetched his combs and other articles of *toilette*.[123]

This behaviour verges on that of the 'gentleman's gentleman': Archibald Hamilton styled himself 'gentleman' and was servant to James Hamilton,

---

121 LMA, DL/C/265 f. 82, Francis Hughes, 5/12/1728; f. 119, Ann Maguire, 22/1/1729; f. 124, Elizabeth Viner, 29/1/1729.

122 Anon., *Plan of a Person of Quality's family*, n.p.; Hecht, *Domestic Servant Class*, pp. 46–8, 104.

123 LMA, DL/C/250 f. 435, James Shortell, 4/6/1709; DL/C/242 f. 252, Richard Oughton, 29/2/1688.

Esquire, of Inner Temple, one of the Gentlemen of the Privy Chamber and, conceivably, a relative. Archibald 'dresseth him and waits on him as his gentleman and does other business for him'; while the ambiguity of 'business' is most unfortunate for the historian, it is known that Archibald claimed a fortune in excess of £100, which he felt entitled him to armigerous status. Deposing in 1712, Thomas Harding, 'a footman to her Majesty [Queen Anne] ever since she came to the crown', was worth between £300 and £400 and also felt able to call himself 'gentleman'. John Lang told the court clerk in 1701 that he 'has lived with the Prince of Denmark for ten years as one of his gentlemen', and claimed enough vicarious status to style himself 'Esquire'. Lang's social origins are too obscure to determine whether he came from an elite family in the first place, but it is conceivable that his fortune of £2,000 was amassed in a decade of royal service rather than inherited.[124]

The measure of higher servant status was the proximity any servant had to the 'person' of his or her employer; but it is crucial that this be seen within the context of household size and structure. Maids-of-all-work serving alone within a small family may have had just as much intimate working contact with their employers, particularly with their mistresses, as waiting women in larger households: they would, for instance, have slept beside their mistresses when their masters were away. But male service was a sign in its own right of an employer's wealth and status and by definition was only found in wealthy middling, professional, gentry or noble households. When Pepys moved to larger premises in Seething Lane in 1660, he immediately hired a footboy 'whose attendance on Pepys in public would mark the new importance of the master of the household'; only eight years later he had really arrived when he purchased a coach and hired a coachman in November, 1668.[125]

Horsework

For these male servant-employing households, and certainly not even all of them, the final major category of service work involved transport and

---

124 PRO, PROB 24/35 f. 292, Archibald Hamilton, 20/10/1696; DL/C/631 f. 312, John Lang, 24/1/1701; DL/C/271 f. 67, Francis Yeo, 19/12/1737; PRO, PROB 24/51 f. 325, Thomas Harding, 20/6/1712.
125 Pepys, *Diary*, I, p. 189, X, p. 194; IX, pp. 377–9, 393; Earle, *English Middle Class*, pp. 218–19; his *City Full of People*, pp. 82, 124; Hecht, *Domestic Servant Class*, pp. 35–8; for French examples see Maza, *Servants and Masters*, pp. 200, 203; Fairchilds, *Domestic Enemies*, pp. 24–5.

especially horses. Such households made a general (though not cast-iron) distinction between indoor and outdoor servants, and those male servants working with horses — coachmen, grooms and postillions — formed the majority of the latter. The *Plan of a Person of Quality's family* distinguished between the last two by noting that grooms 'are to take care of the saddle horses, to feed, dress and clean them; [he] takes care of the horses' furniture and to clean it and to attend whenever the Lord rides abroad', while postillions 'ride when the set of horses goes out with the Lord and Lady, assist the coachman in taking care of the horses, the coaches and harnesses, [and] also wait and attend the chief domestics at table'. In the Duke of York's stables in 1684, the Duchess's postillion 'was busy about his horses', and a servant of the Prince of Denmark's (presumably also a postillion or groom) was 'littering his horses'. It is interesting to note their use of the possessive — not his master's or mistress's horses — which implies a degree of attachment to these animals one might expect from those who worked with them day in, day out: perhaps slightly less problematic a relationship than proximity to the 'person' of the employer.[126]

Such work brought these servants into contact with others through the shared use of stabling. However, it may be that the proprietorial badges of livery and pride in the status of their employers placed barriers in the way of stable solidarity, as when the Duke of Norfolk's groom refused to tell Thomas Shelton, Sir George Savile's groom and huntsman, that the 'three strange horses in the stables' were those of the Duke's. But both of these male servants' work with the horses and resultant distance from the house gave them a degree of independence that allowed Shelton to accept a tip via a stable boy but to refuse to speak to one of his mistress's gentleman lovers directly. Richard Kenarday, coachman to an esquire and his wife, took full advantage of his situation by accepting all the bribes, pecuniary, alcoholic and culinary, from his mistress's lover or his steward, while getting all the necessary information into his hands to make impregnable his trusted position with his master, to whom he related all. These servants played a vital role in transporting their employers to and from their various abodes, to assignations, or to places of leisure like Bath. John Cotton described his former mistress Lady Savile as a 'dutiful and obedient wife' and a 'constant churchwoman . . . which he knows by being coachman and driving her to church'. His mistress 'liked to take the air in the coach to Thoresby park wood in the summer time', and, like others of the

---

126   Anon., *Plan of a Person of Quality's family*, n.p.; LMA, DL/C/241 f. 62, William Richardson, 27/5/1684; f. 62ᵛ, John Stokes, 27/5/1684; Hecht, *Domestic Servant Class*, pp. 57, 59–60.

horse-centred servants in the Savile household, displayed a precise awareness of local distances.[127]

Servants whose work centred around horses had fairly frequent interaction with inns and their stables, particularly when their employers wanted
to travel beyond London. It should therefore come as no surprise to find
them working with innkeepers or hackney carriage operators when out of
place. In 1729 William Black was lodging at the Hole-in-the-Wall and
Magpie public house and maintained himself 'by driving a hackney coach
and being a servant to the producent's husband [the victualler] . . . in water-
ing and looking after his horses'. His previous jobs had been in service
respectively to a lord, a knight and an earl as postillion or second coachman. In 1700, John Harrison was working as coachman to a doctor, but in
the two years before working for him, he had driven a hackney coach. Both
these jobs employed identical skills — driving coaches with teams of horses,
maintaining the 'furniture' (coach, tackle and harnesses), managing a stable
— and were therefore transferable. As Earle notes, 'most [former male
servants] did work which had some logical connection with the training
and experience they had received . . . Knowledge of horses was a valuable
asset'. Leaving service to take up independent operation as a hackney coachman was a question of the man's (and these jobs were always undertaken by
men) relations with his employer, and of capital. Harrison, for instance, had
built up £40 worth of savings in service; but even without the capital, it is
likely that coachmen, postillions and grooms had ample opportunity to
build up contacts with victuallers and innkeepers.[128] Of all the work performed within the sphere of 'idle luxury', these men's labours with horses
form the clearest examples of the development of transferable skills: they
were storing up not just savings but the capital of skill for a life beyond service.

Conclusion

The labour that London domestic servants undertook for their employers
has to be judged in the light of a relatively new literature on work that
embraces more than just the application of economic resources for wages or
profit. All service was remunerated, as Chapter Six demonstrates; but the
dismissal by contemporary commentators or historians of so much service

---

127   LMA, DL/C/271 f. 198, Thomas Shelton, 10/2/1736; DL/C/264 f. 13, Richard
      Kenarday, 24/2/1727; DL/C/271 f. 198, John Cotton, 11/2/1736; f. 152, John
      Redgate; f. 154, John Hooton, both 28/1/1736.
128   LMA, DL/C/266 f. 142, William Black, 9/6/1729; DL/C/631 f. 51ᵛ, John Harrison,
      5/2/1700; Earle, *City Full of People*, p. 85.

work as drudgery or idleness will no longer suffice, because even though many of them may have described their labours as just 'going to service', these domestic servants were definitely working once their activities are analysed closely. However, such an inclusive approach to work poses a problem: if 'work' is to include walking, standing or adopting certain postures while wearing one's employer's livery as well as hard physical labour within the household, how do we make sense of it from the distance of three hundred years? The simple polarity of housewifery and 'idle luxury' is fairly useful, on several levels: housewifery was generally conducted by girls and women while the livery, who provided the bulk of luxurious idleness, were male. In smaller households, domestic service work largely consisted of housewifery, while most 'idle luxury' took place in the households of the gentry and aristocracy. In other words, distinguishing between housewifery and 'idle luxury' seemingly mirrors the sexual division of labour and the fissures of wealth and status that have fractured this history of domestic service, while, ironically, both sides of this opposition have been marginalised by orthodox debates on work. Yet on its own this is too neat a conceptual division, ignoring the nuances in the account above, and it does not tell the whole story.

It is certainly true to say that the sheer cost of employing the livery and upper servants of either sex was beyond the means of most bar the wealthiest households, and Chapter Six emphasises the disproportionate expense of menservants: it was this, as well as the braided and resplendent attire that many of them had to wear, which advertised their employer's higher fortune and status. Horses and carriages were luxuries which could only be afforded by the wealthy and so they performed a similar role in the Veblenesque 'conspicuous consumption of service', in addition to the practical benefits they conferred on their owners as a private mode of transport. The physical impact of waiting, attending and errand-running was likely to be more tedious than onerous upon the domestic servant, and although being at the employer's beck and call at all hours could lend a gruelling aspect to 'idle luxury', Swift's footman-persona thought even this could be circumvented. 'When your master or lady call a servant by name', it states at the beginning of the *Directions to Servants*, 'if that servant be not in the way, none of you are to answer, for then there will be no end of your drudgery: and masters themselves allow, that if a servant comes when he is called, it is sufficient'.[129]

However, as the previous section demonstrated, proximity to the employer's 'person' was as much a function of household size as it was of

---

129 Swift, *Directions to Servants*, p. 7.

servant hierarchy. While it may have conferred status on those servants waiting upon their wealthy employers — and in an earlier section a cookmaid revealed her relative lack of status by her distance from her mistress — maids-of-all-work in the smallest servant-employing households could achieve just such an intimacy by dint of being the only servant present. And all households that employed domestic servants were sites in which the forms of work considered here as housewifery were practised: it simply needs to be recognised that in a clear majority of those households, they were done by the same individuals who ran errands or waited and attended. Social models predicated upon a transition over time from drudgery to idleness, explicit in Veblen but only implicit in theories elaborating the development of 'habitus', fail to appreciate the simultaneity of these modes of work. Yet they were distinct groups of tasks nonetheless, and the delineation of a typology of domestic service work undertaken in this chapter has made it clear that not all such work can be subsumed entirely under a category of housewifery.

Historians should be wary of making conclusions about the change of attitudes or of employment practices over time with this kind of literary evidence, since it was clearly didactic, repetitive and derivative. Best has pointed to the wide range of sources used by Markham: 'The printer of the first edition of *The English Housewife* (1615), Roger Jackson, inserted a note to the "gentle reader", suggesting that Markham had not written or even "collected" the book, but had simply organized it' from writings like those of Richard Surflet, whose *Maison Rustique, or, The Countrey Farme* of 1600 was itself a translation of a French book printed a number of years earlier.[130] But it has been useful in outlining some of the ideas and assumptions that lay behind early modern housewifery, and hinting at changes that may have taken place in perceptions of this social ideal between the early seventeenth and the eighteenth centuries. Earlier in the seventeenth century the concept embraced household tasks, some of which were productive of consumption goods that otherwise would have been provided by the market. This is explained by the manual's apparent rural focus, harking back to the sixteenth-century genre of manuals and an Arcadian ideal of the self-sufficient household. Their London readership, of course, would have ignored items on the processing or manufacture of goods consumed within the household that were readily available in metropolitan markets. Explicitly associated with and aimed at the housewife, it is nonetheless fair to say that a family including servants was assumed by these texts.

---

130 Markham, *English Housewife* (1986), p. xvii: similarity of title and content suggest many of the other books discussed here were 'organized' too.

By the later seventeenth and eighteenth centuries, a certain disaggregation had occurred. There was a burgeoning market in books full of cookery advice and recipes, but despite having been written by former cooks, they never mentioned servants (even though their authors' hands-on experience was one of their key selling points). Housewifery texts had become more explicitly managerial in approach, occasionally resembling personal didactic literature in their instructions to present and future mistresses. *The Accomplish'd Housewife; or, the Gentlewoman's Companion* of 1745, for instance, urged that 'they who are rational creatures should not be treated with the rigour or contempt of brutes . . . a mistress should understand how to do everything with propriety and in season. To employ her servants with so much ease and order, as may make their labour pleasant and their duty desirable'; and the Marchioness de Lambert's *Advice of a Mother to her Son and Daughter* called on mistresses to 'treat your servants with kindness and humanity'.[131] While the cookbook used the highly successful marketing vehicle of the housewifery manual to sell what were in fact extensive collections of recipes, an unravelling of the housewife–servant elision occurred in both directions, towards servants on the one hand and mistresses on the other.

The post-Restoration growth of an eclectic mixture of advice and instruction manuals aimed at servants themselves is well-illustrated by *The Complete Servant-Maid* of 1677. Its frontispiece explicitly directed the text at servants 'to persons of honour or quality', yet was 'composed for the great benefit and advantage of all young maidens'. It advised them 'how they may fit and qualify themselves for any of these employments . . . waiting woman, housekeeper, chamber maid, cook maid, under-cook maid, nursery maid, dairy maid, laundry maid, housemaid, scullery maid'.[132] This literature apparently reflects the growing specialisation of domestic service, particularly in London, visible from the seventeenth century which has been noted by historians like Michael Roberts and Peter Earle.[133] According to the advice literature, then, 'housewifery' had begun the period as a married woman's social role combining a variety of household tasks with managerial status, but by the eighteenth century these functions had become largely separated.

Is there, then, a sense that servants experienced a disaggregation of housewifery and drudgery over our period? In other words, was there a

---

131 Anon., *Accomplish'd Housewife; or, the Gentlewoman's Companion* (London, 1745), p. 428; Marchioness de Lambert, *Advice of a Mother to her Son and Daughter* trans. T. Carte (London, 1737), p. 65.

132 Anon., *Complete Servant Maid* (1677), title page.

133 Roberts, thesis, pp. 172–4; his 'Women and work', pp. 91–3; Earle, *City Full of People*, pp. 111, 126.

process of proletarianisation as skilled household workers — who cooked, dressed meat, bottled fruits and took charge of the marketing, or who washed and mended fine clothing like lace and silk — separated themselves from those performing hard manual labour — like sweeping, scrubbing and scouring, heavy laundry (the 'buckwash') or simple errand-running? It would appear that there was certainly nomenclature-inflation, observable in a range of English urban sources such as wage assessments, but we have seen here how deceptive work-titles could be: this inflation's impact on the working experiences of London domestic servants is more difficult to assess. Both the historians just named acknowledge that London saw a growth in the early modern period 'of specialist jobs', writes Roberts, 'around key practices of sick care, washing, cleaning and even the provision of accommodation'[134]; or, as Earle puts it, 'the increasing employment of living-out washerwomen and char-women was another sign of specialisation within domestic service which reduced the drudgery of the most exhausting tasks'.[135]

We know that most servant-employing families constituted one-servant households, so for the maids-of-all-work within them this growth of external assistance was the crucial factor. What might have been happening — and there are no comparative data from an earlier period to support this convincingly — was that the broad growth in middling employment of servants from the later seventeenth century in London saw a small but significant increase in the number of families of the wealthier middling sorts employing small retinues in emulation of their mercantile or professional superiors, or the landed classes. A complement of only four servants — three female and one male, say — already introduces the possibility for distinct forms of specialisation within the household. The rapidly-growing galaxy of victualling and other retail outlets could be staffed by servants in numbers equivalent to those in a large middling or gentry household; but their mobility between inns, taverns and domestic households, the similarity of much of their work whatever the employer, and the lack of evidence that servant–master relations were any different from those within non-victualling families fails to offer convincing evidence for a transition of the magnitude implied by 'proletarianisation'.

It remains to remind ourselves that the best source for the experiences of London domestic servants, the church court depositions, cannot confirm these suspicions of widespread specialisation with the downgrading of much domestic service, and Pepys's diary in conjunction with the moral agenda inherent in Defoe's commentaries are no substitute for harder evidence.

---

134 Roberts, 'Women and work', p. 93.
135 Earle, *City Full of People*, p. 126.

One sector of the metropolitan market for service that exhibits much more clearly the signs of proletarianisation is that of pauper apprenticeships in housewifery. By the early eighteenth century, when a vibrant service labour market where demand seemed to have outstripped supply proffered a genuine alternative to the more fortunate, there is a sense that this was a convenient device whereby parochial authorities offloaded young people who would otherwise be at their charge; yet these servants must have constituted a small proportion of the total. The overall pattern of change in late seventeenth- and early eighteenth-century London was fragmented rather than unitary.

Finally, to what extent did our period see the rise, implied by the proletarianisation thesis and apparent in the advice literature, of the managerial mistress? A chronology has emerged, whose development into the eighteenth century seemed to be affirmed in the ideal configurations of housewifery employed in the will dispute testimony examined earlier (and, by default, in changing attitudes to pauper apprenticeship). The omnicompetent mistress of Markham's household was apparently unravelled by a growing household specialisation in which the work entailed in housewifery fell to domestic servants, leaving the mistress to adopt a more explicitly managerial role. Over the historical long term, this apparent shift was to be exacerbated by broader changes in the nature of work in the wider economy: 'the prestige of "housework", never high, went into social limbo', writes Corfield, a change over time she ascribes to work becoming 'increasingly defined as paid employment' and taking place 'outside the home', as the home itself 'was left to specialise as residential accommodation, tended by housewives and (up to the mid-twentieth century) by domestic servants'. The term 'housewife', meanwhile, 'remained in use as an occupational designation, but its public acceptance as "real" work was rendered highly uncertain'.[136]

The real questions, of course, are the social depth of that transition, and its timing. The depositions reveal that 'housewifery' was alive and well and living in London in the late seventeenth and early eighteenth centuries. Servants and mistresses undertook a range of tasks within their households — large and small — for the upkeep of the family to which they belonged.[137] Mistresses were often in a supervisory role while servants did the bulk of the drudgery, but in both food preparation and laundry, two of the most time-consuming and important components of housewifery, significant degrees of co-operation between mistress and maid were evident. This is

---

136   Corfield, 'Defining urban work', p. 219 and n. 71.
137   This approximates Davidson's definition of 'housework': *History of Housework*, p. 1.

to deny neither the continued prevalence of unequal power between the parties, since co-operation was far likelier to occur in households with smaller staffs; nor that the chronological shift observed earlier — towards a dis-aggregation of management and labour — did occur over the historical long term. But it is to suggest that change over time will have occurred sporadic-ally and in a fragmented fashion. In the period at issue here, continuity of practice is more evident, and the striking contrast to be found is between women and men, and between larger and smaller households, rather than between 1660 and 1750.

CHAPTER SIX

Wages and remuneration

Introduction

There 'is not one in fifty [footmen] but what over-rates himself; his wages must be extravagant and you can never have done giving him', fumed Bernard de Mandeville in his *Essay on Charity, and Charity Schools* of 1723: 'it is too much money, excessive wages, and unreasonable vails that spoil servants in England'. Daniel Defoe, despite his usual advocacy of a high-wage economy, wrote in 1724: 'I never knew a servant, or a workman in England one farthing the better for the increase of his wages, it is so natural for him to think he deserves it, or else you would not do it; that instead of mending him, it always makes him worse'. As Earle has observed, Defoe 'tended to treat domestic servants as a special case. A rise in wages for anyone was more than likely to lead to vice and insubordination, but this could be accepted as a necessary evil since the resulting consumption helped to sustain the level of employment and prosperity in the economy as a whole'. However, this sub-group of the labouring poor possessed a unique characteristic: 'vice and insubordination in a domestic servant were less easy to condone since they actually occurred in one's own house'.[1]

The debate over wages in the late seventeenth and early eighteenth centuries, part of the development of what historians earlier this century

---

1 B. de Mandeville, 'An Essay on Charity, and Charity Schools', in his *The Fable of the Bees* ed. P. Harth (Harmondsworth, 1970), pp. 308, 309; D. Defoe, *The Great Law of Subordination considered; or, the Insolence and Unsufferable Behaviour of Servants in England duly enquired into* (London, 1724), p. 78; P. Earle, *The World of Defoe* (London, 1976), p. 175.

called 'mercantilism', involved comment on labour as a whole, of course, rather than domestic service *per se*, and a sizeable literature has grown around this debate. But these were not the only views expressed in the period, particularly when one examines writings by those not actively participating in this debate. The language that had resonated from texts of earlier seventeenth-century commentators and divines, like Baxter's injunction that employers of servants should 'allow them their due wages and maintenance, and keep them neither in hurtful want, nor in idleness or sinfulness', could be seen as late as 1745. The anonymous author of an advice manual entitled *The Accomplish'd Housewife; or, the Gentlewoman's Companion* prescribed the following to the employers of servants regarding their remuneration: 'Masters are to give their servants what is just and equal . . . they who are rational creatures should not be treated with the rigour or contempt of brutes. A sufficient and decent provision, therefore, both in sickness and in health, is a just debt to them, besides an exact performance of those particular contracts upon which they were entertained'.[2]

Despite its contractarian overtones (and the evidence on sickness in Chapter Two notwithstanding), this statement appears on the face of it to echo a patriarchal set of attitudes towards the payment of wages in an age which has been seen by historians as one where pre-modern obligations of employer to employee were disappearing. The most pungent account of this transition was expounded several decades ago by E.P. Thompson in a seminal article on the 'moral economy' and its erosion across the eighteenth century. Formulated around the phenomenon of food rioting but with wider implications, Thompson identified a 'notion of legitimation' in crowd action founded on 'the wider consensus of the community'; this exhibited 'a consistent traditional view of social norms and obligations, of the proper economic functions of several parties in the community, which, taken together, can be said to constitute the moral economy of the poor'. But, as he observed in another piece a few years later: 'This was a transitory phase', the first of whose 'prominent features' was 'the loss of non-monetary usages or perquisites, or their translation into monetary payments', a socially significant transformation as these usages 'favoured paternal social control because they appeared simultaneously as economic and as social relations, as relations between persons not as payments for services or things'. Domestic servants' 'vails' (tips), hand-me-down clothing and 'the clandestine perquisites of the surplus of the larder' are explicitly mentioned as examples

---

2   R. Baxter, *Works*, 4 vols (London, 1707), IV, p. 119; anon., *The Accomplish'd Housewife; or, the Gentlewoman's Companion* (London, 1745), p. 428.

of customary, normative payments which would be eroded in the eighteenth century by economic rationalisation.[3]

Recent writing on wages, much of it focusing on London, has yet to resolve the issue of the importance of the moral economy to the labouring poor in the seventeenth and eighteenth centuries. Woodward describes early modern male work and, given the way craftsmen rarely had a single form of getting a living, the resultant mixture of forms of earnings. He has emphasised regional wage variation in the face of the southern English wage orthodoxy established by Phelps Brown and Hopkins, but has stressed that the widening of the wage differential between skilled workers and labourers towards the end of the seventeenth century in northern towns changed through supply and demand rather than through official regulation or custom. Boulton has observed a stasis, perhaps even some convergence of skilled workers' and labourers' wage rates in late seventeenth-century London, re-emphasising regional variation; but supply and demand were again crucial, and he attaches less importance to the effects of custom in the metropolis.[4] Yet while Schwarz has found that eighteenth-century money wages in London were the single most important component of earnings, they were accompanied by a plethora of forms of perquisites and non-cash payments or appropriations which persisted well into the nineteenth century; and Ormrod's investigation into wages in what Gilboy called the 'metropolitan wage area' has shown how difficult it is to map significant eighteenth-century changes in work practices and payment methods by observing shifts in cash wages alone.[5]

There is, then, agreement over the importance of both cash wages and non-monetary remuneration to urban working people, but there is disagreement over their relative importance and the degree to which the period

---

3   E.P. Thompson, 'The moral economy of the English crowd in the eighteenth century', and 'The Patricians and the plebs', both in his *Customs in Common* (London, 1991), pp. 188 and 38 respectively.

4   D. Woodward, 'Wage rates & living standards in pre-industrial England', *Past & Present* **91** (1981); his 'The determination of wage rates in the early modern north of England', *Economic History Review* **47** (1) (1994); and his *Men at Work: Labourers and Building Craftsmen in the Towns of Northern England, 1450–1750* (Cambridge, 1995); E.H. Phelps Brown and S.V. Hopkins, 'Seven centuries of the price of consumables compared with builders' wage rates', *Economica* **23** (1956); J. Boulton, 'Wage labour in seventeenth-century London', *Economic History Review* **49** (2) (1996).

5   L.D. Schwarz, *London in the Age of Industrialisation: Entrepreneurs, Labour Force and Living Conditions, 1700–1850* (Cambridge, 1992); D. Ormrod, 'Real and unreal wages: the experience of labour in the metropolitan region, 1660–1825', I.H.R. seminar paper, Feb. 1992: I am grateful to Dr Ormrod for allowing me to cite his unpublished paper; E.W. Gilboy, *Wages in Eighteenth Century England* (Cambridge, Mass., 1934).

was characterised by change or continuity. Hill has reopened the issue of domestic servants' participation in a Thompsonian moral economy in her recent book on eighteenth-century servants, asserting that the late eighteenth century witnessed a 'transition between paternalism and a contractual wage relationship'. Yet her evidence for the widespread existence of non-wage payments to servants is taken from a period between the last decades of the seventeenth and the first few decades of the nineteenth centuries, and her only evidence of her alleged 'transition' is found in the standard narrative account of the masters' campaign against vails, and footmen's resistance, in the 1760s: even Hill is forced to conclude that 'vails in many households persisted well into the nineteenth century', and that the 'feelings employers had about living-in servants were often paradoxical and contradictory'. But there appears to be little notice taken of regional variation across her huge period, and she fails to present any coherent wage data against which to assess the relative importance of cash wages against the allegedly disappearing customary payments of vails and perquisites. Nor, surprisingly for a historian of women's work, does she offer a gendered analysis of either the availability of such non-monetary payments, or the impact of their selective withdrawal.[6]

This chapter will argue that while money wages remained important to domestic servants (as they always had been), the importance of a mixture of earnings in a customary context — a moral economy of service — persisted for this large and important sector of the London labour force. Contrary to the analysis provided by Hill for servants nation-wide in the eighteenth century, it will be asserted here that such persistence reached well into the nineteenth century in the English metropolis. The account presented below develops themes akin to those (discussed in Chapter Five) of the new history of work; in particular, the gendered nature of remuneration will be highlighted, recognising, in Kessler-Harris's words, 'the rich possibilities contained in the wage conceived as a social rather than as a theoretical construct'.[7] The status- and gender-oriented forces that enable a distinction between drudgery and 'idle luxury' will be seen to have a real bearing on remuneration as well. This chapter will go beyond the construction of wage series alone and attempt to conjecture for real earnings, considering firstly money wages for domestic servants in London between 1670 and 1750 in

---

6   B. Hill, *Servants: English Domestics in the Eighteenth Century* (Oxford, 1996), Chapter 4, esp. pp. 89, 86, 90.

7   A. Kessler-Harris, *A Woman's Wage: Historical Meanings and Social Consequences* (Lexington, 1990), p. 7.

smaller and larger households; secondly, it looks at bed and board, and then the intractable question of perks and vails; finally it offers an analysis of servants' savings.

The importance of money

Cash

Cash wages were extremely important to domestic servants throughout the early modern period. It is important, however, to contextualise their availability, distribution and modes of payment. Wages in the seventeenth century were officially regulated by JPs' (usually annual) wage assessments; but it seems clear that official regulation of domestic service in the capital was ineffective, and by the end of our period largely irrelevant. The modern historian of early modern wage assessments, Michael Roberts, found that 'female wage workers had been subject to statutory wage controls since the fourteenth century', and that 'the single most common category of female work for which wages were assessed was that of the "woman servant"', though none of his data were from London. Certainly, the section in the Statute of Artificers, 1563, allowing masters to compel men and women to work for them may well have forced some into domestic service, but by 1704 judges had ruled that 'the Statute extends only to servants in husbandry, not to gentlemen's servants'. This was probably a belated acceptance of an informality and relative freedom of contract perceptible in urban domestic service that Roberts observes from the late sixteenth century. Boulton cites some London wage assessments under the 1563 Act for the seventeenth century, and one promulgated by Middlesex magistrates after the Restoration; but there is no evidence that such interventions affected wage levels or their movement in the late seventeenth and early eighteenth century.[8]

Wage information in volume for any trade is not easy to come across and in order to construct Table 6.1, three sources balance each other: data from

---

8 M. Roberts, 'Wages and wage-earners in England: the evidence of the wage assessments, 1563–1725', unpublished Univ. of Oxford D.Phil. thesis (1981), pp. 164, 165, 168, 175; 5 *Eliz. c.* 4, sec. iii, repr. in R. Tawney and E. Power, eds, *Tudor Economic Documents* (Oxford, 1924); E. Lipson, *The Economic History of England*, 3 vols, 4th edn (London, 1948), III, p. 263; M. Roberts, 'Women and work in sixteenth-century English towns', in P.J. Corfield and D. Keene, eds, *Work in Towns 850–1850* (Leicester, 1990), p. 92; Boulton, 'Wage labour', p. 272 and n. 34.

Table 6.1 Mean annual money wages of domestic servants, 1670–1795

Year	Hecht, 1700–95[a]				Depositions, 1670–1749[b]				Chelsea, 1700–60[c]	
	Footmen		Maids		Male		Female		Female	
	£/s	n	£/s	n	£/s	n	£/s	n	£/s	n
1670–9					–	0	3/10	2		
1680–9					4/0	1	3/15	7		
1690–9					–	0	3/12	15		
1700–9	4/3	3	–	0	5/0	1	3/9	14	3/0	1
1710–19	5/10	2	–	0	6/0	4	3/19	7	4/0	1
1720–9	5/0	1	–	0	–	0	3/15	4	4/0	2
1730–9	6/8	4	–	0	9/0	1	4/10	2	4/14	5
1740–9	6/6	7	4/13	3	7/0	2	5/0	2	3/16	12
1750–9	8/8	5	5/19	12					6/0	3
1760–9	10/0	20	6/14	25						
1770–9	13/0	15	7/5	25						
1780–9	13/4	12	8/19	30						
1790–5	16/6	18	9/8	16						
Total n		87		111		9		53		26

Sources: [a] Hecht, *Domestic Servant Class*, pp. 144–5, 148–9. [b] London church court depositions. [c] Settlement and Bastardy Examinations, St Luke's Chelsea, 1733–50 (LMA, P74/Luk/121) and 1750–66 (LMA, P74/Luk/122/RI104): I am grateful to Dr Tim Hitchcock for allowing me to make use of this data.

London church court depositions made between 1670 and 1749, settlement and bastardy examinations from the parish of St Luke's, Chelsea taken in the years 1733–50, and data collected by Jean Hecht for his book on eighteenth-century English domestic servants. Hecht collected wages for 25 different ranks of male and 11 female servant from eighteenth-century elite memoirs and newspaper advertisements, mostly from the *Daily Advertiser*.[9] Table 6.1 uses his two groups with the largest number of data, maids of all

9 J.J. Hecht, *The Domestic Servant Class in Eighteenth-Century England* (London, 1956), pp. 141–2: he also used a few late-eighteenth century issues of the *London Chronicle*, *Morning Post*, and *Morning Chronicle*, amongst other manuscript sources.

work and footmen, which also happen to be the two members of the servant hierarchy most prevalent in the metropolis at the time.

Bastardy examinations provide a fairly straightforward source for female servant wages, usually those the woman was earning at the time or shortly before her examination; settlement papers, however, have a few drawbacks. They were often remembered wages, earned years or even decades before a former servant had to avail herself of poor relief; and those who came before the parochial authorities had served at least a year with one of their employers, whether they entered explicitly into a 'yearly hiring' or not. The possibility exists, therefore, that wage levels were affected by faulty memories or the settlement-driven strategy for stability discussed in the Introduction.

The church court deposition data only allow comparison for five of eight decades between 1670 and 1749, but their main drawback lies in the sheer scarcity of wage information in the depositions. Most servants deposed before the London church courts in defamation, matrimonial or testamentary disputes where wages were incidental to the case, so this information was only forthcoming in just over 4 per cent of domestic servants' testimonies. The courts were alive to the problem of bribery, particularly in matrimonial disputes. It is apparent in a few rare cases that litigants kept on certain servants in order to be assured of their testimony or loyalty. But this phenomenon does not appear to have had any significant effect on wage levels: servants from the Savile and Beaufort families (see below) who received bribes to spy or provide information on adulterous employers in the early eighteenth century seem to have received cash lump sums rather than inflated wages.

In Table 6.1 the data are presented as mean annual wages by decade rather than the modal values successfully utilised by Boulton to avoid the dangers of 'prevailing rates'. This is simply because there are too few data and they are overly distorted by taking the most popular values. Nonetheless, the data that result largely fail to confirm recent assumptions about the level of London servant wages: according to Earle, middling employers were paying their maids between £3 and £3 10s per year in the 1670s, and from £5 to £5 10s by the 1710s, whereas the depositional data for the same period suggest stagnation for maidservants in that period. Samuel Pepys only occasionally mentions servant wages in his diary of the 1660s, but in 1662 'my wife and [maid Jane Birch] agreed 3l a year (she would not serve under)'. The following year, 'my wife being troubled . . . for want of a good cook-maid', Pepys employed one at £4 a year. Cookmaids were usually paid more than ordinary maids; however, in Earle's words, 'Pepys was a man in a hurry' and his willingness to pay that much may have had more to do with his upward mobility: 'She did', he wrote, 'live last at my Lord

Monkes house'.[10] Yet Defoe's assertion in 1725 that maids' wages had risen from 30s or 40s a year to £6, or even as high as £8 a year over his life-time, seems (not entirely unpredictably) an exaggeration: any inflation in female servant wages only emerges in the 1730s, and this is affirmed by the parochial examination data; incidentally, Keith Snell's settlement data for eighteenth-century St Clement Danes, the Middlesex parish just beyond the western edge of the City of London, fails to exhibit inflation beyond the £3 15s mark for female servants until the late 1740s. It is possible that wages at the lowest level of men's domestic service were accelerating at the sort of speed about which Defoe was complaining, beginning at a slightly earlier date than the growth of maidservants' wages.[11]

The relative parity in female servant wages between a London-wide source in the depositions and the Chelsea settlements lends a little corroboration to Gilboy's findings of an eighteenth-century metropolitan wage area. This is certainly the case if we compare these data with those given for other parts of the country and beyond — in the depositions, servants who worked their way to London demonstrated the capital's wage supremacy to themselves and the court which heard their testimony: in 1698, for instance, Sarah Blackwell progressed from 50s per year in Ireland, to £3 per year in Somerset, and £4 per year in London. Sharpe has observed that mean urban domestic servant wages in Essex for 1736–40 were at £3, and they failed to return even to that level until the 1780s; while Snell noted that in southern England more generally 'there is much evidence on the awareness of single women of their possibilities in London, particularly in domestic service' in the eighteenth century, as 'London and Middlesex money wages were far higher than those of the surrounding counties'. And this in a period when the cost of living for most of the time was falling.[12]

The clearest finding from the data, and one rarely explored by historians of wages, is the marked gender contrast: at the lower reaches of metropolitan service, menservants were consistently paid at least one-third more than their nearest female counterparts. As Bennett has reminded us, this is akin

---

10 Boulton, 'Wage labour', pp. 275 and 281, Table 2; P. Earle, *The Making of the English Middle Class: Business, Society and Family Life in London, 1660–1730* (London, 1989), p. 220, n. 26; S. Pepys, *Diary*, eds R. Latham and W. Matthews, 10 vols (London, 1971), III, p. 53, and IV, pp. 85–6.

11 D. Defoe, *Everybody's Business is Nobody's Business; or, Private Abuses, Public Grievances* (London, 1725), p. 4; K.D.M. Snell, *Annals of the Labouring Poor: Social Change and Agrarian England 1660–1900* (Cambridge, 1985), p. 416.

12 Gilboy, *Wages in Eighteenth Century England*, Chapter 2; LMA, DL/C/246 f. 43, Sarah Blackwell, 12/7/1698; P. Sharpe, *Adapting to Capitalism: Working Women in the English Economy* (Basingstoke, 1996), p. 115; Snell, *Annals of the Labouring Poor*, pp. 81, 38; Schwarz, *London in the Age of Industrialisation*, pp. 169–72.

to the average gender wage gap that is visible across the labour market in the late fourteenth through to the late twentieth centuries in western Europe. Why does such a differential have a six-century longevity? The answers to that question are many and complex. Orthodox explanations centre on contemporary perceptions of the relative strength of men and women; on the way women's wages were supplementary to their households' incomes; on women's relative lack of clout or bargaining power within the labour market, particularly their early modern exclusion from London livery companies; and on what might be seen as patriarchal norms, where women's work, culturally inferior to that of men and restricted to certain sectors of the economy, was also valued less in pecuniary terms.[13] Can these explanations be applied to the case of domestic servants?

Female service drudgery — scrubbing, polishing, fetching water and coals — was likely to be as arduous as that done by male servants, if not more so, therefore the first explanation holds little water here; and the overwhelming preponderance of unmarried women in service diminishes the importance of the issue of supplementary income. There was no formal corporate body to which male or female domestic servants could belong in London, although contemporaries debated the threat of male servant fraternities, and commentators certainly feared the cabal of wage-inflationary women. Defoe expressed those fears most succinctly when he described the experience of a girl who had arrived in London to take up a place on only three pounds a year: she had

> scarce been a week, nay, a day in her service, but a committee of servant wenches are appointed to examine her, who advise her to raise her wages, or give warning; to encourage her to which, the herb-woman or chandler-woman, or some other old intelligencer, provides her a place of 4 or 5 pounds a year . . . and so gives warning from place to place, 'till she has got her wages up to the tip-top.[14]

There is little other evidence for collective bargaining by female servants; and that by male servants rests on statements like Mandeville's that he was *credibly informed* that a parcel of footmen are arrived to that height of insolence as to have entered into a society together, and made laws by which they oblige themselves not to serve for less than such a sum, nor carry burdens nor any parcel above a certain weight'.[15] The importance of this argument is diminished if the bargaining power granted by a surfeit of

---

13   For references, see the Bibliographical essay.
14   Defoe, *Everybody's Business*, p. 5.
15   Mandeville, 'Essay on Charity', p. 310, my emphasis.

demand over supply (see Chapter One) obviated the need for more overt forms of collective expression. The final explanation exhibits most plausibility: patriarchal social norms ensured that female service was closely associated with housewifery, which slowly degraded over time to the status of 'drudgery', whereas male service could fall under more specialised rubrics or clearly-defined occupational labels that had a tendency to confer higher status, and therefore higher value, at least within the service labour market.

Risking a somewhat circular argument, the association of menservants in London with luxurious consumption is clarified when the wages of those who worked in larger households is examined. Middling employers might have employed several servants, but if there were fewer than four then they were likely all to be women. Even then there could be a hierarchical wage differential: the Nowes family paid a maid £4, a younger waiting woman £5 and a slightly older one £6 in annual wages at the end of the seventeenth century, for instance.[16] But the easiest way to demonstrate both the higher wages, in absolute terms, and the range of wages within large houses is to select examples from the greatest servant-employing households in London in the period.

Wages in large households

The households of Sir George and Lady Savile in the 1730s, and of the Duke and Duchess of Beaufort in the 1740s, are representative of only the largest of the West End great houses of the resident gentry and aristocracy.[17] The nature of the matrimonial disputes that brought them before the London Consistory court render their cases complex, and I have dealt with some of those complexities in my thesis; but they are interesting illustrations of this end of the service market nonetheless. Inevitably, the principal delineating factor in nominal wage payment was gender: remuneration, the range of tasks performed and the chances for advancement within the household clearly separated men from women. Utilising all the wage information at hand (including those wages paid to the same individual when they moved to a different post within the household, and noting the whole range of posts as revealed in the depositions), male average wages approach twice the level of female average wages in both these large families. In the Savile

---

16 LMA, DL/C/246 f. 43, Sarah Blackwell, 12/7/1698; f. 44, Alice Price, 14/7/1698; f. 48, Elizabeth Bailey, 22/7/1698.

17 For more detail on the Beaufort case itself, see L. Stone, *Broken Lives: Separation and Divorce in England 1660–1857* (Oxford, 1993), pp. 117–38; all wage data cited below from the church court depositions.

household, the average wage for the six women was £8 6s, while that for the thirteen men was £15 15s. As one might expect from one of the principal families of the land, the Beauforts paid slightly higher wages, on average £10 10s for their four women, and £18 9s for their menservants.

Of the women, Ann Barker was housemaid to the Saviles, 'first at £4 a year and afterwards to wit about two years before she left her master's service at £5 a year'. Elizabeth Franklin had joined the Beaufort household as under-nursery maid aged 19, on £4 a year, and in 22 years had got as far as chambermaid, on £12 a year. Her mistress's separation was the catalyst for her real leap forward, though, when she was promoted to waiting woman on £20 a year at the age of 41.[18] Within the extensive male side of the servants' hall, a man's fortunes depended on whether he was in the outdoor, stable-centred branch or the fast track of indoor male service. This also affected his access to perquisites and/or 'vails' (tips), which will be discussed later; but even before that consideration it is clear that earnings for men indoors or outdoors were potentially far higher than for women. John Hooton started in the Savile family aged 9, and 'has served Sir George in the capacity of his groom about three years at the yearly wages of £9'; before that he 'used to ride postillion from the time he first came to live there but had no wages for some time', adding that 'his first yearly wages were £7 and then £8'. John Redgate was an outdoor servant and 'was at first hired to serve Sir George [Savile] in the capacity as an husbandman' for four years at £9 a year, then 'served him in the capacity of coachman and the first year had £10, the next £11 and the next £12', arriving at £14 per annum at the time of his deposition.[19]

Indoors, meanwhile, status and therefore pay were largely determined by, as one servant put it, their 'proximity to the person' of the employer. Footmen stood at the lowest rung of the ladder: both of the Beauforts' footmen earned £7 a year (one after serving unpaid for seven years until the age of nineteen looking after their birds).[20] Higher up, Frenchman Samuel Migevan was at first 'only hired as clerk and to wait on the Saviles' son at the rate of £18 per year for the first year and to increase 20 shillings a year so long as his master should think fit'; but two months later his master's valet de chambre ('who was also his book keeper') left so Migevan took over and 'did likewise attend his master as his valet de chambre till he could supply himself with one and on account of his good services and

---

18 LMA, DL/C/271 f. 148; f. 165, Ann Barker, 9/2/1736; DL/C/273 f. 43, Elizabeth Franklin, 25/5/1742.
19 LMA, DL/C/271 f. 152, John Redgate, 28/1/1736; f. 154, John Hooton, 28/1/1736; DL/C/273 f. 17, John Pember, 18/5/1742.
20 LMA, DL/C/273 f. 49, Robert Rivers, 26/5/1742; f. 57, Thomas Pritchard, 28/5/1742.

trouble in attending his master, his wages were advanced to £30'. Robert Croucher had joined the Duke as his confectioner and groom of the chamber in his London mansion on £40 a year, and after twelve years was elevated to be steward of the Duke's estate in Badminton, Gloucestershire, on £50 a year. It is apparent that age, experience and good behaviour were additional factors influencing wage levels in the largest households: Migevan stated that Sir George Savile 'customarily advances all or most of his servants' wages yearly for some time after their coming if they behave well'. But the priority attached to these factors might vary, and could be mitigated by chance occurrences such as the departure or the death of other servants in the household: the same servant also observed that when the Saviles' butler died, the 'under butler was advanced to his place'.[21]

That last example re-emphasises the importance of the hierarchy within large families, which, after gender, was probably the most striking variant of wages within the largest households and is apparent in all the cases cited earlier. The anonymous *Plan of a Person of Quality's family* (probably dating from 1690) differentiated quite clearly between upper male servants and the rest when determining wage levels: 'The yearly salaries of [upper servants] are uncertain, therefore [we] have left blank places to set in their order as the lord and they shall accord'. For the greater mass of the servants, 'it is according to the yearly salary given in England and is frequently more or less as can be agreed between the lord and the domestic'. Upper male servants came to gentlemen's agreements while lower male and most female servants' wages were set at the market rate; yet all servants within the largest households, regardless of their place in the hierarchy, had some room for contractual negotiation with their employers.[22]

To conclude the part of the chapter on money wages, it is clear by now that cash remuneration was of considerable importance to servants, so much so that employers knew that withholding their servants' wages was one of the best coercive tactics they could employ. Nearly all servants were paid wages, and those few that were not — usually the very young and very temporary — received payments in kind which will be discussed shortly. Those wages differed markedly for men and women, but size of household, age and experience were also significant factors. No doubt following conventions at least as old as fourteenth-century attempts to legislate for the control of servants' and labourers' wages, domestic servants, like servants in husbandry, were nominally paid in annual *tranches*. Delayed wage payments

---

21   LMA, DL/C/271 f. 160, Thomas Robertson, 5/2/1736; f. 141, Samuel Migevan, 25/1/1736; DL/C/273 f. 27, Robert Croucher, 20/5/1742.

22   Anon., *Plan of a Person of Quality's family* (c.1690), (n.p.).

had the added benefit for the employer of acting as informal credit from his or her servant; but in reality that pay might have been received by servants in shorter-term chunks, leaving them sheltered from many of the fluctuations in the cost of living, yet able to participate as at least petty consumers as prices by and large fell. Metropolitan domestic servants' frequent mobility meant that they often stayed far shorter terms than a full year, and received wages *pro rata*. So what on the face of it appears to be a clear contrast with the rest of the labour force, who were paid daily or weekly wages, is in fact less significant. And like the rest of the labour force, there were other forms of remuneration that had great significance, the remainder of the moral economy of service.

Non-wage earnings

A moral economy of service?

Since the 1970s, some historians have employed Marxist or modernisation theory to posit the commodification of servant labour. These writers have often assumed that a process of 'monetisation' went on throughout the eighteenth century, where the early modern paternal relationship between master or mistress and servant transformed itself into one between paying employer and wage-earning employee, so that by the nineteenth century, the cash nexus was firmly in the driving seat. Fairchilds did this for eighteenth-century French service, and McBride described the aftermath of this development in nineteenth-century France and England.[23]

Such writers freely acknowledged that their understanding of the eighteenth century owed a debt to the bi-polar model of eighteenth-century social relations, and the notion of the moral economy, posited by E.P. Thompson.[24] But his ideas and those of his followers have come under critical scrutiny in the last few decades: Styles, for one, has noted the changing nature of workers' definitions of customary right and employers' manipulation of the illegality of embezzlement. Sonenscher, in his history of French work and wages, has observed that 'it is very unlikely . . . there was any simple linear trend away from payment in kind to payment in cash' across the eighteenth

---

23 T. McBride, *The Domestic Revolution: the Modernisation of Household Service in England and France 1820–1920* (New York, 1976), pp. 30–31; C. Fairchilds, *Domestic Enemies: Servants and their Masters in Old Regime France* (Baltimore, 1984), pp. 17–18.

24 Fairchilds, *Domestic Enemies*, p. 13 n. 50; S. Maza, *Servants and Masters in Eighteenth-Century France: the Uses of Loyalty* (Princeton, 1983), pp. 237–8; Thompson, *Customs in Common*, Chapters 2, 4 and 5.

century: the wage, he argues, was a 'cipher in which a number of different assumptions were encoded', while customs 'have a misleading appearance of continuity and stability'. Writing about wages in London during the eighteenth and early nineteenth centuries, Schwarz notes that 'there is no serious evidence that payments in kind were less extensive in the nineteenth century than they had been a century earlier'.[25]

Such revisionism notwithstanding, Linebaugh has grafted London domestic servants onto the international proletariat he sees being generated by capital in the eighteenth century, due to their common contestation of employers' attempts to restrict customary earnings (in the servants' case, their vails and perquisites).[26] Yet however viable his model might be for the development of the Atlantic economy more generally, his is a truncated picture of service with undue concentration on the male servants of the very wealthy, a distinct minority of London's domestic servant population but a particular group of men which fits the model more readily. There is something over-determined in Linebaugh's version of events which sets the perk and the wage in opposition, and posits the eighteenth century as the site of once-and-for-all, irreversible change. The following account accepts that the customary practice of giving the full range of exchange entitlements to domestic servants occurred within 'a field of change and of contest, an arena in which opposing interests made conflicting claims', in Thompson's phrase for the mutability of custom.[27] But it will demonstrate the complexity of this question particularly as it relates to the vast majority of London domestic servants, women in small households, and argue not for a commodification or monetisation of service but rather a continuity in customary, mixed remuneration. The moral economy of service was as prevalent in the mid-eighteenth century as it had been in the mid-seventeenth, and arguably as it would remain well into the nineteenth.

Bed and board

One of the defining characteristics of early modern service, an essential component of its life-cycle character, was living in: servants in husbandry,

---

25 J. Styles, 'Embezzlement, industry and the law in England, 1500–1800', in M. Berg *et al.*, eds, *Manufacture in Town and Country Before the Factory* (Cambridge, 1983); M. Sonenscher, *Work and Wages: Natural Law, Politics and the Eighteenth-Century French Trades* (Cambridge, 1989), esp. pp. 194, 174; his *The Hatters of Eighteenth-Century France* (Berkeley, 1987), p. 19; Schwarz, *London in the Age of Industrialisation*, p. 164; his 'Custom, crime and perquisites', *Bulletin of the Society for the Study of Labour History* **52** (1) (1987).

26 P. Linebaugh, *The London Hanged: Crime and Civil Society in the Eighteenth Century* (London, 1991), p. 170 and *passim*.

27 Thompson, *Customs in Common*, p. 6, echoed in Sonenscher, *Work and Wages*, p. 174.

apprentices and nearly but not quite all domestic servants resided in their employers' households as members of their 'families'. If delayed payment of money wages was akin to servants granting their employers long-term credit, then the provision of food and lodging to servants reversed this equation, allowing servants 'to transfer costs of price fluctuations onto their masters' and so avoid changes in the price of food or rent. Sonenscher is referring here to French journeymen, but the point is still relevant; he also notes how masters could pass those bed-and-board credit costs onto victuallers should he board out his servants.[28] How much was this provision worth to servants, and is there any way of arriving at their real earnings?

It is probably correct to assume that servants in middling households ate in Earle's words 'much better than they would ever have eaten with their families before going into service', but quantifying this added nourishment must be indirect. 'Board wages' were paid to those few servants that lived out, 'more often given to men than women', to buy their 'diet' and lodging — in our period 7s a week for menservants and 5s. for maidservants.[29] However, few servants received board wages for very long — they were a temporary expedient — and intuitively, the sums appear to be very high. Bulk food-buying for the whole household must have been cheaper than out-of-doors victuals, so figures have been extrapolated from Earle's *Making of the English Middle Class*. George estimated the cost of renting a cheap room in London in the mid-eighteenth century to be 1s 6d a week, and this was also the price of garret-lodging in the 1730s as related by Johnson to his biographer, Boswell. Late seventeenth-century rents were lower, and single or double rooms could be had (particularly in the East End) for as little as £2 a year, or roughly nine pence a week.[30]

These costs have been separated out, and data are presented in Table 6.2, which outlines total annual values of bed and board, but these figures must be taken as a very high ceiling of 'real' earnings. Estimates of total annual earnings — not including perks and vails, of course — can be calculated by adding in average money wages for the 1680s from the depositions,

---

28   Sonenscher, *Work and Wages*, p. 194.
29   Earle, *English Middle Class*, pp. 279–80 (including a rare documented complaint by a servant of his employers' food); LMA, DL/C/254 f. 205, James Connell, 13/5/1714; DL/C/250 f. 441, Mary Holt, 8/6/1709; see D.A. Kent, 'Ubiquitous but invisible: female domestic servants in mid-eighteenth century London', *History Workshop Journal* **28** (1989), 123; but see P. Earle, *A City Full of People: Men and Women of London, 1650–1750* (London, 1994), p. 169.
30   D. George, *London Life in the Eighteenth Century* (London, 1925), pp. 100–103; J. Boswell, *The Life of Samuel Johnson*, cited in D. Cruickshank and N. Burton, *Life in the Georgian City* (London, 1990), pp. 33, 62: see also Kent, 'Ubiquitous but invisible', 123; Earle, *City Full of People*, p. 169.

Table 6.2 Estimated monetary value of servants' bed and board, 1660–1750

Bed and board (weekly)	Late 17th century	Early 18th century
Rent	9d	1s 6d
Diet (men)	4s	5s
Diet (women)	3s	4s
Annual value, 52 weeks (men)	£12 7s	£16 18s
Annual value, 52 weeks (women)	£9 15s	£14 6s

Sources: see text [Constant board wages, early c.18th (52 weeks): £18 4s (men), £13 0s (women)].

and for the 1730s provided by Hecht for footmen and by the depositions for women (see Table 6.1). These are set against female milliners' wages reported by Campbell in 1747, and Schwarz's estimates of male wages in the building trades in London, in Table 6.3.[31] Of course, most waged work had an element of unpredictability about it, since some was seasonal or intermittent, and a significant proportion of the labour force was under-employed. Service could also be unstable and seasonal, and Schwarz noted that 'servants in the West End were in danger of being unemployed for six months of the year after the aristocracy had left town'.[32] Nevertheless, if earning-equivalents approached the (probably inflated) heights of the figures in Table 6.2, the overall value of such remuneration must have made service attractive for many women, since they were not only guaranteed bed and board but in addition a significant amount of spending money relative to the frequently pauperised needle trades, as can be seen in Table 6.3. It is testimony to the strength of the female life cycle that the female labour market was characterised by a shift from higher-earning service to lower-earning waged labour in women's late twenties and early thirties. Men, however, would have placed a significant emphasis on the non-wage components of their remuneration, since even a builder's labourer notionally earned more in money wages than a footman could earn with bed and board included.

---

31 R. Campbell, *The London Tradesman* (London, 1747), p. 208; Schwarz, *London in the Age of Industrialisation*, p. 170. For Fairchilds's attempts to construct comparative wage series for servants and other lower-order occupations in eighteenth-century France, *Domestic Enemies*, p. 56, Figure 5, and p. 57, Figure 6 and n. 143.
32 Kent, 'Ubiquitous but invisible', 123; Schwarz, *London in the Age of Industrialisation*, pp. 104, 166–8.

Table 6.3 Annual money wages with bed and board compared to select trades, 1680–1750

Waged workers	1680–9	1730–9	mid-*c*.18th
Servants (female)	£13 10*s*	£18 1*s*	
Milliners			£14 6*s*
Servants (male)	£16 7*s*	£23 4*s*	
Skilled building workers			£46 16*s*
Building labourers			£31 4*s*

Sources: see text.

Vails and perks

Anthropologists have shown great interest in the significance of gifts exchanged between members of observed communities, and some historians have utilised these perspectives in the recent development of the history of consumption. Vickery has documented a late eighteenth-century northern gentlewoman's evaluation of, and labour over the goods in her household: 'Clothing received particular attention. It was mended, retrimmed, redyed, converted into household items or cast off to servants'. It was quite clear that 'goods were part of the currency of the mistress–servant relationship', but also that male livery had a much stronger contractual basis than maids' cast-offs, even if Dorothy Cooke told the London Consistory court she had been given clothes by her mistress 'persuant to their agreement'.[33] Sometimes the informal distinction between payment and gift was a contentious area of mistress–maid relations: the mistress's 'gift' was the maid's 'right'. According to Vickery, 'That which was [mistress] Elizabeth Shackleton's to give and her servants' to take was subject to negotiation and reinterpretation', and just as the retention of wages was a strategy employed by the wronged or malicious employer, so too was the withholding of servants' clothes. Mary Hill found this out in 1707, when her former mistress refused to give back some of her clothes: she returned to the household four days later with a friend in tow, and while discussing the matter at the front door,

---

33 M. Mauss, *The Gift* (London, 1970); M. Douglas and B. Isherwood, *The World of Goods: Towards an Anthropology of Consumption* (New York, 1979); A. Vickery, 'Women and the world of goods: a Lancashire consumer and her possessions, 1751–81', in J. Brewer and R. Porter, eds, *Consumption and the World of Goods* (London, 1993), pp. 282, 283; LMA, DL/C/253 f. 43, Dorothy Cooke, 20/11/1712.

a neighbour said to Hill's former mistress, 'Fie, fie, give the poor servant her clothes, what do you keep them for?'.[34]

The permeable boundary between gift and payment is highlighted in the depositions. In 1681, for instance, Mary Thompson was accused of stealing some flame-red fabric called flamming, 'enough to make a petticoat', from her mistress, the wife of a churchwarden and victualler. She was sacked from the household when she got toothache badly enough to prevent her from working, and when she 'left suddenly with it [the flamming] under her apron' her mistress denied ever having given it, and the housekeeper insisted on looking into her trunk. She beat Mary and took from her a bible, a 'little book with her name in it', which she had in fact lent the housekeeper, an 'alamode' hood, two ells of lace (roughly seven-and-a-half feet of cloth), six handkerchiefs, an apron, a fan, several pieces of black ribbon, and a pair of black gloves the housekeeper had given her when Mary had attended her son's funeral. Some of these things were gifts from the housekeeper as well as her mistress, but both of them were in the position to manipulate the blurred gift–payment boundary. These two may have given such gifts when 'feeling bountiful, fond or grateful', or as a gesture of favouritism, but they could be removed when those feelings were reversed.[35]

In the largest households, menservants will have had their clothing provided for them by their employer, but for many of them — especially footmen and postillions — it will have been in the form of uniform 'livery' which for the servants of noble employers was traditionally scarlet. There is some evidence that many lower servants wearing the badge of livery felt it emphasised their servile status. The ever-more-frequent sight of blue or other non-noble livery on the backs of menservants to bourgeois employers with inflated social pretensions demonstrated just how little account employers took of their lower male domestic servants' wishes on the sartorial front, but also how enduring a status symbol livery was. Pepys, for instance, clothed his footboy in a livery first of 'black and gold lace upon grey', which later was changed to 'green lined with red'.[36]

---

34 Thompson, 'Moral economy', p. 78; J. Rule, *The Labouring Classes in Early Industrial England* (Harlow, 1986), p. 116; Styles, 'Embezzlement, industry and the law', p. 186; Vickery, 'Women and the world of goods', p. 283; LMA, DL/C/249 f. 409, Mary Hill, 13/10/1707.
35 LMA, DL/C/240 f. 150, Mary Thompson, 15/12/1681: a list not too far removed from the 'checklist of plebeian female consumer longing' of two young northern women in the late eighteenth century in J. Styles, 'Clothing the north: the supply of non-elite clothing in the eighteenth-century north of England', *Textile History* **25** (2) (1994), 158; Vickery, 'Women and the world of goods', p. 284.
36 D. Marshall, 'The domestic servants of the eighteenth century', *Economica* **9** (25) (1929), 18, 22; LMA, DL/C/253 f. 43, Dorothy Cooke, 20/11/1712. Pepys, *Diary*, III, p. 50, and IX, p. 372.

Clothes substituted for some servants' cash wages, particularly the youngest or most temporary, and their value meant that poor servants could be bribed with them; this was appreciated by the Consistory court to the extent that proctors frequently asked servant witnesses whether 'the clothes she now wears are her own'. Linebaugh has rightly pointed out that 'clothing represented a store of wealth for many people: the circuits of clothing might intersect with circuits of money', and this statement is reinforced by Lemire's research on the second-hand clothing trades in London during the later eighteenth century.[37] In our period servants' relative wages were reasonable, and it was because the importance of bed and board was undiminished that money wages were in effect disposable income in a period of low price inflation. London offered unrivalled opportunities for consuming clothing — first and second hand — and manufactured goods at the turn of the eighteenth century, and Mary Thompson's list of gifts and purchases mentioned earlier suggests much low-level servant consumption.[38] So, to what extent did servants consider clothing as simply another form of remuneration? The question can be asked more broadly of 'perquisites' and 'vails'. They present two related problems of significance to historians, the first of definition and the second of extent.

The general meanings of perquisite and vail have traditionally been taken to be, respectively, employees' customary profits arising from the use of materials directly related to the nature of their employment, and cash gratuities (tips). Perquisites were part and parcel of the cook's expected earnings, for instance, for she or he could sell the fat dripping and other left-overs from running a kitchen.[39] Literary evidence, at least, suggests that those who did the household's marketing and shopping were often presented with opportunities for profit and, highlighting the contested nature of many of these non-wage earnings, some of the prescriptive literature warned against such behaviour. In a section of her *Present for a Servant-Maid* of 1743, entitled 'The Market-Penny', Eliza Haywood battled against unofficial credit for servants and wrote them the following advice: 'To purloin

---

37 For instance, LMA, DL/C/242 f. 65, Joanna Glover, 16/6/1687; DL/C/248 f. 18, Mary Butler, 22/1/1703; DL/C/252 f. 328, Mary Shackbolt, 8/6/1711, who borrowed her mistress's cap but had otherwise clothed herself; Linebaugh, *London Hanged*, p. 254; B. Lemire, 'Developing consumerism and the ready-made clothing trade in Britain, 1750–1800', *Textile History* **15** (1) (1984); her '"A good stock of cloathes": the changing market for cotton clothing in Britain, 1750–1800', *Textile History* **22** (2) (1991); D. Marshall, *The English Domestic Servant in History*, Historical Association General Series 13 (London, 1949), pp. 19–20.

38 Earle, *City Full of People*, Chapter 1.

39 Hecht, *Domestic Servant Class*, p. 157; Maza, *Servants and Masters*, p. 102; Fairchilds, *Domestic Enemies*, pp. 26–7.

or secrete any part of which is put into your hands to be laid out to the best advantage, is as essentially a theft as though you took the money out of the pockets of those who entrust you'. She continued: 'Do not imagine that by taking pains to find out where you can buy cheapest you are entitled to that overplus you must have given in another place', by implication an 'overplus' also obtained from traders giving discounts to regular servant customers.[40]

The importance of perquisites to male servants — the amount of 'card money' garnered from employers' guests at the gaming table, for instance — was such that they sometimes quitted their posts if their expectations of reward via perquisites were not met. Vails made up a large part of the manservant's wages, although they were shared with the female servants in some households, and frequently were given for servants who ran errands or delivered letters. Defoe believed that vails could double a maidservant's wages, and they occasionally seem to have had the expectation of some recompense that way: her mistress told Elizabeth Taylor 'she would pay her wages for her service after the rate of £4 a year if her vails did not amount to as much'.[41] But for men their potential was far more lucrative — in 1741, a gentleman's servant (about to be hanged for stealing a watch from Lord Mordington's cook) told the Ordinary of Newgate, the prison's resident cleric, that he had collected over £100 in tips within two years from a job whose wage was only £4 a year. His employer clearly had wealthy and profligate guests, or perhaps this servant was an expert extortionist — either way this sort of bounty was only available in the largest or wealthiest households, and largely to male rather than female domestic servants.[42]

The Great Vail Controversy surfaced just beyond the temporal scope of this book, in the late 1750s and 1760s, when gentry and noble masters engaged in a concerted attempt to prevent servants in their households demanding large tips from guests. 'Representing an aggressive minority', wrote Hecht, 'they seem to have adopted a course of militant action whenever the welfare of the occupational group appeared to be threatened'. He was referring to the male servants, of course, most notorious among whom were the footmen, who resisted their masters' militancy with vigour, and in London, footmen rioted in Ranelagh gardens in 1764. Marshall suggests

---

40   J. Swift, *Directions to Servants*, in *The Prose Writings of Jonathan Swift*, eds H.J. Davis and
     I. Ehrenpreis (Oxford, 1968) vol. 13, p. 38; Mandeville, 'Essay on charity', pp. 309–10;
     Marshall, 'Domestic servants', 28–9; [E. Haywood], *Present for a Servant-Maid; or, the Sure
     Means of Gaining Love and Esteem* (London, 1743), p. 24.
41   Marshall, 'Domestic servants', 28; Defoe, *Everybody's Business*, pp. 10–11; LMA,
     DL/C/255 f. 318, Elizabeth Taylor, 8/7/1715: is the expectation that Taylor's vails
     would not suffice?
42   Linebaugh, *London Hanged*, p. 251; Marshall, 'Domestic servants', 27.

that 'vails had become a very necessary part of servants' wages, and that they went in many cases, not to satisfy the claims of debauchery, but the necessities of the recipient'.[43]

To what extent did servants consider perks (including clothing) and tips simply as other forms of remuneration, part of the moral economy of service? Linebaugh reinforces his point over the intersection of circuits of cash and clothing by quoting a penny ballad that described a sorry tale of servant theft leading inexorably to Tyburn. He observes that the ballad had 'no nicely discerned distinctions between vails and perquisites': given the London second-hand trade in clothing (and in just about everything else), perquisites had exchange value and could be converted into their cash equivalent if required; and secondly, there was no distinction in the plebeian mind between material gains of office and cash tips — both, Linebaugh alleges, were seen as customary entitlements as of right.[44]

There is evidence that contemporary usage mirrored this. Servants involved in marketing may have gained benefit in kind from the shopkeepers they patronised, but Haywood's fears over the 'market-penny' seem to have revolved around money. Given the sorts of things young women in particular might have wanted to purchase, and maidservant Mary Thompson's hoard of treasures (listed above) is suggestive, cash will have been much more useful. However, clothing was different. Menservants' livery will have been directly associated with their employer and therefore very difficult to sell, or at the very least its exchange value will have been distinctly limited, even if bourgeois livery was increasingly popular. But male servants not in livery will have been extremely interested in their clothing, and many female servants saw the clothes they had been given as valuable in their own right; indeed, for women who waited on their mistresses in 'company of the best fashion', good clothes were obligatory.[45] The perquisite of clothing may not simply be reduced to its cash value.

The evidence appears to demonstrate that perks and tips were vital components in the moral economy of service. But this brings us to the question of access: for whom were perks and tips realistic and regular sources of income? Perquisites were available to waged workers in most

---

43 Hecht, *Domestic Servant Class*, p. 87; Marshall, 'Domestic servants', 35–7; her *English Domestic Servant*, p. 19.

44 Linebaugh, *London Hanged*, pp. 250, 255; J. Beattie, 'London crime and the making of the "Bloody Code", 1689–1718', in L. Davison *et al.*, eds, *Stilling the Grumbling Hive: The Response to Social and Economic Problems in England, 1689–1750* (Stroud, 1992), pp. 49–76; Lemire, 'Developing consumerism'; for the exchange of stolen fabric and clothes into cash in northern England, see Styles, 'Clothing the north'.

45 LMA, DL/C/271 f. 158, Margaret Tweedy, 5/2/1736.

Table 6.4 Assets or 'fortune' of London domestic servants, 1669–1752

Asset (£)	Male servants	Female servants	Male + Female
'Little' or 'Nothing'	34	152	186
50s–£10	5	34	39
£11 and over	29	33	62
Other	8	31	39
Total *n*	76	250	326

Sources: London church court depositions.

aspects of economic life within the metropolis, as Schwarz and others have recognised. While Schwarz himself stresses the abiding importance of the money wage, they were at the very least a supplement to many Londoners' earnings.[46] As far as servants are concerned, perks and vails may have constituted a significant and sometimes lucrative non-wage component of their remuneration. But the impact of these additions to the wage is extremely difficult to quantify since it has to be examined in terms of opportunity as much as value. For maidservants on average wages, the relative impact of a large tip or irregular perk will have been great; but the opportunity to receive such emoluments will have been far more prevalent for those (usually male) servants with certain types of tasks and in certain, especially larger, households. The conclusion that the moral economy of service was both gendered as well as socially stratified is inescapable.

Did the servants who worked within the metropolitan high-wage area in our period also save significantly more? A little more than one-fifth of servant witnesses at the London church courts (in gender proportions akin to the sample as a whole) were asked 'how much they were worth', or in other words, the extent of their savings or fortune. The findings, displayed in Table 6.4, suggest that saving while in London service was difficult, if not impossible, for most: just over 60 per cent of female, but fewer than half of male, servants stated explicitly that they were worth little or nothing. Looking at it from the opposite direction, an eighth of female, but almost two-fifths of male, servants declared their worth at over £10. Henry Smith was master cook to William III and claimed to be worth £1,000, while Joanna

---

46 Linebaugh, *London Hanged*, Chapter 5; M. Rediker, *Between the Devil and the Deep Blue Sea: Merchant Seamen, Pirates and the Anglo-American Maritime World, 1700–1750* (Cambridge, 1987), pp. 117, 125–32; Schwarz, *London in the Age of Industrialisation*, pp. 158, 163–4 and *passim*.

Parker, who had been wet-nurse in Admiral Benbow's household, was worth £400. But she appears to have returned to service in widowhood, at quite a different stage in her life cycle compared to most maidservants.[47] Although marginally over a quarter of the female servants had managed to accumulate what for most was at least one year's wages, the typical London servant would have informed the court that she was only worth a small amount, if anything at all. Overall, these figures confirm the gender differential in servant wealth, and suggest that in London most servants would not or could not accumulate for the next phase in their lives.

Conclusion

Defoe and Mandeville were in some senses right to be worried: attempts by JPs and other members of the social elite in statutory and non-statutory capacities were failing to regulate wages for London domestic servants in the late seventeenth and early eighteenth centuries. The operation of the metropolitan wage market drew young people into the capital through its decisively higher wages, and for the minority of male servants, ensured that their wages rose fairly steeply after 1700. These commentators were wrong in that the female majority of domestic servants' money wages generally remained stable, as they did for most other wage-earners in the period; but this allowed them to shelter behind their employers if and when cost of living fluctuated, letting them take advantage of generally falling prices in London's vast market for consumer goods. The data on fortunes certainly points to most servants as consumers rather than life-cycle savers.

It is also clear that custom was particularly influential for domestic servants, and recognising the importance of the money wage should not draw us away from the vitality of the moral economy of service. But Thompson's dictum must be adjusted: 'non-monetary usages . . . appeared simultaneously as economic and social relations, as relations between people' *and also* 'as payment for services and things'.[48] Perquisites, clothing and tips were exceptionally important: to male servants they probably constituted more, sometimes much more, than half of their overall earnings, while female servants may have received small regular additions to their wages, and the occasional windfall would have made a marginal difference. Clothing,

---

47   PRO, PROB 24, 36 f. 203, Henry Smith, 14/4/1697; 60 f. 376, Joanna Parker, 15/7/1723.

48   Thompson, 'The patricians and the plebs', in his *Customs in Common*, p. 38.

however, cannot simply be assessed for its cash worth, as its value as a gift in the anthropological sense varied with the nature of the servant–employer relationship. Further, the moral economy of service showed no signs of petering out mid-century: the well-publicised and highly theatrical confrontation over vails in the 1750s and 1760s was not the first occasion in which customary earnings had been contested by employers of servants — it neither marked the beginning of the end of mixed forms of earnings, nor the end of the beginning of the money-wage's supremacy.

Finally, it remains to emphasise the operation of gender in this moral economy. It ensured that the divergence between female domestic servants, mostly in smaller households with little opportunity in the short term for wage-enhancing promotion, and male, mostly in larger households where such promotion was a distinct possibility, grew wider in this period. Menservants' cash wages were greater and accelerated faster and earlier than those for women; the value of their non-monetary remuneration was higher and access to it was easier; and their savings were potentially much larger. Female servants may have been better off than women working in the sweated trades, and in general relatively well remunerated for the female labour force in London; but their position relative to their male colleagues was distinctly disadvantaged and getting worse. It would be macro-economic fluctuations in the late eighteenth and early nineteenth centuries that demonstrated the financial vulnerability of female servants, not the demise of custom.

CHAPTER SEVEN

Conclusion

Domestic servants living and working in London households during the long period chosen for this book, between the year in which Samuel Pepys began writing his diary and the middle of the following century, experienced mixed fortunes. It would be foolhardy to characterise their diverse lives in a single sweeping judgement, given the variety of their origins, the potential for delight as well as distress in their relations with employers, and the fact that for many domestic servants — particularly female — this was an important but transient phase in their life cycles, the gateway to their adult lives. Those historians who have tried to pass definitive judgement on domestic servants risk building walls around the diversity found in the chapters here. This final account will survey very briefly the conclusions drawn in previous chapters — each chapter had its own sub-conclusion and there is no fun in labouring points already made in summary more than is absolutely necessary — and will end with the judgements that can be made with some degree of certitude.

London was presented in the Introduction as a unique location for the study of pre-modern domestic service: both the strength of demand for service and its sheer scale present the historian with unrivalled opportunities for investigation and discovery that elude smaller towns. As Britain's greatest metropolis, London and this vital part of its labour force cannot be representative of the British experience as a whole, but the conclusions from this study are instructive nonetheless. In the first chapter, it could be seen that the politics of 'place' ensured domestic service was conducted within a patriarchal context of order and authority in which mastery was not questioned, but where it had to be exercised under the curious and sometimes censorious gaze of neighbourhood, parish and even metropolis. The managerial role of the mistress was a long-term component of household authority, and not only its timing but the proximity of mistress and maid in most servant-employing households makes this aspect of 'separate spheres' look decidedly shaky.

The discussion of household relations in Chapter Four demonstrated that simply characterising servants in terms of degrees of vulnerability denied them the agency over their lives that they were able to exercise much of the time. While servant sexuality could sometimes be characterised by coercion and rape, in no way could these terms stand for the totality of the servant experience. That agency in matters sexual served to emphasise further the inadequacy of 'privacy' and its alleged growth in the period: as a spatial phenomenon the evidence failed to offer support to conventional theses of change, and as the *leitmotif* for relations within households it was deeply inadequate. The 'Gormenghast' model of servant seclusion or invisibility cannot survive even the most cursory glance at the interaction between servants and their employers or fellow-household dwellers, neighbours and Londoners; likewise, the 'threshold' perspective placing servants on the cusp between employer and plebeian worlds does not do that level of contact justice. While London was admittedly unique in the English context in terms of scope and scale, urban domestic service thrust the predominantly young people in service, willingly or otherwise, into the maelstrom.

The chapter on service as work sought to offer a perspective on domestic servants that rarely emerges from other historical accounts: they were household workers engaged in sometimes strenuous labour, and unlike most premodern working people, they were engaged for this part of their life cycles in one form of livelihood-earning activity. The latest literature on the history of work allowed service to be understood as meaningful labour in a cultural as much as economic sense, and also to categorise it as either housewifery or 'idle luxury' depending upon task, and while a certain circumspection must be used when analysing the prescriptive literature, there seems to have been some reflection in the depositions of the work specialisation evident in household manuals. The final substantive chapter on wages and remuneration further emphasised that point by showing how diverse the range of earnings could be in households in which specialisation was found. But it also pushed home the points made throughout the book, but most clearly articulated in Chapters Five and Six, that the servant experience in London was powerfully cross-cut by household size and gender. Most female servants worked in small households on their own or with one or two fellow servants in close proximity with their mistresses (and even masters); their working lives differed considerably from those of menservants, most of whom worked in larger households in which earning potentials were far greater, only certain servants had any real proximity to the employer's person, hierarchies were steeper and consequently chances for promotion and long-term employment were higher.

Chapter Six concluded that a moral economy of service could be seen in operation in metropolitan households, in which cash wages were important but, particularly for menservants, a mixture of earnings was a crucial customary component of servant remuneration. But this moral economy differed in two significant ways from the Thompsonian model: firstly, there did not appear to be decisive change as the eighteenth century wore on, and while this book only covers the period up to 1750, it seems likely that a moral rather than a strictly cash, market economy held sway for domestic servants well beyond the turn of the nineteenth century. Secondly, this was not a monolithic entity, but one — and it bears repeating — torn by gender: the way earnings were mixed, the opportunities for significant boosts to earnings from perks and vails, and therefore the relative importance of the cash wage, were different for women and men. Overall, these were factors characterised by continuity, and this theme has been present throughout the book in the chapters on household relations as much as those on work and wages: as the moral economy persisted, so too did a diverse set of relationships between servant and employer that the 'separation of spheres' and 'growth of privacy' fail to encompass. What is clear, however, is the relative good fortune servants experienced in this period as opposed to those periods immediately before or afterwards. Demography and economy, allied to the expansion of London, created a range of working opportunities for domestic servants in the metropolis and empowered them in the service labour market in ways which may have begun to be undermined even before this book's period had ended. It remains to be said that the ways modern historians have attempted to account for change so far — admittedly in the face of inadequate histories of pre-modern domestic service — will not suffice.

Domestic service has been examined here through a variety of lenses. But in general, an attempt has been made to gaze through them with the eyes not of employers, whose dominant view has distorted the subject for too long, but of the servants themselves. No claims are made here for the universality or omniscience of the church court depositions which have provided the bulk of servants' own words: they sometimes result (like all social history based on court records) in a crisis-riven perspective in which day-to-day living can be obscured, and it is possible that the lowliest of servants have sometimes been excluded because they or their places were deemed too base for testimony in the courts. But the view offered here, however partial, is intended as the antidote to the traditional employer's eye view: it is the nearest we have so far to a servant's perspective on life in early modern domestic service.

APPENDIX I

Bibliographical essay

The literature on domestic service during the 'long' eighteenth century is far from extensive. This essay attempts to provide the student of the subject with lists of further reading, thematically arranged roughly according to the book's chapters. But it will soon become clear that those serious about investigating domestic service in greater depth will have to turn their attention to the available primary sources in their locality: depositions from the archdeacon's or bishop's consistory courts; parish settlement and bastardy examinations; correspondence, ledgers and household accounts from great houses and families who have deposited such records locally; diaries or journals (much more likely to come from employers rather than servants themselves in this period); and other as yet undiscovered delights. Only then will a patchwork of local studies emerge to fill the vast gaps in our knowledge of those thousands of people who spent part or much of their lives as pre-modern domestic servants.

General domestic service

D.M. Stuart insisted in the foreword that her survey of domestic service across six centuries, *The English Abigail* (London, 1946), was 'not a history of domestic service in England; it is nothing so ambitious — or so controversial' (v). In which case, there are only very few works that address English domestic service directly in our period: a start can be made with D. Marshall, 'The domestic servants of the eighteenth century', *Economica* **9** (25) (1929); the same author's *The English Domestic Servant in History*, Historical Association General Series 13 (London, 1949), which surveys the sixteenth through to the nineteenth centuries; J.J. Hecht, *The Domestic Servant Class in Eighteenth-Century England* (London, 1956), still the only full-blown monograph on the subject for eighteenth-century England; D.A. Kent, 'Ubiquitous

210

but invisible: female domestic servants in mid-eighteenth century London', *History Workshop Journal* **28** (Autumn, 1989), a stimulating short piece utilising Westminster settlement examinations; and the essays in B. Hill, *Servants: English Domestics in the Eighteenth Century* (Oxford, 1996).

M. Waterson, *The Servants' Hall: A Domestic History of Erdigg* (London, 1980) is a fully-illustrated account of a National Trust restoration, the history of a country house and the servants of a family almost obsessed with their welfare; M. McIntosh, 'Servants and the household unit in an Elizabethan English community', *Journal of Family History* **9** (1984) is a useful demographic study of servants in small-town and rural Elizabethan Essex; while A. Kussmaul, *Servants in Husbandry in Early Modern England* (Cambridge, 1981), is the now-classic study of rural service-in-husbandry. While many urban historians make reference to servants — see for instance N. Goose, 'Household size and structure in early-Stuart Cambridge', *Social History* **5** (1980); J. Boulton, *Neighbourhood and Society: A London Suburb in the Seventeenth Century* (Cambridge, 1987) especially Chapter 5; and M. Roberts, 'Women and work in sixteenth-century English towns', in P.J. Corfield and D. Keene, eds, *Work in Towns 850–1850* (Leicester, 1990) — few have tackled them head on. I.K. Ben-Amos, 'Service and the coming of age of young men in seventeenth-century England', *Continuity and Change* **8** (1988) (more concerned with apprenticeship than domestic service), and G. Mayhew, 'Life-cycle service and the family unit in early modern Rye', *Continuity and Change* **6** (2) (1991) are both useful, while for the earlier period see P.J.P. Goldberg, 'Marriage, migration and servanthood: the York cause paper evidence', in his edited *Woman is a Worthy Wight: Women in English Society c.1200–1500* (Stroud, 1992); and his *Women, Work and Life Cycle in a Medieval Economy: Women in York and Yorkshire c.1300–1520* (Oxford, 1992).

Domestic service in London

For London, in addition to Boulton's and Kent's works, the following are essential: P. Earle, *The Making of the English Middle Class: Business, Society and Family Life in London, 1660–1730* (London, 1989), Chapter 8; his 'The female labour market in London in the late seventeenth and early eighteenth centuries', *Economic History Review* **42** (3) (1989); and his *A City Full of People: Men and Women of London, 1650–1750* (London, 1994), Chapters 3 and 4. For the medieval period, see J.M. Bennett, 'Medieval women, modern women: across the great divide', in D. Aers, ed., *Culture and History 1350–1600: Essays on English Communities, Identities and Writing* (Brighton, 1992); for the sixteenth and early seventeenth centuries, see L. Gowing, *Domestic Dangers: Women, Words and Sex in Early Modern London* (Oxford, 1996); and V. Brodsky Elliott, 'Single women in the London marriage market: age, status and mobility, 1598–1619', in R.B. Outhwaite, ed., *Marriage and Society: Studies in the Social History of Marriage* (London, 1981): her forthcoming *Mobility and Marriage: The Family and Kinship in Early Modern London* will no doubt be worth the wait. L.D. Schwarz, *London in the Age of Industrialisation: Entrepreneurs, Labour Force and Living Conditions, 1700–1850*

(Cambridge, 1992) is excellent in setting domestic service in a very long eighteenth-century context, and the evergreen *London Life in the Eighteenth Century* (London, 1925), by M.D. George, remains required reading. The essays in A.L. Beier and R. Finlay, eds, *London 1500–1700: the Making of the Metropolis* (Harlow, 1986) provide a wide-ranging context, while R. Porter, *London: A Social History* (Harmondsworth, 1996), Chapters 4–7, presents a readable recent background account of metropolitan expansion.

European domestic service

European works are readily available, and O. Hufton's magisterial *The Prospect Before Her: A History of Women in Western Europe Vol. I, 1500–1800* (London, 1995) Chapter 2 is the best general introduction, while for the earlier period see C. Klapisch-Zuber, 'Women and the family', in J. Le Goff, ed., *The Medieval World* trans. L.G. Cochrane (London, 1990). France in particular has spawned a fascinating literature: C. Fairchilds, 'Masters and servants in eighteenth-century Toulouse', *Journal of Social History* **12** (3) (1979) and her *Domestic Enemies: Servants and their Masters in Old Regime France* (Baltimore, 1984); S. Maza, 'An anatomy of paternalism: masters and servants in eighteenth-century French households', *Eighteenth Century Life* **2** (1) (1981) and her *Servants and Masters in Eighteenth-Century France: the Uses of Loyalty* (Princeton, 1983). For those who read French, see J-P. Gutton, *Domestiques et serviteurs dans la France de l'ancien régime* (Paris, 1981). The French metropolitan context is provided by D. Roche, *The People of Paris: An Essay in Popular Culture in the Eighteenth Century* (Leamington Spa, 1987); D. Garrioch, *Neighbourhood and Community in Paris, 1740–1790* (Cambridge, 1986); and A. Farge, *Fragile Lives: Violence, Power and Solidarity in Eighteenth-Century Paris* (Cambridge, 1993).

For the Dutch Republic, a useful introductory piece comparing prescriptive literature to notarial records is M. Carlson, 'A Trojan horse of worldliness? Maidservants in the burger household in Rotterdam at the end of the seventeenth century', and R. Dekker's reply, in E. Kloek, N. Teeuwen, and M. Huisman, eds, *Women of the Golden Age: An International Debate on Women in Seventeenth-Century Holland, England and Italy* (Hilversum, 1994), while A.T. Van Deursen, *Plain Lives in a Golden Age: Popular Culture, Religion and Society in Seventeenth-Century Holland* trans. M. Ultee (Cambridge, 1991) provides the social context. The history of youth in early modern Europe has much to say about service in general: J.R. Gillis, *Youth and History: Tradition and Change in European Age Relations, 1770–Present* (New York, 1974) is dated now, but M. Mitterauer, 'Servants and youth', *Continuity and Change* **5** (1) (1990), and his *A History of Youth*, trans. G. Dunphy (Oxford, 1992) are far more up to date. A classic on contemporary social attitudes to the young is K. Thomas, 'Age and authority in early modern England', *Proceedings of the British Academy* **62** (1976). The most comprehensive work for this country is P. Griffiths, *Youth and Authority: Formative Experiences in England, 1560–1640* (Oxford, 1996), containing much material from London though its focus is pre-Civil War; while I.K. Ben-Amos, *Adolescence* *and Youth in Early Modern England* (New Haven, 1994) is more broad-brush but valuable particularly for its analysis of autobiographies.

Domestic service in the nineteenth and twentieth centuries

Modern domestic service has a vast and growing literature, and the account originally influential in linking Victorian domestic servant-employment with middle-class formation was J.A. Banks, *Prosperity and Parenthood* (London, 1954); but for works on England the best place to start are those by Leonore Davidoff: 'Mastered for life: servant and wife in Victorian and Edwardian England', *Journal of Social History* **7** (1974); her 'The rationalization of housework', in D. Barker and S. Allen, eds, *Exploitation in Work and Marriage* (London, 1976); and 'Class and gender in Victorian England', in J. Newton, M. Ryan and J. Walkowitz, eds, *Sex and Class in Women's History* (London, 1983); which should be read alongside C. Hall, 'The history of the housewife', reprinted in her *White, Male and Middle Class: Explorations in Feminism and History* (New York, 1992). With Hall she penned the most influential work linking gender and class (at whose centre was the interaction of mistress and servant), *Family Fortunes: Men and Women of the English Middle Class, 1780–1850* (London, 1987). The impact these feminist/Marxist works had can be appreciated best by then going back to P. Horn, *The Rise and Fall of the Victorian Domestic Servant* (Dublin, 1975), whose almost anecdotal approach looks very old-fashioned now; and T. McBride, *The Domestic Revolution: the Modernization of Household Service in England and France 1820–1920* (New York, 1976), a sociological text that seemed to credit domestic service (apparently in female guise an invention of the nineteenth century) with the phenomenon of urbanization.

However, the voyeuristic mock-horror of the Munbys' diaries, which detail the life of an upper class man with a fascination for working women who married his domestic servant and were brought most effectively to light by Davidoff, has arguably stunted the feminist vision of nineteenth-century service. A useful antidote is F. Barret-Ducrocq, *Love in the Time of Victoria: Sexuality, Class and Gender in Nineteenth-Century London* trans. J. Howe (London, 1991), which presents different perspectives on the mistress/maidservant relationship. Overly-schematic views of service and class have been usefully challenged by Higgs's intense scrutiny of the nineteenth-century censuses: see in particular E. Higgs, 'The tabulation of occupations in the nineteenth century census with special reference to domestic servants', *Local Population Studies* **28** (1982); his 'Domestic service and household production', in A.V. John, ed., *Unequal Opportunities: Women's Employment in England 1800–1918* (Oxford, 1986); his *Domestic Servants and Households in Rochdale, 1851–1871* (New York, 1986), a valuable local urban study; and his 'Women, occupations and work in the nineteenth-century censuses', *History Workshop Journal* **23** (1987).

The Americas have also seen a burgeoning of works on modern domestic service, usually focusing on class relations between servants and their employers. For a comprehensive list of works to 1989 on both sides of the Atlantic (despite the title) see M.L. Smith's bibliography in E.M. Chaney and M.G. Castro, eds, *Muchachas No More: Household Workers in Latin America and the Caribbean* (Philadelphia,1989). A selection of American texts would include F.E. Dudden, *Serving Women: Household Service in Nineteenth-Century America* (Middletown, Conn., 1983); P. Palmer, *Domesticity and Dirt: Housewives and Domestic Servants in the US, 1920–1945* (Philadelphia, 1989); and S.L. Graham, *House and Street: The Domestic World of Servants and Masters in Nineteenth-Century Rio de Janeiro* (Cambridge, 1988).

Service, slavery and patriarchy

Returning to the earlier period, Chapter One discussed the 'otherness' of slavery and contemporary attitudes to the exotic, and in addition to the works cited there, see J.J. Hecht, 'Continental and colonial servants in eighteenth-century England', *Smith College Studies in History* 40 (Northampton, Mass., 1954). Also extremely useful is A.J. Frantzen and D. Moffat, eds, *The Work of Work: Servitude, Slavery, and Labour in Medieval England* (Glasgow, 1994), while attitudes to servility and disorder are tackled in A.L. Beier, *Masterless Men: The Vagrancy Problem in England, 1560–1640* (London, 1985). Many of the works already cited here deal with the complex question of employer–servant relations; two that deserve mention on domestic violence are J.A. Sharpe, 'Domestic homicide in early modern England', *The Historical Journal* **24** (1) (1981), in which he examines the lenient treatment meted out to murderers of servants in Essex; and F.E. Dolan, *Dangerous Familiars: Representations of Domestic Crime in England, 1550–1700* (Ithaca, 1994), where the author dissects the pamphlet, dramatic and other popular literature on perceived enemies within the household, especially Chapter II in which she discusses literary representations of the petty treasons committed by servants in usurpation of patriarchal authority. S.D. Amussen, *An Ordered Society: Gender and Class in Early Modern England* (Oxford, 1988) deals with patriarchal social and domestic relations more generally, albeit from a slender evidential base. Two very recent books, one a collection of essays and the other a textbook, have sought to reassess gendered relations and in particular to challenge Davidoff and Hall's influential 'separate spheres' paradigm: see H. Barker and E. Chalus, *Gender in Eighteenth-Century England: Roles, Representations and Responsibilities* (Harlow, 1997), and particularly R.B. Shoemaker, *Gender in English Society: The Emergence of Separate Spheres?* (Harlow, 1998). The latter's Chapter 4 is a thorough summary of current historical publication on the household.

Anyone writing on work in the seventeenth and eighteenth centuries cannot avoid E.P. Thompson, whose rallying-cry in his *The Making of the English Working Class* (Harmondsworth, 1963) to 'rescue the poor stockinger . . . from the condescension of posterity' gave inspiration to a generation of social historians determined to renew interest in plebeian and other non-elite groups of people. Yet it is interesting to note how he and the Warwick School inspired by his supervision and example have paid little attention to servants. Both Thompson and Malcolmson quote didactic literature aimed at or about servants to illustrate eighteenth-century social divisions, yet servants themselves are only discussed in the context of the plebeian life cycle: E.P. Thompson, 'The patricians and the plebs', in his *Customs in Common* (London, 1991); R.W. Malcolmson, *Life and Labour in England, 1700–1780* (London, 1981). Rule has discussed apprenticeship but is not really interested in domestic service despite its importance in the urban (and even parts of the rural) labour market: J. Rule, *The Experience of Labour in Eighteenth-Century Industry* (London, 1981); his *The Experience of Labour in Eighteenth-Century England* (London, 1986); and his *The Labouring Classes in Early Industrial England, 1750–1850* (London, 1987). Of this group, only Linebaugh has given the subject sustained discussion, but his view is unfortunately rather one-dimensional, since domestic servants in the metropolis are coerced into the formation of an international proletariat without their particular historical experiences being considered: P. Linebaugh, *The London Hanged: Crime and Civil Society in the Eighteenth Century* (London, 1991).

Gendered work and wages

The Marxist-feminist debate on household labour was centred around histories of the nineteenth century, and spawned a substantial literature. Apart from the references cited in Chapter Three, the following will be useful: H. Hartmann, 'The family as the locus of gender, class and political struggle: the example of housework', *Signs* **6** (1981); Hall, 'The history of the housewife'; E. Malos, *The Politics of Housework* revised edition (London, 1982); and R.E. Pahl, *Divisions of Labour* (Oxford, 1984). He edited a collection of essays that dealt comprehensively with the many sides of this debate, and his introductory paragraphs before each section are helpful: *On Work: Historical, Comparative and Theoretical Approaches* (Oxford, 1988). The key texts in understanding the debate over the way women's work changed over time remain A. Clark, *Working Life of Women in the Seventeenth Century* (London, 1919), arguing that the fortunes of women declined from the end of the seventeenth century; and I. Pinchbeck, *Women Workers and the Industrial Revolution, 1750–1850* (London, 1930), who saw the industrial revolution as a largely positive experience for women. However, the relative paucity of coverage both gave to domestic service helps to explain the limited literature on it for the pre-modern period.

The following texts have gone some way to redress the balance and stress long-term continuities in women's subordinate work: Earle, 'Female labour market'; Bennett, 'Medieval women, modern women'; and her ' "History that stands still": women's work in the European past', *Feminist Studies* **14** (2) (1988). B. Hill, *Women, Work and Sexual Politics in Eighteenth-Century England* (Oxford, 1989), discusses domestic service and housework within a traditional Clarkian, pessimistic mould, while P. Sharpe, *Adapting to Capitalism: Working Women in the English Economy, 1700–1850* (Basingstoke, 1996) does so in the context of a more sophisticated local study of the relationship between the Essex and London labour markets largely in the late eighteenth and early nineteenth centuries. Meanwhile, our understanding of male work has been greatly enhanced by texts like those of D. Woodward, *Men at Work: Labourers and Building Craftsmen in the Towns of Northern England, 1450–1750* (Cambridge, 1995); J. Ward, *Metropolitan Communities: Trade Guilds, Identity and Change in Early Modern London* (Stanford, 1997); and by R.C. Davis, 'Venetian shipbuilders and the fountain of wine', *Past and Present* **156** (1997), and his earlier *Shipbuilders of the Venetian Arsenal* (Baltimore, 1991). In these authors' different ways, one through the detailed analysis of probate inventories, the second of London livery companies, and the third through the case study of a particular (albeit enormous) place of work, they have exposed the rich cultural contexts within which male work took place. Their researches ensure that dichotomous contrasts between men's and women's work require more nuanced gendered contexts. Michael Roberts has already demonstrated some of what is possible in his ' "Words they are women, and deeds they are men": images of work and gender in early modern England', in L. Charles and L. Duffin, eds, *Women and Work in Pre-industrial England* (Beckenham, 1985), and his forthcoming book on early modern work is eagerly awaited.

Chapter Six grappled with the problem of servants' remuneration and the gender wage differential, and one of the two angles of enquiry in Marshall's classic article was to test contemporary claims that servants' wages had risen radically: Marshall, 'Domestic servants of the eighteenth century'. But as Sharpe has written recently, 'Women's wages, and indeed, other aspects of women's work were subject to traditional, local cultural differences which it is only possible to penetrate by producing detailed case studies of early modern communities' (*Adapting to Capitalism*, p. 150). Her work, and that of others, is enabling historians to create a more satisfactory and complex picture. To start with, see D. Woodward, 'Wage rates and living standards in pre-industrial England', *Past and Present* **91** (1981). For rural wages, A. Hassell Smith, 'Labourers in late sixteenth-century England: a case study from north Norfolk' parts I and II, *Continuity and Change* **4** (1) and (3) (1989); M. Roberts, 'Sickles and scythes: women's and men's work at harvest time', *History Workshop Journal* **7** (1979); and C. Middleton, 'The familiar fate of the *famulae*: gender divisions in the history of wage labour', in Pahl, ed., *On Work*. London-based studies include Bennett, 'Medieval women, modern women'; Earle, 'Female labour market'; S. Rappaport, *Worlds within Worlds: Structures of Life in Sixteenth-Century London* (Cambridge, 1989); Schwarz, *London in the Age of Industrialisation*; and J. Boulton, 'Wage labour in seventeenth-century London', *Economic History Review* **49** (2) (1996). The early modern debates over wages have a large (if old-fashioned) literature, but for the best recent summary, see J. Hatcher, 'Labour, leisure and economic thought before the nineteenth century', *Past and Present* **160** (1998).

Sources for London domestic service

Finally, readers may wish to enquire further into the nature of the principal sources used in this book. While some of them are relatively inaccessible, these works detail the church courts' formal procedures: H. Consett, *The Practice of the Spiritual or*

Ecclesiastical Courts (London, 1685); J.T. Law, *Forms of Ecclesiastical Law; or, the mode of conducting suits in the Consistory courts, being a translation of the first part of Oughton's Ordo Judiciorum* (London, 1831) — Oughton was one of the leading proctors, or civil lawyers practicing in the church courts during the period covered by this book; and, more approachable, D.M. Owen, *The Records of the Established Church in England, Excluding Parochial Records* (London, 1970). A number of studies in the last few decades allow the historian to see these courts in action: R.A. Marchant, *The Church Under the Law: Justice, Administration and Discipline in the Diocese of York, 1560–1640* (Cambridge, 1969); R. Houlbrooke, *Church Courts and the People During the English Reformation, 1520–1570* (Oxford, 1979); and the best of these is M. Ingram, *Church Courts, Sex and Marriage in England, 1570–1640* (Oxford, 1987), which moves beyond the institutional study and into historical anthropology. For a stimulating case-study of one aspect of the church courts' work, see J.A. Sharpe, *Defamation and Sexual Slander in Early Modern England: the Church Courts at York*, Borthwick Papers 58 (York, 1980). The following recent works have employed London church court records: for the late medieval period, see R.M. Wunderli, *London Church Courts and Society on the Eve of the Reformation* (Cambridge, Mass., 1981); for the early seventeenth century, Gowing, *Domestic Dangers*; and for the period under scrutiny here, Earle, 'Female labour market', and his *City Full of People*; L. Stone, *Road to Divorce: England 1530–1987* (Oxford, 1990) and the accompanying volumes of testimony, *Uncertain Unions: Marriage in England 1660–1753* (Oxford, 1992), and *Broken Lives: Separation and Divorce in England 1660–1857* (Oxford, 1993); and T. Meldrum, 'A women's court in London: defamation at the Bishop of London's Consistory Court, 1700–1745', *London Journal* **19** (1) (1994).

INDEX

adolescence 4, 7, 18, 48, 61–2
apprentice, parish 7, 14, 162–4, 180–1
apprenticeship 7, 8, 18, 27, 32, 33, 61, 89, 131, 132, 161–4, 180–1
Arches, Court of 8
authority (*see* mastery, parish authority) 4, 33, 36–7, 44–6, 49, 61, 65–7, 68, 87, 106

Baxter, R. 38–9, 48, 49, 129, 184
Beattie, J. 53, 64, 111
Bedfordshire 19, 20
Belgravia 1
Ben-Amos, I.K. 7, 60, 89, 161–2, 163
Bennett, J. 13, 38, 190–1
Berkshire 19
Blackstone, W. 25–6, 44
Boulton, J. 62, 185, 187, 189
Brewer, J. 64, 71
Bristol 14, 89, 96, 161, 163
Brodsky Elliott, V. 19, 161
Buckinghamshire 19
Burns, R. 39

Cambridgeshire 14, 19
canon law 8
Canterbury 20
census 6, 13, 14, 74
chamberlain 86, 133, 155–6, 157
chambermaid 34, 35, 59, 80, 86, 98, 118, 120, 150–1, 164, 179, 193
character 17, 50, 51–65, 66, 99, 101, 115, 165
City of London 8, 13, 14–16, 20, 29, 61, 65, 81, 91, 114, 157, 190
Clark, A. 41, 134–5
Clark, P. 20, 21
Collinson, P. 38
Commissary court 8
consumption 13, 32, 55, 95, 164–7, 177–8, 183, 192, 199–201
contract (-ual) 6, 25–6, 31–2, 70, 73–6, 89–91, 126, 163, 184–6, 194, 199–200, 205–6

cook (-ery) 1, 98, 132, 133, 140–6, 153, 164, 170, 173, 179, 201–2, 204
cookbooks 140–2, 153, 179
cookmaid 30, 49, 56, 59, 60, 80, 81, 85, 88, 108, 143, 149, 172, 178, 189–90
Corfield, P. 76–7, 138, 165, 181
Co. Carlow, Ireland 20
Coutts Bank 1, 3
Coventry 32

Dalton, M. 62
Davidoff, L. 6, 41, 42, 71, 72–3
Davis, N.Z. 6
Davison, L. 21
defamation 8, 9, 51, 59, 97–100, 112, 115–16, 121 (Table 4.1), 122, 160, 189
Defoe, D. 55, 58, 60, 63–4, 130, 148, 158, 164, 180, 183, 190, 191, 202, 205
domestic
  interiors 34
  labour 1, 3, 11, 38–9, 44, 47, 48, 56, 59, 106, 134–7, 165–6, 208
  slavery 26
  violence 9, 76, 91–4, 96, 100, 104, 107–8, 112, 121 (Table 4.1)
domesticity 70, 72–4, 76

Earle, P. 9, 10, 13, 14, 23, 28, 73, 80, 139, 163, 176, 179, 180, 183, 189, 197
ecclesiastical jurisdiction 8, 51, 97
economy, moral 11, 48, 123, 184–6, 195–206, 209
Edinburgh 20
Essex 19, 20, 105, 190

Fable of the Bees 2, 130, 164, 171, 183, 191
Fairchilds, C. 57–8, 74, 102, 112–13, 117, 195, 198 (n.31)
family-household 11, 35, 66, 70, 71–6, 77, 84, 124, 128, 135, 164, 196–7
favouritism 87–8, 90, 99, 119, 127, 172, 200
femininity 1, 136
feminisation 6, 10, 16, 74
feminism 6, 41, 71–4, 134–5, 166

218

INDEX

5–7, 89

, 151–3, 170, 179, 193

36, 37–51, 61–2, 64–7, 68, 2, 172

2–4

er) 133 (n.17), 155–6
e 14, 155, 174–6, 193

rity (*see* authority, order) 35, 66, 117, 124, 126, 161–4, 207
88–9, 91, 151
and E. 52, 57, 60, 70, 80, 92, –10, 125–6, 130, 142–3, 147, 8–50, 174, 180, 189–90, 200, 207
1, 20, 49, 184–5, 186, 193, 196, 99–205, 205–6, 209
of a Person of Quality's Family 86, 133, 143, 148, 168, 171, 173, 175, 194
tax 13
rter 34, 169
orter, R. 13, 104
rerogative Court of Canterbury 8, 144
privacy 11, 41–2, 53, 70, 71–83, 84, 85, 101–2, 120, 124–5, 141, 151, 167, 208–9
problem, servant 1, 3, 5, 61
profession 12, 22, 23, 29, 131, 174, 180
Public Record Office 8

rape 93–4, 100–1, 103–4, 107–8, 116, 124, 126, 208
Reims 32
remuneration 11, 30, 32, 121 (Table 4.1), 122–3, 176 (Chapter 6)
Revolution, French 6
Roberts, M. 61, 111, 129–30, 140, 144 (n.52), 179–80, 187
Rogers, N. 113–16
Roman law 8
Rutland 19

St Bride's, City of London 80
St Giles in the Fields, Middlesex 100–2, 147, 154, 156
St Mary le Bow, City of London 15
St Michael Bassishaw, City of London 15
St James's, Westminster 19, 57, 101, 147

Schwarz, L.D. 13, 185, 196, 198–9 (Table 6.3), 203–4
'separate spheres' 37, 41–2, 66, 124–5, 136, 208–9
servant-in-husbandry 21, 27, 61, 162, 187–8, 194, 196–7
'servant problem' 1, 3, 5, 61
settlement 10, 23, 25, 62, 101, 188–9 (Table 6.1), 190
Sharpe, J.A. 51, 110–11
Sharpe, P. 136, 190
Shoemaker, R.B. 13, 42, 63–5, 99, 160
slander 9, 35, 51, 66, 97–8, 121 (Table 4.1), 122–3, 160
slavery 25–7, 33
Sonenscher, M. 133–4, 195–6, 197
Souden, D. 14, 21
Southampton 14
Snell, K.D.M. 21, 162, 190
Stepney, Middlesex 31
Stone, L. 8, 14, 77–81, 82–3, 93, 102, 118–19, 192 (n.17)
Styles, J. 64, 195, 200 (n.35), 209 (n.44)
Suffolk 19
Surrey 19, 20, 156
Sussex 19, 111
Swift, J. 171–2, 177

Tadmor, N. 72
tapster 133 (n.17)
Thompson, E.P. 57, 184–5, 195–6, 205, 209
Thompson, P. 135
threshold 69–70, 124–5, 142, 168, 208
tips (*see* vails) 11, 20, 97, 145, 175, 184, 193, 199–205

vails 11, 20, 171, 183, 184, 186, 193, 196, 199–205, 206, 209
Vickery, A. 42, 73, 199
violence, domestic 9, 76, 91–4, 96, 100, 104, 107–8, 112, 121 (Table 4.1), 124
vulnerability 69, 101–4, 111–12, 124, 126, 160, 171, 206, 208

Warwickshire 20
West End 14, 29, 63, 113, 114, 143
Westminster 19, 51, 57, 64, 101, 113–15
wet-nurse 42–3, 152

youth 6, 7, 10, 62
York 32, 168